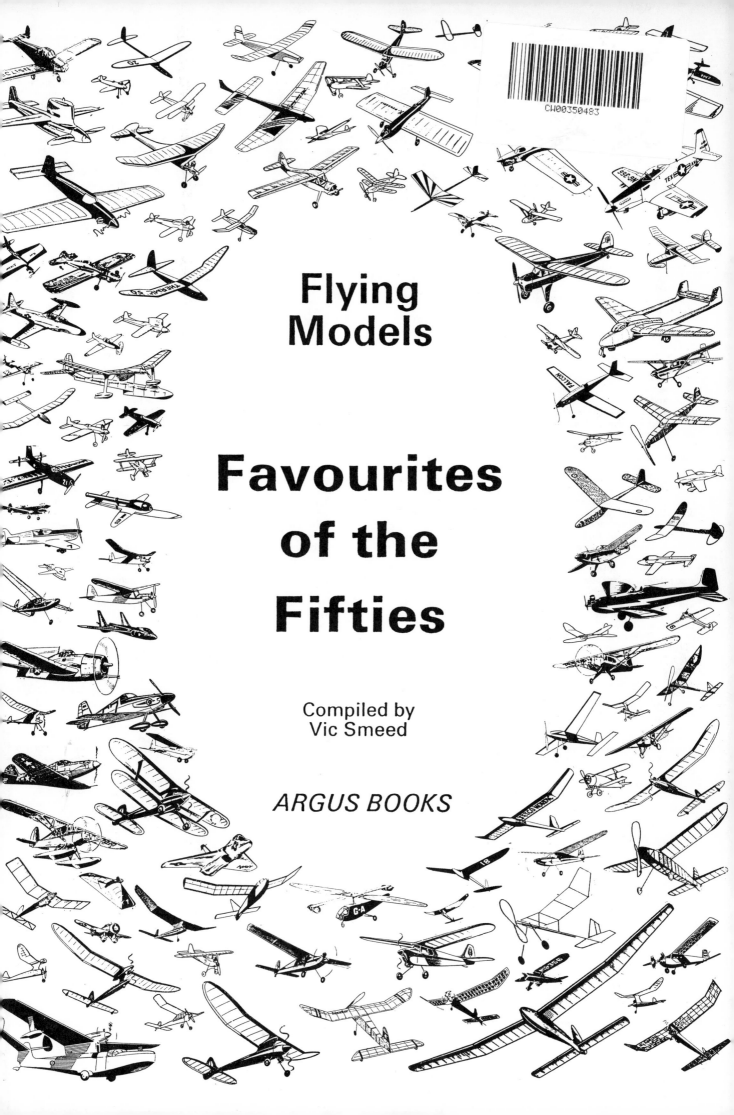

Flying Models

Favourites of the Fifties

Compiled by
Vic Smeed

ARGUS BOOKS

INTRODUCTION

What constituted the "golden years" of any activity will to a great extent depend on the age and experience of the participant, but it is safe to say that a majority would agree to the 1950s as the golden years of aeromodelling. The outbreak of World War 2 in 1939 had brought international events to a halt and, with the exception of the U.S.A., organised model flying was to be very low key until, effectively, 1947, when world-wide demobilisation was nearing completion and supplies of modelling materials were becoming more freely available.

For most of the world the period 1946-1949 ushered in three basic changes, two of which, i.e.-engined free flight and control-line flying, were due to the rapidly growing availability of small engines; the third was the enormous increase of interest in towline gliders. From being the only inexpensive and widely available source of power for free-flight models, rubber became one of three ways of achieving flights of acceptable duration and as a result began to lose its dominance. Nevertheless, at the beginning of the 1950s the Wakefield Cup, for rubber-powered models, was still regarded as far and away the most important and prestigious international competition. This applied even in America, where power flying was extensive due to mass production of model motors from 1934 until temporary interruption in 1942; America was, interestingly, the last major country to accept towline gliders on a large scale.

Control-line flying, seen in very basic form in France in 1911 and developed in Britain as a novelty in the 1920s, was patented in the U.S.A. and commercially launched in 1940 as an alternative form of competition for gasoline models as so many free-flight models were being lost under existing rules. Methods of terminating flights – dethermalisers – were not heard of until 1942/3. Much development in power model flying took place in America in the years between 1937 and 1945, when few motors were to be found in other countries and for most of which time petrol-engined models were banned. At this time the Germans and Scandinavians, in particular, were developing gliders and the miniature so-called diesel was evolving in Switzerland, Austria, Italy, France and Germany.

When active modelling was resumed in the post-war years there was thus much to digest and many new avenues opening. Innovation was continual – pulse jets, the glowplug, Jetex, ducted fans, CO_2 motors are some examples – and there were always new challenges and new directions. When C/L stunt and speed began to get too specialised team racing appeared, for example, to be followed by rat-racing, mouse-racing and combat.

The beginning of the fifties saw the Nordic or A2 class of sailplane begin to catch on world-wide but it soon became necessary to halve the permitted towline length to make it more difficult to achieve a maximum flight. Alterations to the Wakefield and power rules were also made in an attempt to *reduce* performances, a process which still continues!

Most significant, however, was the arrival of commercial radio control equipment on a wide scale. Early gear was almost always single-channel, which called for ingenuity to achieve more than rudder-only control. The unreliability of some of the gadgetry allied to the temperament of the soft-valve circuitry meant that several seasons had to pass before the average modeller without radio knowledge could buy and use reliable, lightweight equipment. Even in 1957 an American article suggested that multi-channel radio was "too expensive for the average modeller and likely to remain so."

In the 50s scale modelling substantially increased its following. There had always been interest but rubber is not the ideal form of power for scale models and the constant output of an i.c. engine, and the ability to match output closely to model requirements, meant that a much higher success rate was achievable. Flying on control lines encouraged the inclusion of more and finer detail, which influenced F/F models; radio offered little help initially but as multi-function equipment grew lighter, more reliable and less of a financial mountain scale subjects began to appear more often. The first national R/C

scale competition was in the U.S.A. in 1958 but it was several years later that proportional control ushered in the forerunners of the remarkably detailed scale masterpieces that we see today.

There have always been specialist clubs but in 1950 the *average* British club had a wide range of interests and the average member pursued several of them. Thus more than half the membership would be flying F/F sports power models and probably two-thirds trying their hands with gliders. One third would fly rubber regularly, perhaps a fifth F/F competition power, one third control-line, mostly sport and stunt. One in ten might be interested in scale and there would have been one or two intrigued by the possibilities of radio control. Probably two thirds built from kits, a quarter from magazine plans and the remainder from own or club designs. Rubber models would be sport designs or competition lightweights, gliders all shapes and sizes, and F/F power designs mostly under 2½cc.

On a wider scale – and there were at least 25 active non-club enthusiasts for every club member – interest was largely in small (up to 2cc) sport power and C/L models plus, inevitably, the extensive assortment of small and inexpensive scale rubber kits and slightly larger gliders. To give an idea of volume, the largest U.K. manufacturer in the early 50s was KeilKraft, who in 1953 had a range of 103 models and sold in the year well over a million kits. Half of these were 5/- (25p) or under, but 5/- more than covered a 24in. rubber model. Typical prices are shown on page 9.

In the other major modelling country, America, the early 50s were notable for the introduction of a whole selection of tiny engines, made possible by Ray Arden's successful adaptation of the hot coil ignition system to model-size motors. The CO_2 motor, popular around 1907, reappeared, in small form. These new, small motors led to a flood of new kits, with the emphasis on F/F, thus partly redressing the balance, since control-liners had virtually taken over up till 1949.

There were a fair number of rubber kits, quite a selection of F/F power, but very few gliders. A list of kits being advertised at the beginning of the period is included, but a number of these appeared at the time only in America's Hobby Center adverts and manufacturers were not included; given time they could no doubt all have been traced or hesitant recollections confirmed, but . . .

Magazines provided a continual flow of plans, often full-size or with full-size parts for tracing, covering all aspects of aeromodelling. Most issues included at least three designs and for a spell *Flying Models* was running as many as five mostly full-size plans in each issue. During the period all the mags. not already doing so introduced mail order full-size plans for larger models.

The impression received by onlookers without direct experience of American activities was of a number of prominent clubs associated with major cities around the country, each with several top-level expert members. Because of the distances involved many of these clubs never got to meet, while between them were spread thousands of air-minded youngsters and occasional mature and experienced modellers, sometimes forming little groups but often operating entirely alone. In centres of relatively high population annual contests might be sponsored by non-modelling concerns: the Mirror Model Flying Fair, run by a New York newspaper, is an example. This meeting accepted only the first 1000 entries but reckoned on 250,000 spectators!

European countries still tended to follow individual paths in 1950, partly because of limitations on imports, but during the following decade increasing international contact influenced every country's approach. English-speaking countries such as Australia, New Zealand and South Africa had always paralleled American and British progress but their own manufacturing capacities increased when they too found importation restricted by the currency problems of the period.

In other countries, in Asia and South America, awareness of model flying was only awakening, with the exception of a few individual enthusiasts, for example in Argentina, who achieved remarkably high standards despite almost total isolation, and the few Japanese manufacturers who had played a small but significant part in pre-war modelling. For modellers in these countries the expression "the golden years" is perhaps inappropriate, but such models as were built in the 50s would undoubtedly have originated from, or have been heavily influenced by, designs from American and British sources.

This book sets out to illustrate popular models, or at least popular types of models, widely flown in the 1950s by average modellers. Ideally a good many plans of kit models of the time should have been included, but this presents obvious difficulties and the best that can be done is to attempt to list those British and American kits available early in the period, together with motors, and to illustrate some of them. Relatively few designs from non-English-speaking sources were generally available, except for competition winners, usually published in U.K. and/or U.S. and in any event not really classifiable as popular with average modellers.

As with *Fifty Years of Aeromodeller* and *Model Flying – the First Fifty Years*, it has not always been possible to include deserving models because of reproduction difficulties. Nevertheless, a sufficient variety appears to awake nostalgia in older modellers and to show younger ones the sort of machines we had fun with at the time when model flying was experiencing the greatest period of growth in its 85 year history.

FLYING MODELS - FAVOURITES OF THE FIFTIES
is published by
ARGUS BOOKS LTD.,
Wolsey House,
Wolsey Road,
Hemel Hempstead,
Hertfordshire HP2 4SS
England

© Argus Books Ltd. 1988
(with acknowledgements to
publications listed)

ISBN 0 85242 964 9

Phototypesetting by Multiform, Cardiff.
Printed and bound by Richard Clay Ltd., Chichester, Sussex.

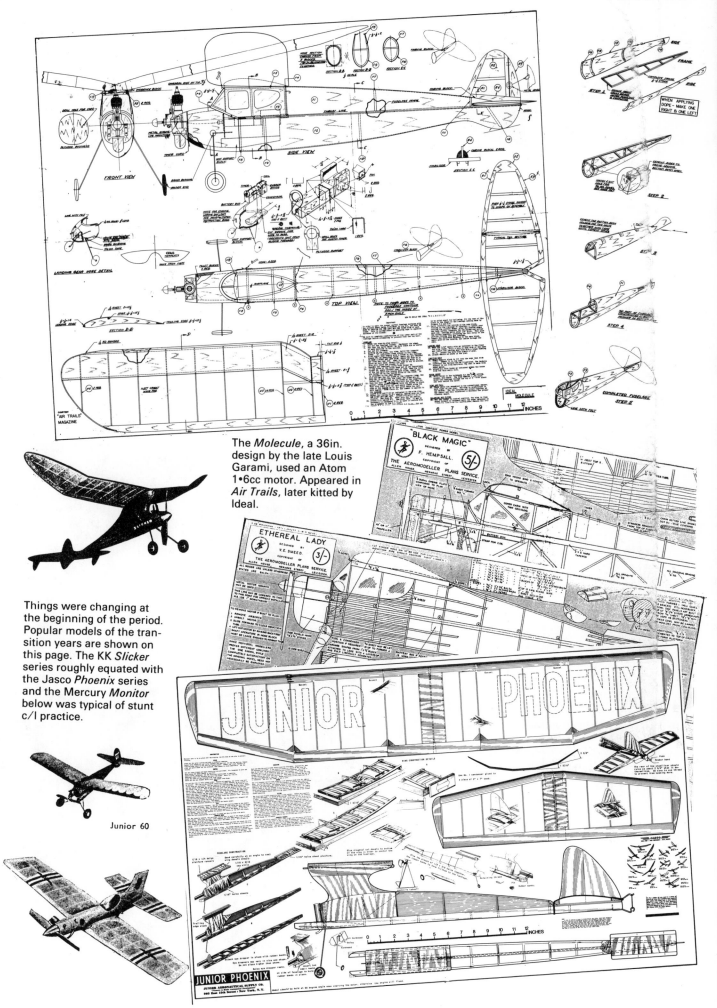

The *Molecule*, a 36in. design by the late Louis Garami, used an Atom 1•6cc motor. Appeared in *Air Trails*, later kitted by Ideal.

Things were changing at the beginning of the period. Popular models of the transition years are shown on this page. The KK *Slicker* series roughly equated with the Jasco *Phoenix* series and the Mercury *Monitor* below was typical of stunt c/l practice.

Junior 60

3

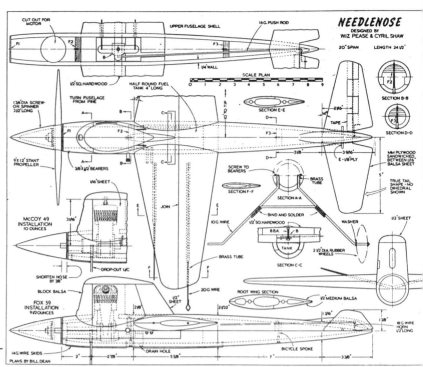

Control-line speed was in its hey-day in the early '50s. Prominent British exponents were Cyril Shaw and Wiz Pease whose *Needlenose* (Class 5) was fastest in Britain in 1949 at 119•7mph.

Below, rubber-powered helicopters attracted enthusiasts for the unorthodox at the beginning of the period but real success with engine power was ten years or more away. (Air Trails 1949).

Stunt control-line was much more popular than speed. The Brian Hewitt design below was kitted by KeilKraft; the original was designed for the very noisy but powerful Yulon 30. Smaller models as opposite appealed more to average modellers. Rubber was still well supported with *Tiercel* an outstanding example. (All drawings appeared in the Ian Allan Model Aviation series but also elsewhere

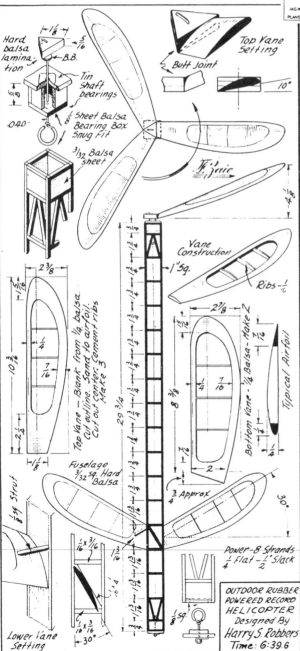

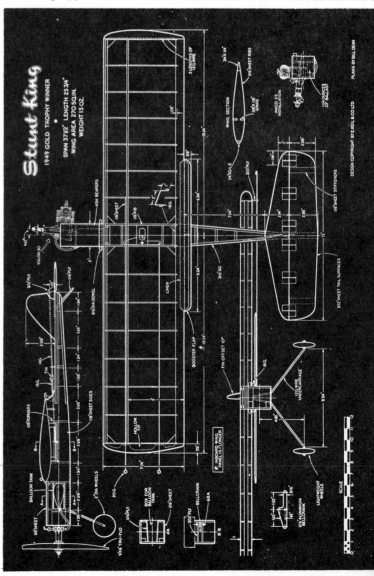

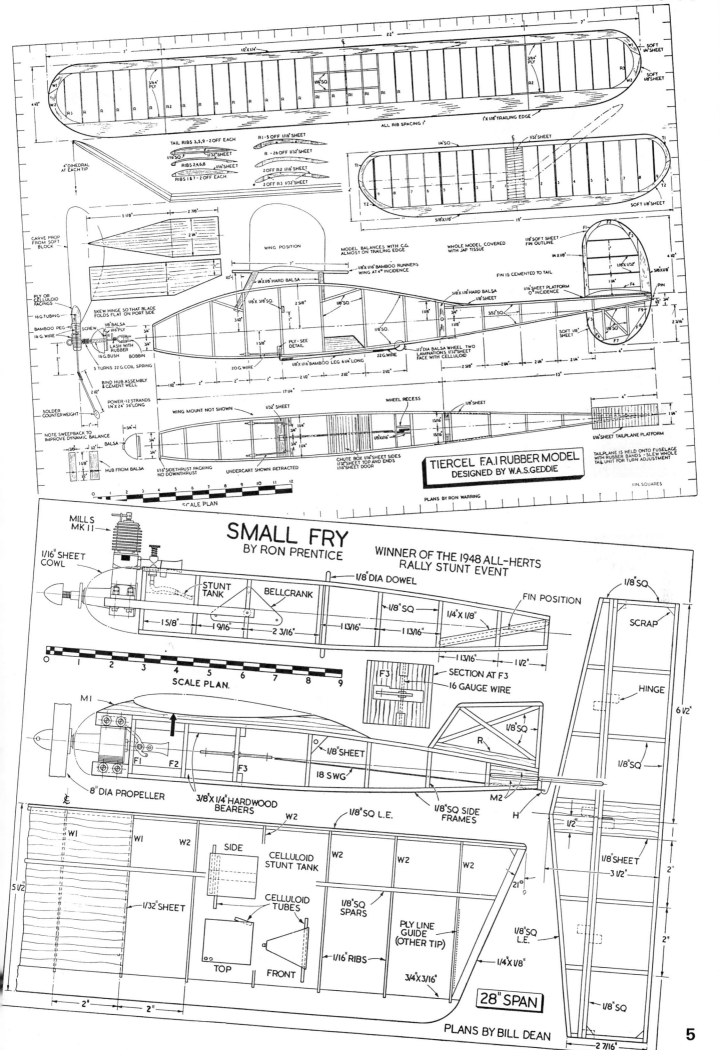

TIERCEL F.A.I RUBBER MODEL
DESIGNED BY W.A.S.GEDDIE

PLANS BY RON WARRING

SMALL FRY
BY RON PRENTICE

WINNER OF THE 1948 ALL-HERTS
RALLY STUNT EVENT

28" SPAN

PLANS BY BILL DEAN

5

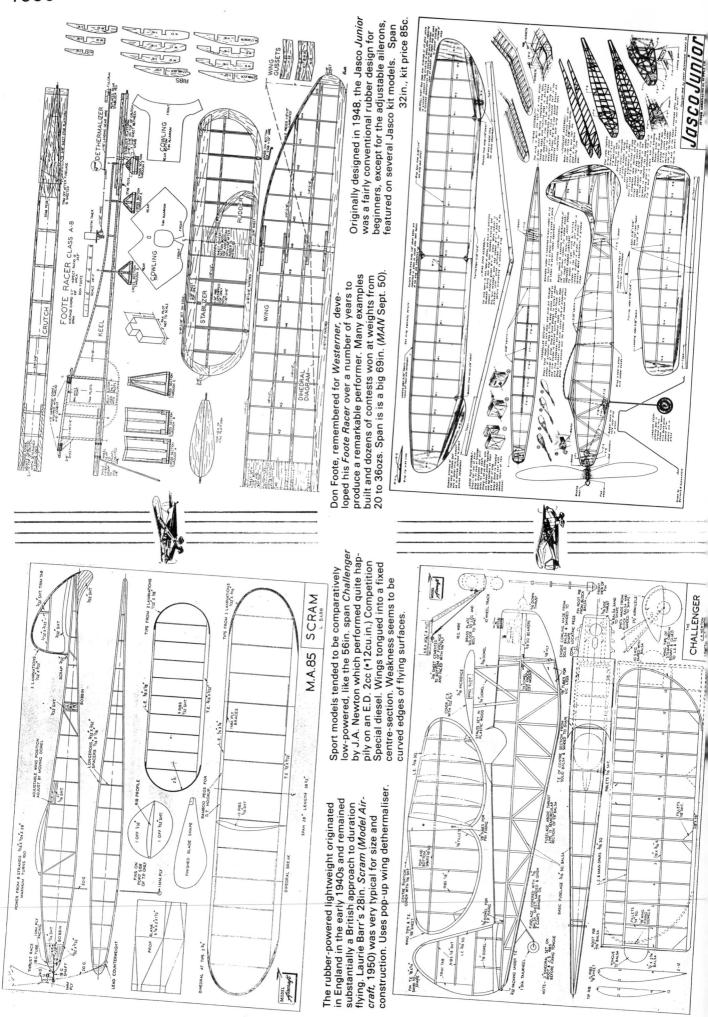

Don Foote, remembered for *Westerner*, developed his *Foote Racer* over a number of years to produce a remarkable performer. Many examples built and dozens of contests won at weights from 20 to 36ozs. Span is is a big 69in. (*MAN* Sept. 50).

Originally designed in 1948, the Jasco *Junior* was a fairly conventional rubber design for beginners, except for the adjustable ailerons, featured on several Jasco kit models. Span 32in., kit price 85c.

The rubber-powered lightweight originated in England in the early 1940s and remained substantially a British approach to duration flying. Laurie Barr's 28in. *Scram* (*Model Aircraft*, 1950) was very typical for size and construction. Uses pop-up wing dethermaliser.

Sport models tended to be comparatively low-powered, like the 56in. span *Challenger* by J.A. Newton which performed quite happily on an E.D. 2cc (•12cu.in.) Competition Special diesel. Wings tongued into a fixed centre-section. Weakness seems to be curved edges of flying surfaces.

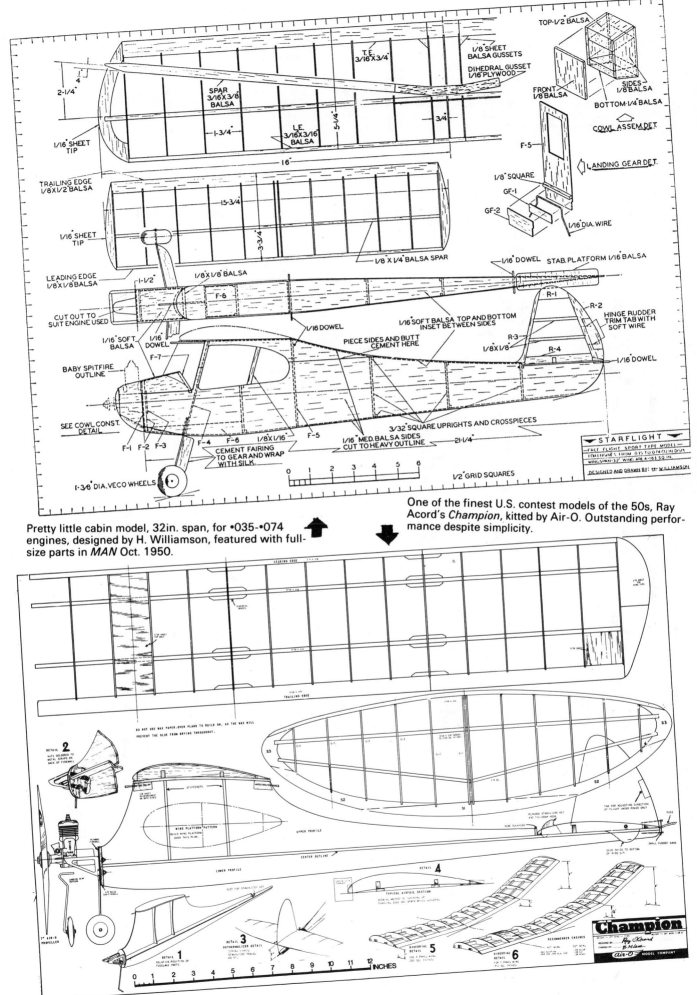

Pretty little cabin model, 32 in. span, for •035-•074 engines, designed by H. Williamson, featured with full-size parts in *MAN* Oct. 1950.

One of the finest U.S. contest models of the 50s, Ray Acord's *Champion*, kitted by Air-O. Outstanding performance despite simplicity.

The following lists of British kits show, apart from the nostalgia factor, just what a range was available and from what a variety of manufacturers. Note that no scale models are included; there were a good few scale C/L and F/F power from all sorts of firms, large and small, plus scores of rubber scale kits from Skyrova/Skyleada (British Model Aircraft) and Airyda and other fondly-remembered firms as well as survivors such as Keil and Veron (Model Aircraft, Bournemouth).

The lists were compiled in 1950 for *Model Aircraft* magazine by Ron Warring, who normally used a typewriter as his hand-writing could be difficult. It is likely that the glider list on this page was hand-written as there are several errors, including line 21 – COMET, W.A. Dean, line 26 – V-tail, line 38 – THREE-FOOTER, Profile Fuselage, line 44 – SUNNANVIND, line 47 – TERN, line 48 – VANDA, line 56 – F.A.I., line 64 – MINIMOA and lines 73 and 75 – A2 Contest.

GLIDER KITS

This table embraces glider kit models manufactured in reasonable quantities since January, 1947, and those kits known to be now out of production or not normally available are indicated. Whilst every care has been taken to make this table as complete as possible, no responsibility can be accepted for errors or ommissions.

Span ins.	Model	Designer	Manufacturer	Type	Special Features	Price
12	ATO ELF*	—	Ato Model Crafts	Solid	Chuck-Glider	2/-
12	ZIPPER	—	Halfax Models	Solid	Chuck-Glider	1/3
12	TOMTIT	—	Model Aircraft (Bournemouth)	Solid	Chuck-Glider	1/6
12	VEGA	W. A. Dean	E. Keil & Co.	Solid	Chuck-Glider	1/3
12-18	TRIPLET	C. H. Saunders	21st Century Products	3 alternative designs	—	4/-
12½	SPOOK	W. A. Dean	E. Keil & Co.	Solid	Tailless Chuck-Glider	1/6
14	MIDGE*	R. H. Warring	British Model Aircraft	Semi-Solid	Profile Fuselage	1/3
16	DART*	J. R. Vanderbeek	International Model Aircraft	Solid	Chuck-Glider	2/6
16	GNAT	W. A. Dean	Elite Model Airplane Supplies	—		2 6
18	SWIFT*	—	Model Aircraft (Bournemouth)	Solid	Tailless Chuck-Glider	1/9
18	SQUIRREL	—	Don Models	Solid	Chuck-Glider	2/6
20	SWIFT*	—	British Model Aircraft	Solid	Chuck-Glider	2/6
20	JEEP*	J. Paterson	British Model Aircraft	Semi-Solid	Cabin	3/6
20	WIZARD	—	Halfax	Solid	Chuck-Glider	2/6
20	POLARIS	W. A. Dean	E. Keil & Co.	Solid	Chuck-Glider	2/6
20	CUB	W. A. Dean	E. Keil & Co.	Cabin	Also Jetex " 50 " Powered	2/-
21	GREMLIN	—	—	—	Twin Fin	3/-
22	WREN*	—	Model Aircraft (Bournemouth)	Solid	Chuck-Glider	3/-
24	WIZARD*	R. H. Warring	British Model Aircraft	Pod & Boom	Built-up Wings	3/-
24	MAGPIE	H. J. Nichols	Mercury Models	Cabin	Begginer's Model	3/9
24	COMFIT	W. A. Dran	E. Keil & Co.	Solid	Chuck-Glider, Polyhedral Wag	3/6
26	HI-FLY*	R. Calvart	Hi-Fly	Semi-Solid	Alt. Single or Twin Fin	10/-
27	BENNY	—	Don Models	High Wing	Slabsider	3/6
30	HERON*	—	Elite Model Airplane Supplies	Cabin	Gull Wing	5/-
30	SUNBEAM	—	Warneford	Tailless	Built-up	5/6
30	WAGTAIL	—	Model Aircraft (Bournemouth)	Pod & Boom	U-Tail	5/-
30	ATO " 30 "*	—	Ato Model Crafts	Cabin	Slabsider	4/6
30	WARRIER*	C. H. Saunders	Worcraft	Cabin	—	6/-
30	CADET	W. A. Dean	E. Keil & Co.	Cabin	—	4/-
30	FAIRY	J. R. Vanderbeek	International Model Aircraft	Cabin	—	7/6
30	ELITE NO. I.	R. H. Warring	Elite M.S.A.	Beginners	Triangular fuselage	6/-
31	BEAU GLIDER*	A. H. Lee	Model Airport (Bristol)	Cabin	Short Moment Arm	5/6
31	BABY GULL–	R. F. L. Gosling	Aeromodels	Cabin	Semi-streamlined	8/3
32	VENTURA	E. Chasteneuf	Chas. Models	F.A.I.	Streamliner	12/-
34	MANX CAT	—	Airyda	Tailless	—	10/-
34	NORTH WIND	—	Airyda	—	—	5/-
36	WEST WIND	—	Airyda	—	—	6/-
36	3-ROUTER	R. H. Warring	British Model Aircraft	Solid	Propue Fuselage	5/(-
36	SOARER BABY	C. H. Saunders	E. Keil & Co.	Cabin	—	5/-
36	SOUTHERN SLOPER	L. Heath	Southern Junior Aircraft	Pylon	Diamond Fuselage	6/6
36	DIANA	C. T. Buffery	International Model Aircraft	Cabin	—	5/6
36	CORINTHIAN	—	Warneford	Cabin	Polyhedral Wing	5/6
38	PEEWIT	A. E. Peters	A. E. Peters	—	Lightweight	10/6
39	SUNNAWIND	A. H. Dadd	Paramount Model Aviation	Contest	Lightweight	10/6
40	SAILPLANE*	—	Chingford Model Aerodrome	—	—	12/6
40	INVADER	L. Heath	E. Keil & Co.	Cabin	Twin-Fin	6/6
40	TARN	R. F. L. Gosling	Halfax Models	Cabin	High Tail	10/-
40	UANDA	J. R. Vanderbeek	International Model Aircraft	Cabin	—	9/6
40	SUNDUSTER	—	Airyda	—	—	7/6
40	ROMA	J. Magson	Halfax Models	Hatchet	Lightweight Contest	7/6
40	BEAU GLIDER*	A. H. Lee	Model Airport (Bristol)	Cabin	Short Moment Arm	7/6
40	ASCOT	E. Chastenuef	Chas. Models	Lightweight	Streamliner	8 6
40	ARNHEM GLIDER	Aeromodeller	E. Law & Sons	Beginners	Slabsider	14/6
40	GAMMA	—	Chingford Model Aerodrome	Lightweight	Diamond Parasol	12 6
42	ALBATROSS	—	Model Shop, Newcastle	Pod & Boom	Semi-scale	10/6
42	GILI-CHOPPER	P. Guilmont	Mercury Models	Hatchet	R.A.I. Contest	12/6
42	KIWI*	—	Model Aircraft (Bournemouth)	Tailless	—	18/6
42	MARLIN*	—	Model Aircraft (Bournemouth)	Cabin	—	8/6
44	GULLDUN	—	Don Models	Cabin	Gull Wing	7/6
48	SOARER MINOR	C. H. Saunders	E. Keil & Co.	Cabin	—	8/-
48	FORTUNA	C. T. Buffery	International Model Aircraft	Contest	Shoulder-Wing	—
48	CLUB CONTEST*	—	Model Aerodrome	—	—	15/6
50	BEAU GLIDER*	A. H. Lee	Model Airport (Bristol)	Cabin	Short Moment Arm	9/6
50	MINIMOD	C. H. Saunders	E. Keil & Co.	Scale	Gull-Wing	7/-
50	WRAITH*	R. H. Warring	Shaws Model Aircraft	Contest	Shoulder-Wing	25/-
52	ATO " 52 "*	—	Ato Model Crafts	—	Shoulder-Wing	18/-
52½	20-MIN GLIDER*	E. Chasteneuf	Premier Aeromodel Supplies	Contest	Shoulder-Wing	19/4
56	WANDERER*	D. Cookson	Elite Model Airplane Supplies	Contest	Shoulder-Wing	11/1
60	SOARER MAJOR	C. H. Saunders	E. Keil & Co.	Cabin	—	11/6
60	CONTEST GLIDER*	R. H. Warring	Shaws Model Aircraft	Contest	Slabsider	10/6
60	BUZZARD*	—	Model Aircraft (Bournemouth)	Slabsider	High-Wing	13/6
60	PRINCE	C. T. Buffery	International Model Aircraft	Cabin	Streamliner	—
—	NORSEMAN	P. Guilmont	Mercury Models	Hatchet	A-Z Contest	17/6
—	GIPSY II	C. H. Phillips	Premier Aeromodel Supplies	Shoulderwing	—	15/10
64	CHIEF	W. A. Dean	E. Keil & Co.	Cabin	A-Z Contest	—
66	ALBATROSS	H. Austwick	Halfax Models	Cabin	High Aspect Ratio	25/-
84	WINDJAMMER*	R. Slcuer	Premier Aeromodel Supplies	Cabin	High Tailplane	30/-
94	ALBATROSS II*	R. Munney	Luton Model Aircraft Supplies	Contest	High Aspect Ratio	36/-

* No longer in production.

RUBBER-DRIVEN MODEL KITS

This table has been compiled to include all rubber model kits produced between 1948 and the present date, June, 1950, but restricted to sport and contest types only. Flying scale models are not included. Whilst every effort has been made to make these data as complete as possible we can accept no responsibility for errors or omissions.

Span in.	Model	Weight oz.	Designer	Manufacturer	Type	Specification	Price
15	PICKANINNY	—		Aeromodels	Slabsider	High Wing	6/3
15	GILEY	—	C. A. Shaw	Shaws Model Aircraft	Cabin	High Wing	3/9
16	MIDGE	—		Elite Model Airplane Supplies	Slabsider	High Wing	2/6
16	SNARGASHER	—	D. Jackson	J's Model Centre	Biplane	Stick Fuselage	5/-
16	SKYROVA	—		British Model Aircraft	Slabsider	High Wing	1/6
18	LITTLE GEM	—		Premier	Slabsider	—	2/6
18	SAURUS	—		Aeromodels	Solid	Flying Wing	4/-
18	JUNIOR	—	A. H. Lee	Model Airport (Bristol)	Slabsider	High Wing	4/11
19	SKAT	—		Don Models	Slabsider	High Wing	3/6
20	ELF	—		Elite Model Airplane Supplies	Slabsider	High Wing	4/3
20	PIXIE	—		"	—	—	4/3
20	BEE	—		"	—	—	4/3
20	WINNER	—	C. H. Saunders	Worcraft	Cabin	High Wing	3/6
20	PLAYBOY	—	W. A. Dean	E. Keil & Co.	Cabin	High Wing	3/3
20	MINOR	—		Halfax	Slabsider	High Wing	3/3
20	GOBLIN	1½	P. H. Smith	Model Aircraft (Bournemouth)	Diamond	Shoulder Wing	3/3
20	SNIPE	1¾	P. H. Smith	Model Aircraft (Bournemouth)	Cabin	High Wing	5/-
20	GNAT Mk I	2	T. R. Kennedy	Model Shop (Newcastle)	Cabin	High Wing	4/6
21	PUP	—	A. H. Lee	Model Airport (Bristol)	Slabsider	High Wing	5/9
21	ZIP	—		Paramount	Cabin	High Wing	6/6
21	SKYLARK	1	P. H. Smith	Model Aircraft (Bournemouth)	Cabin	High Wing	4/6
22	ATO "22"	—		Ato Model Crafts	Slabsider	High Wing	5/6
22	GREYHOUND	—		M.S.S.			
22	FALCON	—		British Model Aircraft	Cabin	High Wing	3/6
22	FANTAIL	1¾	P. H. Smith	Model Aircraft (Bournemouth)	Shoulder Wing	Pusher	5/-
23	ORION	—	A. Hatfull	E. Keil & Co.	Slabsider	Shoulder Wing	3/6
24	ACHILLES	—	L. Heath	E. Keil & Co.	Cabin	High Wing	4/-
24	EAGLET	—	W. A. Dean	E. Keil & Co.	Cabin	High Wing	4/6
24	GOBLIN	—	C. T. Buffery	International Model Aircraft	Cabin	High Wing	4/9
24	FLEDGELING	2¼	P. H. Smith	Model Aircraft (Bournemouth)	Slabsider	High Wing	6/9
24	RASCAL	1¾	P. H. Smith	Model Aircraft (Bournemouth)	Cabin	High Wing	4/6
24	MIDGE	2¼	F. R. Kennedy	Model Shop (Newcastle)	Low Wing	Semi-scale	5/6
24	SPRITE	—	E. A. Ross	International Model Aircraft	Slabsider	High Wing	—
24	COMMANDO	—		Halfax	Slabsider	High Wing	5/-
24	SCOOTER	—	L. Heath	Southern Junior Aircraft	Parasol	Diamond Fuselage	4/-
24	PETREL	—		Elite Model Airplane Supplies	Cabin	High Wing	6/-
24	CADET	—		British Model Aircraft	Slabsider	High Wing	5/6
24	HAWK	—		British Model Aircraft	Cabin	High Wing	4/6
24	ROVA	—		Worcraft	Cabin	High Wing	4/11
24	SKIPPER	—		Don Models	Cabin	High Wing	4/6
26	ALPHA	—		Chingford Model Aerodrome	Cabin	High Wing	10/6
26	GNAT Mk II	3	T. R. Kennedy	Model Shop (Newcastle)	Cabin	High Wing	6/6
26	SPUPSTER	1⅝		Model Shop (Newcastle)	Parasol	Semi-scale	10/6
29	SKYROCKET	—	C. H. Saunders	Elite Model Airplane Supplies	Parasol	Slabsider	7/-
30	AJAX	—	L. Heath	E. Keil & Co.	Cabin	High Wing	6/-
30	MAJOR	—		Halfax	Slabsider	High Wing	5/6
30	KEELBILD	3½		Model Shop (Newcastle)	Parasol	Streamliner	14/6
30	DRAGONFLY	1⅞		Model Shop (Newcastle)	Cabin	High Wing	10/6
30	CABIN COUPE	3		Model Shop (Newcastle)	Cabin	High Wing	12/6
30	CRUISER PUP	—	C. A. Rippon	Premier	Cabin	Low Wing	9/11
30	SATURN	—	J. R. Vanderbeek	International Model Aircraft	Cabin	Semi-scale	10/6
30	CAVALIER	—		British Model Aircraft	Parasol	Slabsider	5/6
30	EAGER BEAVER	—	I. Lewis	Shaw's Model Aircraft	Parasol	Slabsider	10/6
30	BABY DURATION	—	C. A. Bowden	Worcraft	Cabin	High Wing	10/6
30	LYNX CUB	—		M.S.S.			
30	WIDGET	—		Don Models	Parasol	Diamond Fuselage	6/9
30	PHANTOM	—		Avlon			10/-
31	LINNET	—	A. H. Lee	Model Airport (Bristol)	Slabsider	High Wing	9/6
32	PHANTOM	—		Elite Model Airplane Supplies	—	Flying Wing	5/6
32	PYM	—		Don Models	Slabsider	High Wing	6/-
32	COMPETITOR	—	W. A. Dean	E. Keil & Co.	Cabin	High Wing	7/-
33	JUNIOR CONTEST	—		Elite Model Airplane Supplies	Slabsider	—	10/-
34	SENTINEL	2⅝	P. H. Smith	Model Aircraft (Bournemouth)	Cabin	High Wing	10/-
34	PARATROUPER	—		Masco	Cabin	High Wing	12/6
34	MONITOR	—		Airyda	Slabsider	—	8/6
35	MAJOR PUP	—	C. A. Rippon	Premier	Cabin	Low Wing	13/4
36	WITCH	—	C. T. Buffery	International Model Aircraft	Hex. Fuselage	High Wing	—
36	JAKE	—		Power Models	—	—	13/6
36	CLUB CONTEST	—		Model Aerodrome	Slabsider	High Wing	12/-
36	SETTER	—	A. H. Lee	Model Airport (Bristol)	Slabsider	Low Wing	13/9
36	THERMAL KING	—	A. H. Dadd	A. E. Peters	Slabsider	—	12/6
36	JUPITER	—	C. T. Buffery	International Model Aircraft	Cabin	Low Wing	15/-
36	LANCER	—		Halfax	Slabsider	High Wing	15/-
36	QUESTER	—		Southern Junior Aircraft	—	—	10/6
37	STARDUST	—	J. R. Vanderbeek	International Model Aircraft	Parasol	Slabsider	10/6
37	ST. GEORGE	—	C. A. Rippon	Premier	Parasol	Diamond Fuselage	21/-
37½	AIR CADET	—	C. A. Rippon	Premier	Slabsider	High Wing	15/4
37¾	NORTHERN STAR	4¼	R. Copland	Premier	Slabsider	High Wing	19/4
38	HI-CLIMBER	8¼	P. H. Smith	Model Aircraft (Bournemouth)	Cabin-pylon	Slabsider	25/-
38	PANDA	—		M.S.S.			
38	VENUS	—	A. A. Judge	International Model Aircraft	Shoulder Wing	Streamliner	15/-
40	GIPSY	8	W. A. Dean	E. Keil & Co.	Cabin	High Wing	10/6*
40	DURACADET	5	C. A. Rippon	Premier	Slabsider	High Wing	21/-
40	NORTHERN ARROW	5	I. Hall	Premier	Slabsider	High Wing	19/4
40	LIBRA	5	C. A. Rippon	Premier	Shoulder Wing	—	19/4
40	SENIOR	—		Airyda	—	—	9/6
40	DROME	—		Model Aerodrome	Cabin	High Wing	12/6
40	BETA	—		Chingford Model Aerodrome	Slabsider	High Wing	17/6
40¼	LYNX	—		M.S.S.	—	—	—
40¼	G.H.91	8¼	G. W. W. Harris	Cartwrights	Slabsider	High Wing	12/6
42	STRATOSPHERE	6	A. E. Ross	International Model Aircraft	Parasol	Streamliner	17/6
44	KORDA	8	R. Korda	British Model Aircraft	Cabin	High Wing	17/6
44	JAGUAR	8¼	E. W. Evans	Halfax	Mid-wing	Diamond Fuselage	21/-
44	TAURUS	8¼	R. H. Warring	Astral	Cabin	High Wing	21/-
45	G.B.3.	9	R. Copland	Premier	Streamliner	Shoulder Wing	33/6
45	MASTERPLANE	6	R. Copland	Premier	Stream-slabsider	Shoulder Wing	32/-
45	MASTER	—		Airyda	Slabsider	—	22/6
45¼	WARRING'S WAKEFIELD	8¼	R. H. Warring	Paramount	Stream-slabsider	Shoulder Wing	29/6
45¼	CONTESTOR	8	W. A. Dean	E. Keil & Co.	Cabin	High Wing	23/6
46	CLIPPER	8	E. W. Evans	Super Model Aircraft Supplies	Diamond	Shoulder Wing	8/6†
48	FLYING MINUTES	8	L. Stott & N. Lees	Halfax	Streamliner	Parasol	21/-
50	SUPER CRUISER	12	C. A. Rippon	Premier	Cabin	Low Wing	29/3
52	Q. CUP WINNER	12	P. H. Smith	Model Aircraft (Bournemouth)	Cabin-pylon	High Wing	10/-†

* Dry Kit. † Plan and printed sheet only.

FREE-FLIGHT POWER KITS

Whilst every care has been taken to make these tables as complete as possible, up to March, 1950, no responsibility can be taken for omissions or errors contained therein.

Span in.	Kit	Price	Manufacturer	Type	Class	Suitable Motors (Design motors in bold type)
30	ZEPHYR	10 6	E. Law & Sons	Pylon	A	**Frog 100**
31	JUNIOR ZIPPER	14 6	British Model Aircraft	Hatchet Fuselage	A	**E.D. Bee**, Mills II, etc.
32	AIRFLO MITE	8 6	Shaw's Model Aircraft	Cabin-Pylon	A	**Amco .87**, Mills .75
32	SOUTHERNER MITE	11 6	E. Keil & Co.	Cabin	A	**Mills .75**, Amco .87
32	SLICKER MITE	10 6	E. Keil & Co.	Developed Pylon	A	**Mills .75**, Amco .87, CO₂
33	TRIUMPH "33"	16/-	Aeromodels	Pylon	A	**Frog 100**, E.D. Bee, Mills .75, Amco .87
34	PIRATE	13 6	E. Keil & Co.	Cabin	A	**E.D. Bee**, Amco .87, Mills .75, Arrow
35	SCARAB	15 -	Worcraft	Shoulder Wing	A	Amco .87, Mills .75, E.D. Bee, Frog 100
36	YOLANDE	10 6	E. Law & Sons	Cabin	A	E.D. Bee, Mills .75, Mills II, etc.
36	MARTINET‡	21 -	Model Aircraft (Bournemouth)	Cabin	A	Mills .75, Mills II, E.D. Bee, etc.
36	VIXEN	12 6	International Model Aircraft	Cabin	A	Mills .75, Amco .87, E.D. Bee, Frog 100
34	FIREFLY	*	International Model Aircraft	Biplane	A	**Frog 100**, 160, 180, Mills II, E.D. Bee, Javelin, Arrow
37	STREAKER	19 9	Model Aircraft (Bournemouth)	Pylon	A	Amco .87, Mills .75, E.D. Bee, Frog 100, Javelin, Arrow
40	HELL'S ANGEL	15 -	Shaw's Model Aircraft	Pylon	A	Frog 100, E.D. Bee, Mills II, Frog 100, Javelin, Arrow
40	ENVOY	14 9	Shaw's Model Aircraft	Cabin, Tricycle U/C.	A	**E.D. Bee**, Amco .87, Mills .75, Mills II, Javelin, Arrow
40	FOX	*	International Model Aircraft	Pylon	A	**Frog 100**, Amco .87, Mills .75, E.D. Bee, Mills II, Javelin, Arrow
41½	HERMES	15 6	Halfax Models	Cabin	A	E.D. Bee, Mills II, Mills .75, Javelin, Arrow, Frog 100
42	SOUTHERN DRAGON	25/-	Southern Junior Aircraft	Cabin	A	**Mills II**, E.D. Bee, Frog 100, 160, 180
42	HORNET	19 6	Model Shop (Newcastle)	Semi-Scale Parasol	A	**Mills .75**, Amco .87, E.D. Bee, Mills II, Javelin, Arrow
42	WASP	22 6	Model Shop ,, ,,	Biplane Version of Hornet	A	**Mills .75**, Amco .87, E.D. Bee, Mills II, Javelin, Arrow
42	STRATO-D	15/-	International Model Aircraft	Pylon	A	Frog 100, 160, 180, E.D. Bee, Mills II, Elfin 1.5
42	SLICKER	22 6	E. Keil & Co.	Developed Pylon	A	**Mills II**, E.D. Bee, Frog 100, 160, 180, Elfin 1.5
44	SCORPION	37 6	E. Keil & Co.	Cabin	A-B	Mills II, E.D. Comp., Allbon, Elfin, etc.
44	AIRFLO BABY	18 6	Shaw's Model Aircraft	Cabin-Pylon	A	**Mills II**, Frog 100, 160, 180, E.D. Bee
44	BANTAM	25 -	British Model Aircraft	Cabin	A-B	Mills II, Mills 2.49, E.D. Comp., etc.
44	JANUS	15 -	International Model Aircraft	Shoulder Wing	A	**Frog 100**, 160, 180, E.D. Bee, Javelin, Arrow, Elfin 1.5
44	ZIPPER	21 -	British Model Aircraft	Hatchet Fuselage	A-B	E.D. Comp., Mills 2.49, Allbon, etc.
44	BANDIT	21/-	E. Keil & Co.	Cabin	A-B	Mills 2.49, E.D. Comp., E.D. III, etc.
45	HAMMERHEAD	14 6	Shaw's Model Aircraft	Hatchet Fuselage	A-B	E.D. Comp., Mills 2.49, Elfin, Allbon
45	FROG "45"	27 6	International Model Aircraft	Cabin	A	Frog 100, 160, 180, Mills II, E.D. Bee, Javelin, Arrow, Elfin 1.5
48	MALLARD	*	Mercury Model Aircraft Supplies	Pylon	A	Elfin 2.49, Elfin 1.5, Mills 2.49, E.D. III, Amco 3.5, Javelin, Arrow, Elfin 1.8
48	RAPIER	22 6	Halfax Models	Hatchet Fuselage	A-B	E.D. Comp., E.D. III, Elfin, Mills 2.49, etc.
48	POWAVAN	25/-	International Model Aircraft	Pylon : High Thrust	A	**Frog 100**, 160, 180, Mills II, Javelin, Arrow, E.D. Bee
48	CIRRUS	*	International Model Aircraft	Pylon	A	**Frog 160**, 180, 250, Mills II, Javelin, Arrow, Elfin 1.5, Elfin 1.8
50	SLICKER "50"	32 6	E. Keil & Co.	Developed Pylon	A-B	E.D. II, E.D. III, E.D. Comp. Allbon, Elfin 2.49, Mills 2.49
50	OUTLAW	27 6	E. Keil & Co.	Cabin	A-B	E.D. Comp., Elfin, Allbon, E.D. III, etc.
54	PACEMAKER	37 6	Premier Aeromodel Supplies	Cabin	A-B	Mills 2.49, E.D. III, Allbon, etc.
59	CUMULUS	*	E. Keil & Co.	Developed Pylon	B-C	Eta 19, Mills 2.49, E.D. III and IV, Frog 500
60	SPARTAN	45 -	Halfax Models	Cabin	A-B	Mills 2.49, E.D. III, Allbon, etc.
60	CENTURION†	59 6	International Model Aircraft	Cabin	A-B	Frog 180, 250, Mills 2.49, etc.
60	SUPER SLICKER	47 6	E. Keil & Co.	Developed Pylon	A-B	Mills 2.49, etc., up to Frog 500
60	SOUTHERNER†	47 6	E. Keil & Co.	Cabin	A-B	**Mills 2.49**, E.D. III, Eta, Yulon, Frog 500
60	JUNIOR "60"†	39 6	E. Keil & Co.	Cabin		E.D. III, Wildcat, Frog 500, E.D. IV, Eta 29, Yukon
72	STENTORIAN†	69 6	Model Aircraft (Bournemouth)	Cabin	B-C	Frog 500, Yulon, etc.
90	RADIO QUEEN†	98 6	Electronic Developments	Cabin	B-C	E.D. IV, etc.
96	FALCON†	117 6	E. Keil & Co.	Cabin	C	Nordec, Rowell, etc.

* Price not yet announced.   † Suitable for Radio Control.   ‡ Convertible to Control-line.

FREE-FLIGHT POWER KITS FOR JETEX MOTORS

Span in.	Kit	Price	Manufacturer	Type	Jetex Motor	Span in.	Kit	Price	Manufacturer	Type	Jetex Motor
18	Min-o-Jet	3/-	Veron	Solid	50	30	Air-o-Jet	7 6	Veron	Pod & Boom	100
18	Skyjet "50"	3/9	Keilkraft	,,	50	32	Skyjet 200	7 6	Keilkraft	,,	200
21	Mijet	5/6	Jetex	,,	50	33	Widjet	6 6	Southern Jun. Aircraft	,,	200
24	Skyjet "100"	5/6	Keilkraft	Pod & Boom	100	35	Cir-o-Jet	10 6	Veron	,,	200
26	Flying Wing	5/-	Jetex	Tailless	50 or 100	36	Durajet	14/6	Jetex	Parasol	350

SPEED AND TEAM RACER KITS
Compiled to December, 1950

Class		Span(ins.)	Model	Designer	Manufacturer	Price	Motor
Speed III	...	12	Speedwagon 20	H. deBolt	Mercury Models	12/6	Amco 3.5, E.D. III
„ V	...	15	„ 30	„	„ „	14/6	Yulon 29, Frog 500, Eta 29
„ V-VI	...	20	„ 60	„	„ „	29/6	Yulon 49, Nordec
„ I	...	12	Midge	C. A. Shaw	„ „	5/6	Javelin, Arrow, Elfin 1.49
„ I	...	18	Orbit	—	E. Law & Sons		Mills II, Javelin, Elfin 1.49
„ I	...	18	Sabre	J. T. London	Halfax Models	16/6	Mills II, Javelin, Elfin 1.49
Team A	...	24	Ranger	W. A. Dean	E. Keil & Co.	—	Elfin 1.49, Javelin, Elfin 2.49, etc.
„ A-B	...	24	Midget Mustang	P. C. Smith	Model Aircraft (Bournemouth)	21/-	Amco 3.5, All motors 1-5 c.c.
„ B	...	24	Mk. I	J. Nunn	Mercury Models	17/6	Frog 500, 2.5-5 c.c.
„ B	...	20	Scout	W. A. Dean	E. Keil & Co.	22/6	Eta 29, Amco 3.5, Yulon 29, Frog 500
„ B	...	25½	Philibuster	P. L. Smith	Model Aircraft (Bournemouth)	—	Amco 3.5, 2.5-5 c.c.

STUNT CONTROL LINE KITS

The following tables have been compiled to include all current stock and production kit models, as up to April, 1950. Whilst every effort has been made to ensure that these tables are as complete as possible we can take no responsibility for any errors or omissions. Allocation into the two main groups—Stunt and Sport—has been based on our own estimates of performance. The fact that a particular design is included in the "Sport" category does not necessarily mean that it is not stuntable, but rather that the model has been designed for sport flying rather than pure aerobatics. We should also like to point out that no flying scale models are included. These will be the subject of a later survey.

Whilst every care has been taken to make these tables as complete as possible, up to March, 1950, no responsibility can be taken for omissions or errors contained therein.

Span	Kit	Price	Manufacturer	Type	Max. Line Length	Suitable Motors (Design motors in heavy type)
20	COMET	11/6	British Model Aircraft	Low Wing	—	E.D. Bee, Mills II, Frog 100-160, 180, etc.
22	BEE BUG	11/6	Model Aircraft (Bournemouth)	Semi-scale	—	E.D. Bee, Mills .75, Amco .57, Mills II, etc.
24	STUNTER	19/6	„ „ „	Biplane	45-50 ft.	Mills II, Javelin, Frog 160, etc.
24	AEROBAT	10/6	Super Screw	Low Wing	—	0.75 c.c.-1.8 c.c.
24	SWIFT	25/-	Airyda	Biplane	—	Elfin 1.8, Frog 160, Javelin, etc.
25	DRAGONFLY	23/6	Premier	Biplane	70 ft.	Eta 29, Elfin 2.4, E.D. III, E.D. IV, Amco 3.5.
26	DE BOLT S-BIPE.	29/6	Mercury	Biplane	70 ft.	Eta 29, E.D.IV, Yulon, Frog, etc.
26	VANDIVER	12/6	International Model Aircraft	Mid-Wing S S	55 ft.	Frog 100, 150, Elfin 1.8, etc.
26	SKYSTREAK "76"	9/6*	Keil	Low Wing S S	—	E.D. Bee, Amco .57, Mills .75, etc.
26	NIFTY	12/6	Don Models	Low Wing	—	E.D. Comp, Elfin 1.8, Elfin 2.4, etc.
26	MARLIN MITE	14/6	Mercury	Low Wing S/S	—	E.D. Bee, Amco .87, Mills .75
28	DERUSH	19/6	Shaws Model Aircraft	Semi-Scale	55 ft.	Mills II, Elfin 1.8, Frog 160, Javelin, etc.
28	SOUTHERN STOOGE	18/6	Southern Junior Aircraft	Low Wing	55 ft.	Mills II, Elfin 1.8, Frog 100, Javelin, etc.
28½	SUPALUPA	25/-	Aeromodels	Pod & Boom	—	E.D. Comp, Elfin 1.8, Elfin 2.4, etc.
29	KAN DOO	25/-	Kan Doo Products	Profile	55 ft.	E.D. Comp, Elfin 2.4, Mills 2.4, etc.
30	STUNTMASTER	19/6	Keil	Profile	60 ft.	Mills II, All 1.5, 3.5 c.c.
30	JNR. MONITOR	14/6	Mercury	L/W Short Coupled	60 ft.	Elfin 2.49, etc.
30	WILDCAT	30/-	Davis-Charlton	Low Wing	—	Wildcat, Frog 500, E.D. IV, Eta 29, Yulon.
30	PLAYBOY	17/6	Shaws Model Aircraft	Mid Wing	55 ft.	Mills II, Elfin 1.5, Javelin Arrow etc.
31	SKYLARK	17/6	Roadway Models	Mid Wing	70 ft.	Elfin 1.8 up to Amco 3.5.
32	MILLS BOMB II	18/6	Halfax	Low Wing	55 ft.	Mills II, Elfin, Javelin, etc.
32	MARLIN	19/6	Mercury	L/W Semi-Scale	60 ft.	Elfin 1.8, Frog 160, Elfin 2.9, etc.
36	BABET	25/-	Super Screw	Low Wing S S	—	Amco 3.5, E.D. IV, Eta 19, etc.
37½	STUNT KING	18/6	Keil	High Wing	70 ft.	Yulon, Frog 500, Eta 29.
38	MONITOR	27/6	Mercury	L/W Short Coupled	70 ft.	Amco 3.5, E.D. IV, Yulon, Eta 29, Frog 500.
40	VANFIRE	—	International Model Aircraft	Mid Wing S/S	70 ft.	Frog 500, Yulon 29, E.D. IV, Eta 29.
40	SKYSTREAK "40"	10/6†	Keil	Low Wing S/S	70 ft.	Frog 500, Yulon, Eta 29.
40	MUSKETEER	19/S	Mercury	L/W Short Coupled	70 ft.	Frog 500, Yulon, Eta 29.

* Dry kit.   † Basic kit.

SPORT CONTROL LINE KITS

Span	Kit	Price	Manufacturer	Type	Max. Line Length	Suitable Motors (Design motor in heavy type)
—	SHUFTI	10/6	Astral		—	0.75-1.5 c.c.
16	PHANTOM MITE	11/6	Keil	Low Wing S/S	35 ft.	Amco .87, 0.75-1.5 c.c.
17	NIPPER	9/6	Model Aircraft (Bournemouth)	Low Wing S/S	35 ft.	Amco .87, 0-75-1.5 c.c.
18	NANCY	14/6	J's	High Wing	—	Mills II, 1-2 c.c.
18	NANCY BIPLANE	15/6	J's	Biplane	—	1.2 c.c.
18	SWALLOW	12/-	Airyda	—	—	1-2 c.c.
18	PUSHER PUP	19/6	Don Models	Pusher	—	Amco .57, 0.75-2.c.c.
18	NIPPER	13/6	Roadway Models	—	—	1-2.5 c.c.
20	SCOUT	22/6	Keil	Biplane	35 ft.	Mills II, 1-2 c.c.
21	PHANTOM	18/6	Keil	Low Wing S, S	35 ft.	Mills II, 1-2.5 c.c.
22	RADIUS	17/6	International Model Aircraft	Mid Wing	—	Frog 100, 1-2.5 c.c.
—	WIZARD	17/6	Shaws Model Aircraft	High Wing	45 ft.	Mills II, 1-2.5 c.c.
22	RIVAL	10/6	Don Models	High Wing	—	Mills II, 1-2.5 c.c.
—	SWIFT	25/-		Biplane	—	E.D. Comp, 1.5-2.5 c.c.
22	MINX	25/-	Normans	Low Wing S S	—	E.D. Comp, 1.5-2.5 c.c.
23½	RINGMASTER	25/-	Royles	Biplane	—	E.D. Comp, 1.5-2.5 c.c.
—	GOBLIN	15/-	Shaws Model Aircraft	Shoulder Wing	45 ft.	Mills II, 1.0-2.5 c.c.
24	SPEEDEE	17/6	Model Aircraft (Bournemouth)	Twin Boom Pusher	45 ft.	Mills II, 1.0-2.5 c.c.
26½	MONARCH	17/6	Wurcraft	Low Wing S/S	45 ft.	E.D. Comp, 1.8-3.0 c.c.
26¾	MAGNETTE	25/-	Mercury	Mid-Wing S/S	45 ft.	E.D. Comp, 1.8-3.0 c.c.
29	TRAINER	20/-	Halfax	Shoulder Wing	45 ft.	E.D. Comp, 2-3.5 c.c.
30	JINKER	†	Watkins	Low Wing	45 ft.	Mills II, 1.5-2.5 c.c.
30	THUNDERBIRD	22/6	British Model Aircraft	Mid Wing	—	E.D. Comp, 1.5-3.5 c.c.
33	ANITA	19/6	J's	Flying Wing	50 ft.	Elfin 1.8, 1.8-3.5 c.c.
36	FLYING WING	25/-	British Model Aircraft	Flying Wing	—	2-3.5 c.c.
45	GOSHAWK	79/6	Model Aircraft (Bournemouth)	Low Wing S/S	70 ft.	5-10 c.c.

† Plan pack.

1950

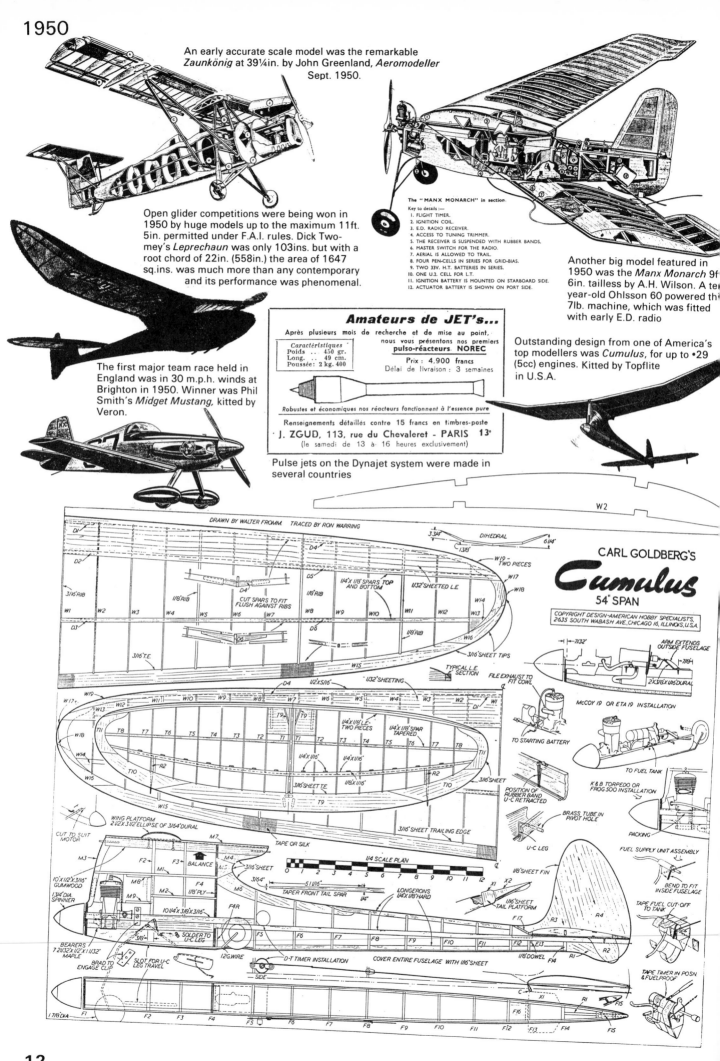

An early accurate scale model was the remarkable *Zaunkönig* at 39¼in. by John Greenland, *Aeromodeller* Sept. 1950.

The "MANX MONARCH" in section.
Key to details:—
1. FLIGHT TIMER.
2. IGNITION COIL.
3. E.D. RADIO RECEIVER.
4. ACCESS TO TUNING TRIMMER.
5. THE RECEIVER IS SUSPENDED WITH RUBBER BANDS.
6. MASTER SWITCH FOR THE RADIO.
7. AERIAL IS ALLOWED TO TRAIL.
8. FOUR PEN-CELLS IN SERIES FOR GRID-BIAS.
9. TWO 33V. H.T. BATTERIES IN SERIES.
10. ONE U.2. CELL FOR L.T.
11. IGNITION BATTERY IS MOUNTED ON STARBOARD SIDE.
12. ACTUATOR BATTERY IS SHOWN ON PORT SIDE.

Open glider competitions were being won in 1950 by huge models up to the maximum 11ft. 5in. permitted under F.A.I. rules. Dick Twomey's *Leprechaun* was only 103ins. but with a root chord of 22in. (558in.) the area of 1647 sq.ins. was much more than any contemporary and its performance was phenomenal.

Another big model featured in 1950 was the *Manx Monarch* 9f 6in. tailless by A.H. Wilson. A te year-old Ohlsson 60 powered th 7lb. machine, which was fitted with early E.D. radio

The first major team race held in England was in 30 m.p.h. winds at Brighton in 1950. Winner was Phil Smith's *Midget Mustang*, kitted by Veron.

Amateurs de JET's...
Après plusieurs mois de recherche et de mise au point, nous vous présentons nos premiers **pulso-réacteurs NOREC**

Caractéristiques	
Poids	450 gr.
Long.	49 cm.
Poussée	2 kg. 400

Prix : 4.900 francs
Délai de livraison : 3 semaines

Robustes et économiques nos réacteurs fonctionnent à l'essence pure

Renseignements détaillés contre 15 francs en timbres-poste
J. ZGUD, 113, rue du Chevaleret - PARIS 13ᵉ
(le samedi de 13 à 16 heures exclusivement!)

Pulse jets on the Dynajet system were made in several countries

Outstanding design from one of America's top modellers was *Cumulus*, for up to •29 (5cc) engines. Kitted by Topflite in U.S.A.

CARL GOLDBERG'S
Cumulus
54" SPAN

COPYRIGHT DESIGN-AMERICAN HOBBY SPECIALISTS, 2635 SOUTH WABASH AVE., CHICAGO 16, ILLINOIS, U.S.A.

DRAWN BY WALTER FROMM. TRACED BY RON WARRING

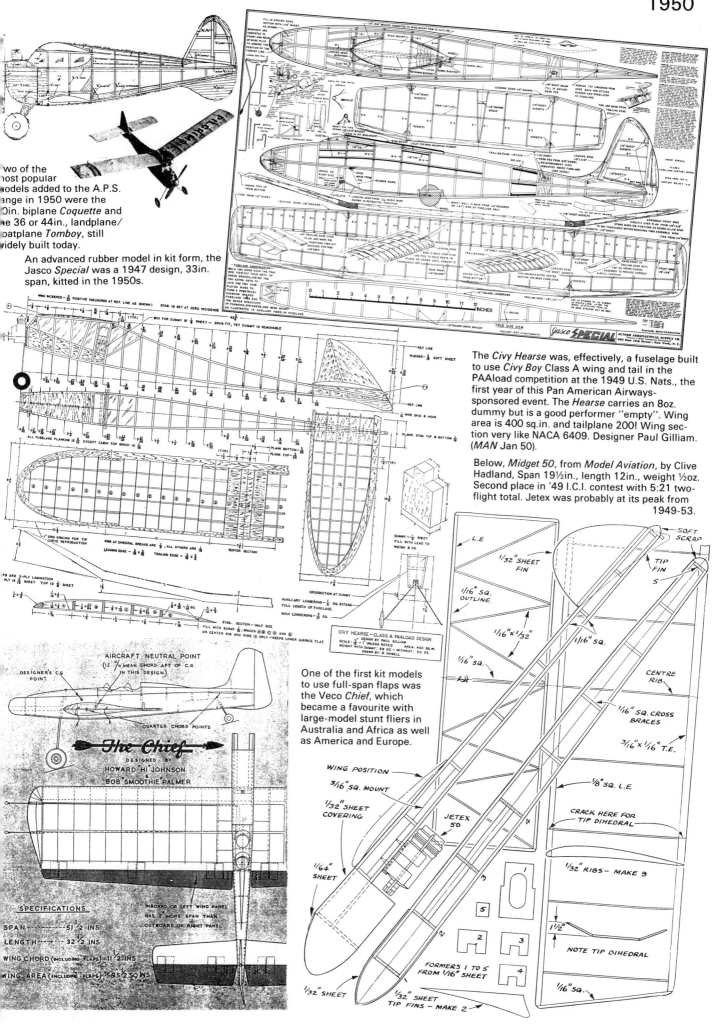

wo of the
most popular
models added to the A.P.S.
ange in 1950 were the
0in. biplane *Coquette* and
e 36 or 44in., landplane/
oatplane *Tomboy*, still
idely built today.

An advanced rubber model in kit form, the
Jasco *Special* was a 1947 design, 33in.
span, kitted in the 1950s.

The *Civy Hearse* was, effectively, a fuselage built
to use *Civy Boy* Class A wing and tail in the
PAAload competition at the 1949 U.S. Nats., the
first year of this Pan American Airways-
sponsored event. The *Hearse* carries an 8oz.
dummy but is a good performer ''empty''. Wing
area is 400 sq.in. and tailplane 200! Wing section very like NACA 6409. Designer Paul Gilliam.
(*MAN* Jan 50).

Below, *Midget 50*, from *Model Aviation*, by Clive
Hadland, Span 19½in., length 12in., weight ½oz.
Second place in '49 I.C.I. contest with 5:21 two-
flight total. Jetex was probably at its peak from
1949-53.

One of the first kit models
to use full-span flaps was
the Veco *Chief*, which
became a favourite with
large-model stunt fliers in
Australia and Africa as well
as America and Europe.

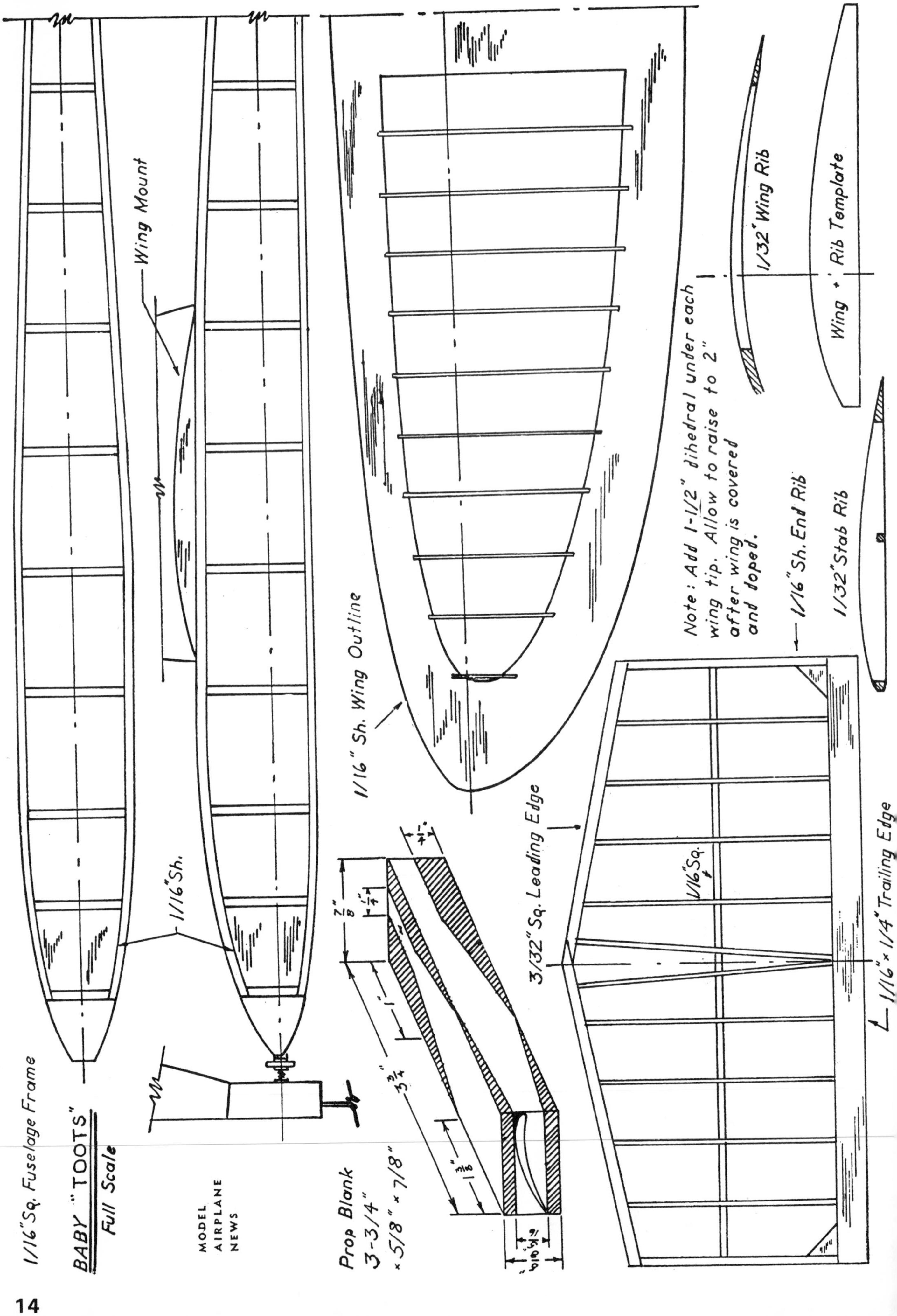

1/16"Sq. Fuselage Frame

BABY "TOOTS"
Full Scale

MODEL
AIRPLANE
NEWS

Wing Mount

1/16"Sh.

1/16 " Sh. Wing Outline

1/16" Sh. Wing Outline

Note: Add 1-1/2" dihedral under each wing tip. Allow to raise to 2" after wing is covered and doped.

1/32"Wing Rib

Wing ' Rib Template

1/16 "Sh. End Rib

1/32"Stab Rib

Prop Blank
3-3/4"
× 5/8" × 7/8"

7/8"

1/4"

1"

3 1/8"

3/4"

3 1/8"

9/16"

3/32" Sq. Leading Edge

1/16"Sq.

1/16" × 1/4" Trailing Edge

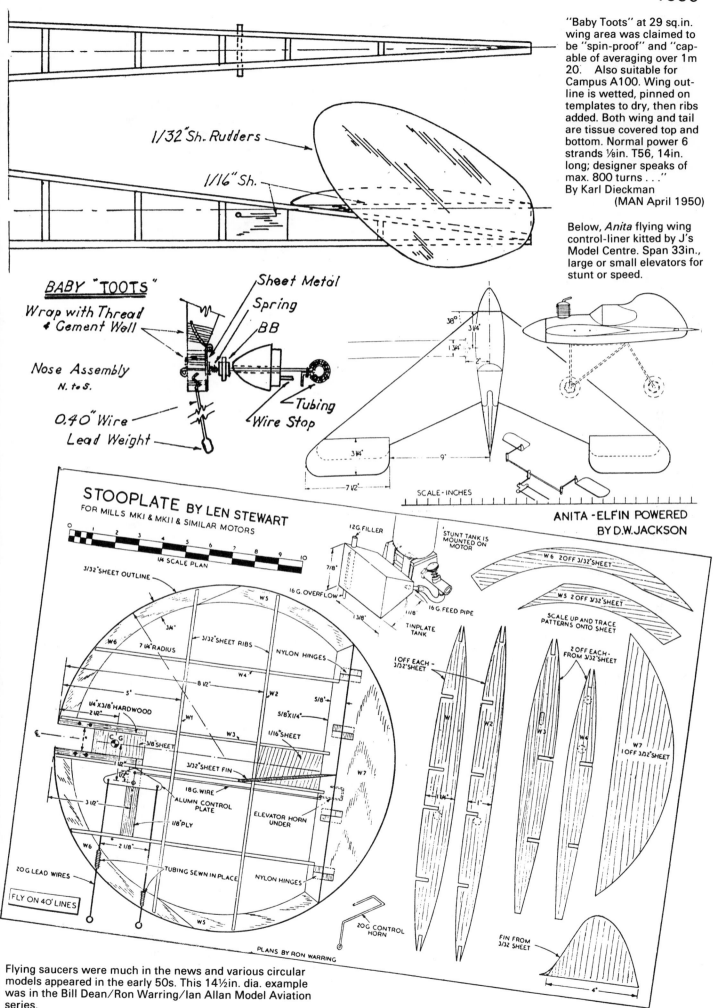

"Baby Toots" at 29 sq.in. wing area was claimed to be "spin-proof" and "capable of averaging over 1m 20. Also suitable for Campus A100. Wing outline is wetted, pinned on templates to dry, then ribs added. Both wing and tail are tissue covered top and bottom. Normal power 6 strands ⅛in. T56, 14in. long; designer speaks of max. 800 turns . . ." By Karl Dieckman
(MAN April 1950)

Below, *Anita* flying wing control-liner kitted by J's Model Centre. Span 33in., large or small elevators for stunt or speed.

1/32" Sh. Rudders

1/16" Sh.

BABY "TOOTS"

Wrap with Thread & Cement Well

Sheet Metal
Spring
BB

Nose Assembly
N. to S.

0.40" Wire
Lead Weight

Tubing
Wire Stop

ANITA - ELFIN POWERED
BY D.W. JACKSON

38°
3 1/4"
1 3/4"
2"
3 1/4"
9"
7 1/2"
SCALE - INCHES

STOOPLATE BY LEN STEWART
FOR MILLS MK.I & MK.II & SIMILAR MOTORS

1/4 SCALE PLAN

3/32" SHEET OUTLINE
W5
3/4"
W6
7 1/4" RADIUS
3/32" SHEET RIBS
NYLON HINGES
W4
8 1/2"
W2
5/8"
5"
5/8" X 1/4"
1/4" X 3/8" HARDWOOD
2 1/2"
W1
W3
1/16" SHEET
1/8" SHEET
3/32" SHEET FIN
18 G. WIRE
ALUMN CONTROL PLATE
1/8" PLY
W7
3 1/2"
ELEVATOR HORN UNDER
W6
2 1/8"
20 G. LEAD WIRES
TUBING SEWN IN PLACE
NYLON HINGES
FLY ON 40' LINES
W5
PLANS BY RON WARRING

12 G. FILLER
7/8"
16 G. OVERFLOW
1 3/8"
'STUNT TANK IS MOUNTED ON MOTOR
1/8"
16 G. FEED PIPE
TINPLATE TANK

W6 2 OFF 3/32" SHEET
W5 2 OFF 3/32" SHEET
SCALE UP AND TRACE PATTERNS ONTO SHEET

1 OFF EACH - 3/32" SHEET
2 OFF EACH - FROM 3/32" SHEET
W1
W2
1 1/4"
1"
W3
W4
W7 1 OFF 3/32" SHEET

20 G. CONTROL HORN

FIN FROM 3/32" SHEET
4"

Flying saucers were much in the news and various circular models appeared in the early 50s. This 14½in. dia. example was in the Bill Dean/Ron Warring/Ian Allan Model Aviation series.

1950

American Kits

The following lists are of U.S.-produced kits which *were being advertised* at the beginning of 1950, grouped into Glider, Rubber, Control-line, Pee Wee and Free Flight categories. Each group is also broken down into manufacturers; mail order houses frequently omitted manufacturers and each category therefore ends with a list of unidentified models, where time has not permitted us to confirm the makers of kits appearing only in mail order lists. Some advertisers do not even include the span or other indication of model size, especially for U-control models, where engine classification was obviously felt sufficient information.

Advertisements at the time tended to list kits for the relatively new "pee wee" or ½A motors separately and this practice has been followed. Flying scale rubber kits have not been detailed, only the number in a range, to save space.

Motor categories in cubic inches and rounded cubic centimetre equivalents are: A •19cu.in. (3•2cc), B •29 (5•0), C •49 (8•0) and D •61 (10). AA or ½A included up to •099 (1•6) but this tended to sub-divide into •020 (•32), •049 (•8) and •061 (1•0).

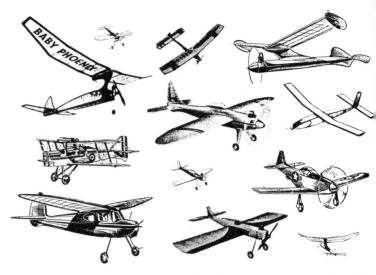

GLIDERS

	span, ins.
Berkeley Sinbad	50
Super-Sinbad	62
Cleveland Condor	72
Eaglet	48
Baby Condor	36
Albatros	120
Jasco Thermic 20	20
Thermic 30	30
Thermic 50	50
Thermic 70	70
Thermic 72	72
Thermic 100	100
Trooper	40
Sailwing	50
Floater	72
Scientific Zenith	33
Imperial	72

RUBBER

Berkeley

Buccaneer Junior	26
Musketeer Junior	26
Flying Cloud Junior	26
Chieftain	26
Powerhouse Junior	26
Brigadier Junior	26
Skybuggy Junior	26
Sportsman	30
American Ace	30
Buccaneer	30
Conqueror	30
Executive	40
Flying Cloud	44

Plus nine rubber scale mostly around 35in. including Henry Struck's Nationals-winning Interstate Cadet and Stinson Sentinel.

Capitol

Five scale rubber, most 30in.

Cartercraft

Three WWI models 12-14in.

Cleveland

Fleetster	32
Lancer	30
Thermalier	30
Sixteen f.s.r. at	30in.
Seven f.s.r. at	36in.
Eight f.s.r. assorted	18-29in.
Six f.s.r. at	20in.
Thunderjet	16
Stinson Station Wagon	43
B26 Marauder	48
P61 Black Widow	49
B25 Mitchell	55
Douglas DC3	70

Comet

Eight f.s.r. ca.	15in.
Eight f.s.r.	20in.
Piper Cub	40
Taylorcraft	54
Dipper	20
Skyrocket	20
Stratus	20
Sparky	32

Jasco

Thermal Traveller	36
Thermal Cruiser	36
Special	33
Kid	–
Senior	–
Junior	–
R.O.G.	12
Modelcraft Pacific Ace	30

Monogram

Six f.s.r. at	18in.
Prowler	28
Pirate	31

Miniature Aircraft Corp.

Stearman PT17	22
Curtiss Hawk FIIC4	32
Grumman F3FI	32
Grumman Hellcat	42
Vought Corsair	40
Seversky P35	32
P&C Cookie	24

Scientific

Windsor	25
Hornet	25
Ranger	25
Major	25
Bantam	25
Royal	25
Thunderbolt	25
Mustang	30
Cub Grasshopper	30
All American	45
Spartan	42
Zephyr	42
Olympic	42
Victory	32
Gold Star	32
Clarion	30
Miss World's Fair	30
Miss World's Fair	50
Whippet	30
Bullet	30
Yellowbird	30
Miss America	40
Firefly	36
Flea	36

CONTROL-LINE KITS

A.H.S.

Glo-bug	A-B-C	27
Nifty	A-B-C	23
Trainee	B	30
Zing	B-C-D	24
A-J. Fireball	B-C-D	36

Berkeley

Bat	C-D	32
Bearcat	C-D	35
Bee	B	24
Bug	A	17
Buster	B-C	24
Cessna	A-B	36
Hawker Super Fury	A-B	24
Key	B-C	29

Key – Det	A	18
Lil' Duper Zilch	A-B	42
Minnow	A-B-C	28
Navion	A	25
P-47 Thunderbolt	C-D	40
P-51 Mustang	A-B	37
Pee Wee Zilch	A	32
Senor Puddle Jumper	A	25
Super Squirt	Jet	21
Super Duper Zilch	C-D	52
Super Zilch	C-D	52
Swee' Pea Racer	A-B-C	24
T28 Trainer	A-B	30
Cavacraft Fly Boy	A-B	24

Cleveland

Tether Streak	C-D	22
Topper II	A-B	16
Topper III	B-C	20

Comet

Flying Circus	B	28
Piper Cub	A-B	35
Rookie Trainer	B-C-D	36

Consolidated

Hell Razor	C-D	17
Hell Razor	B	14
Hell Razor	A	14
Contest Craft So Lo	A-B	–

Dmeco

Bipe Stunt Trainer	B-C-D	22
Special	C-D	24
Special Junior	A-B-C	16
Speedwagon 20	A	12
Speedwagon 30	B	15
Speedwagon	C-D	19
Sportwing	A-B-C	36
Stuntwagon 30	B-C	44
Stuntwagon	D	58
Super Bipe	B-C-D	28

Drone

Dronette	A-B	–
Guided Missile	A-B	36
Hot Rock	A-B	–
Navion	A-B	–
Secret Weapon	A-B	–

Duro-Matic

Invader	A	11
Invader	B	17

Enterprise

Baby Era	A	18
New Era	A-B-C	28
Phantom	A-B	28
Pirate	B-C-D	40
Tuckette	C-D	38

F. & B.

Baby Skybox	A-B	36
Piper Vagabond	A-B-C	36
Skybox Stunt	B-C-D	42
Skybox Trainer	B-C-D	36
Super Skybox Stunt	C-D	47

Guillow

Trixter Invert Junior	A-B	40
Trixter Invert Profile	B	28
Trixter Profile	A-B	32
Trixter Profile	B-C	38
Trixter Trainer	A-B	25

Miniature Aircraft Corp.

Curtiss P-40	B-C	48
Fokker D8	B-C	39
Piper Cub	B-C	52
Republic P47D	B-C	36
Vought F4UI	B-C	40

Model Aeronautics

Cessna 140	C	49
Culver V	C	43
Stearman	B	32

Monogram

Aeronca Sedan	A-B-C	35
Piper Cub Special	A-B-C	35
Whirlwind Jnr.	A	19
Whirlwind Snr.	B-C-D	30

P.D.Q.

Corsair	B-C	36
Flying Clown	A-B-C	28
Junior	A-B	24
Sportcoupe	A-B	24

Scientific

Atomic	B	14½
Beechcraft 17	A-B	24
Circle King	A-B	30
Cyclone	B-C-D	36
Dynamic	A-B	26
Kingpin	A-B-C	28
Stunt Ace	A-B-C	40
Stuntmaster	B-C	40
Trail Blazer	B-C-D	24

Stanzel

Baby V-Shark	A-B	20
Shark G5	B-C-D	30
Super V-Shark	B-C-D	24
Tiger Shark	C-D	36
Tuffy	AA-A	24

Sterling

Howard Pete	B-C-D	30
Maverick	A-B	24
Monocoupe	B-C	36
Mr. Mulligan	B-C	32

Testor

Freshman Trainer	A	24
Freshman 29	B	36
Junior 19	A	34
Junior 29	B	40
Sophomore 19	A	33
Sophomore 29	B	39

Thomas Associates

PIA	B	31
Republic Seabee	C	38

Veco

Brave	A-B-C	36
Papoose	A	32
Squaw	A-B-C	39
Warrior	A-B-C	36
Chief	A-B-C-D	51½

Baby Cinch	B-C	30
Baby Misbehave	A-B	24
Beechcraft	B-C-D	40
Big Cut-up	B-C	48
Buster	A	-
Butch Trainer	B-C-D	28
Buzz	C-D	30
Cadet	A-B	33
Casalaire	C	48
Cessna	B-C	36
Chupp Autogiro	B-C-D	34
Competitor	C-D	26
Dreamer	B-C-D	20
Dynastreak	Jet	24
Flicker	A-B	24
Flipper	B-C	32
Flivver	B-C	24
Flying Saucer (Lecke)	A-B	18
Fokker Triplane	A	-
Greyhound	A-B-C	16
Hellcat F6F4	B-C-D	42
Hot Dog	A-B	17
Hot Rock	B-C-D	38
Howard Ike	B-C	24
Jeepers	A-B	-
Jester	B	-
Jiggers	B	-
Joker	C	-

Laird–Turner Meteor	A-B	18
Liquid Dynamite	A-B	13
Little Cut-up	A-B	36
Little Rhody	B-C	32
Lockheed Sirius	B	-
Madman Jnr.	B	-
Madman Snr.	C	-
Miss Behave (A.M.E.)	B-C-D	34
Mite Bee	A-B	24
Mr. Mulligan	A	22
Perky Flier	A	18
Piper Skycycle	B-C-D	30
Presto Liner	A-B-C	20
PT Trainer	A-B	26
Ryan Fireball	A-B-C	22
S.E.5	B	-
Sharpy	C-D	47
Skystreak	A-B	16
Snafu Ercoupe	C-D	45
Snorky	A-B-C	24
Stardust	B	26
Stinson 150	A-B	26
Stinson Station Wagon	B-C-D	43
Streamliner	B-C-D	25
Super Cinch	B-C	36
Super Snorky	C-D	40
Super Solution	A	18
TC2 Trainer	B	31
Texan Jnr.	A-B	28
Texan Snr.	C-D	36
Time Flies	A	22
Topping 100	B-C-D	21
Vee Gee (Modelcraft)	B-C-D	18
Waco	B-C	33
Whippet	A-B-C	21
Wildfire	B-C-D	23
Wing Ding	A-B	18
Winnie Mae	A-B	24
Woodchopper	A-B-C	32
Yo-Yo	B-C-D	22

'PEE WEE' C/L & F/F/ KITS

Air-O Small Fry	F/F	-
Austin-Craft Civy Boy 24	F/F	24
Civy Boy 31	F/F	31
Berkeley Mini-Zilch	C/L	20
Powerhouse 33	F/F	33
Profile Powerhouse	F/F	24
Puddle Jumper	C/L	19
Cleveland Minnow	F/F	-
Comet Flying Circus Jnr.	C/L	16
Contest Craft So Lo Jnr.	C/L	13
Dmeco Infant Wagon	C/L	20
Speedster	C/L	12
Enterprise Baby Era	C/L	18
Baby Era Bipe	C/L	-
Shadow	F/F	32
Guillow Trixter Babe	C/L	20
Trixter Piper Cub	F/F	29
Trixter Pixie	F/F	26
Jasco Sport Prince	F/F	35
J.P. Pee Wee Pursuit	C/L	16
Stunt Runt	C/L	16
Midwest Sniffer	F/F	29
Modelcraft Baby Bi-Line	C/L	-
Little Butch	C/L	-
Pup	F/F	-
Swee' Pea	C/L	-
P. & C. Gremlin	F/F	-
Skippy	C/L	20
Scientific Baby Ace	C/L	18
Little Bipe	C/L	16
Little Devil	C/L	18
Sterling Hawk	F/F	27
Maverick	C/L	24
Testor Baby TC2 Trainer	C/L	18
Sophomore 9	C/L	26
Junior 9	C/L	27

Bambino	F/F	-
Cub Special	F/F	29
Sweet Pea	F/F	17
Termite	F/F	25

FREE FLIGHT KITS

A.H.S. Cumulus	A-B	54
Air-O Champion	A	50
Zeek	A-B	-
American Ace	A	36
American Ace	B	54
Berkeley Brigadier	A	38
Brigadier	B	58
Buccaneer	A	36
Buccaneer B Spl.	B	54
Buccaneer C Spl.	C-D	72
Buccaneer Standard	C-D	66
Buccaneer Super	D	90
Cavalier	C-D	60
Cavalier Custom	D	108
Cavalier Custom Twin	D	108
Musketeer	A	42
Musketeer Standard	C-D	72
Powerhouse	A	41
Powerhouse	B	56
Powerhouse	C	62
Sin-Jet	A	24
Super Brigadier	B	58
Swisher	Jetex 50	-
Cleveland Luscombe Sedan	D	76
Playboy Jnr.	B	55
Playboy Snr.	C-D	70
Comet Interceptor	A-B	42
Zipper	A	32
Zipper	B	54
Contest Craft So Hi	A	-
Ehling Ent. Super Phoenix	-	-
Guillow Trixter Cub	A-B	29
Jasco Baby Phoenix	A	36
Jet	Jetex 100	
Junior Phoenix	A	36
Midwest Porky	CO$_2$	-
Min. Aircraft Taylorcraft	C	108
Scientific Coronet	A-B	46
Humdinger	B	52
Stanzel Interceptor	A-B	58

Flamingo	D	72
Honey Bee	B	60
Jiffy	A	36
Larkey	B	50
Luscombe Silvaire	A-B	43
Miss Tiny	A-B	48
Runt	A-B	44
Skybo	C-D	66
Skybuggy	B-C	42
Skyrocket	A	36
Spook	A-B	48
Sunduster Special	D	88
Varsity	B	50
Wanderer	B-C	54
Wog	C	60

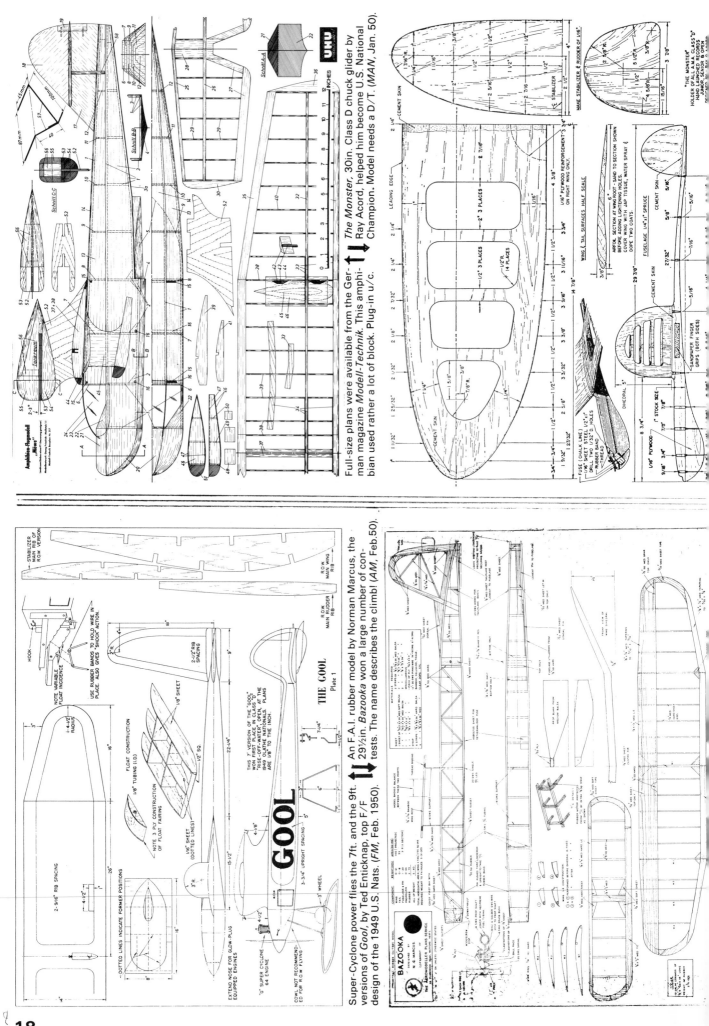

The Monster, 30in. Class D chuck glider by Ray Acord, helped him become U.S. National Champion. Model needs a D/T. (MAN, Jan. 50).

Full-size plans were available from the German magazine Modell-Technik. This amphibian used rather a lot of block. Plug-in u/c.

Super-Cyclone power flies the 7ft. and the 9ft. versions of Gool, by Ted Enticknap. top F/F design of the 1949 U.S. Nats. (FM, Feb. 1950).

An F.A.I. rubber model by Norman Marcus, the 29½in. Bazooka won a large number of contests. The name describes the climb! (AM, Feb.50).

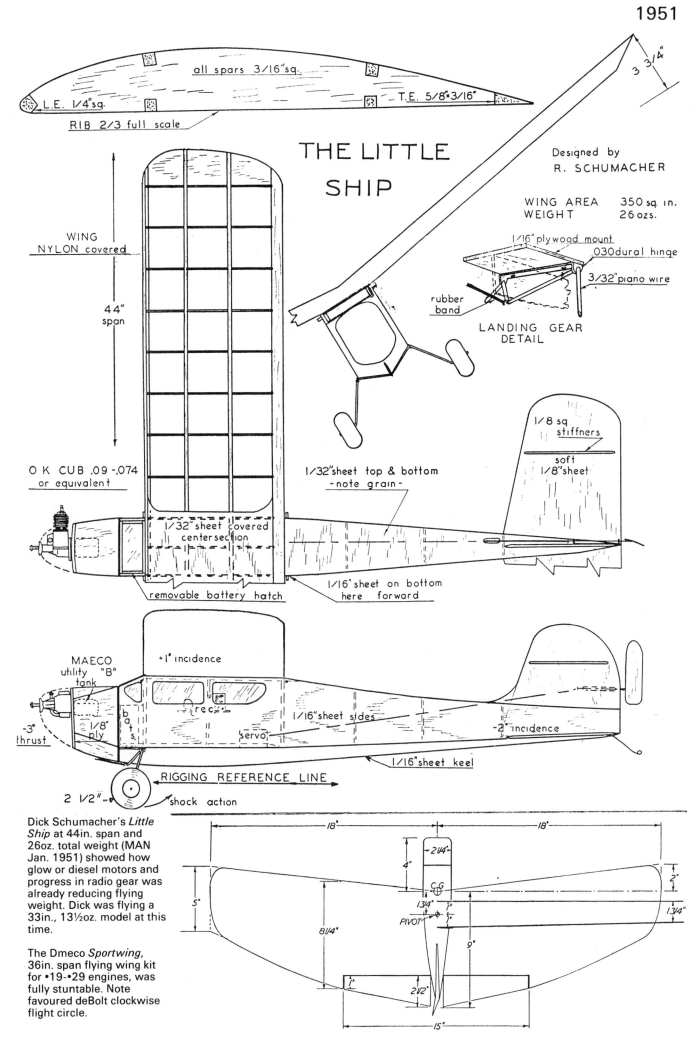

all spars 3/16"sq.

L.E. 1/4"sq.

T.E. 5/8"×3/16"

RIB 2/3 full scale

3 3/4"

THE LITTLE SHIP

Designed by
R. SCHUMACHER

WING AREA   350 sq. in.
WEIGHT   26 ozs.

1/16" plywood mount
030 dural hinge
3/32" piano wire
rubber band

LANDING GEAR DETAIL

WING
NYLON covered

44"
span

O K CUB .09 -.074
or equivalent

1/32" sheet covered centersection

1/32" sheet top & bottom
-note grain-

1/8 sq stiffners
soft 1/8" sheet

removable battery hatch

1/16" sheet on bottom
here forward

MAECO
utility "B"
tank

+1° incidence

1/8" ply

bats.

rec

servo

1/16" sheet sides

-3° thrust

-2° incidence

1/16" sheet keel

RIGGING REFERENCE LINE

2 1/2"

shock action

Dick Schumacher's *Little Ship* at 44in. span and 26oz. total weight (MAN Jan. 1951) showed how glow or diesel motors and progress in radio gear was already reducing flying weight. Dick was flying a 33in., 13½oz. model at this time.

The Dmeco *Sportwing*, 36in. span flying wing kit for •19-•29 engines, was fully stuntable. Note favoured deBolt clockwise flight circle.

18"   18"

2 1/4"
4"
2"
C.G
1 3/4"
1 3/4"
PIVOT
5"
8 1/4"
9"
1"
2 1/2"
15"

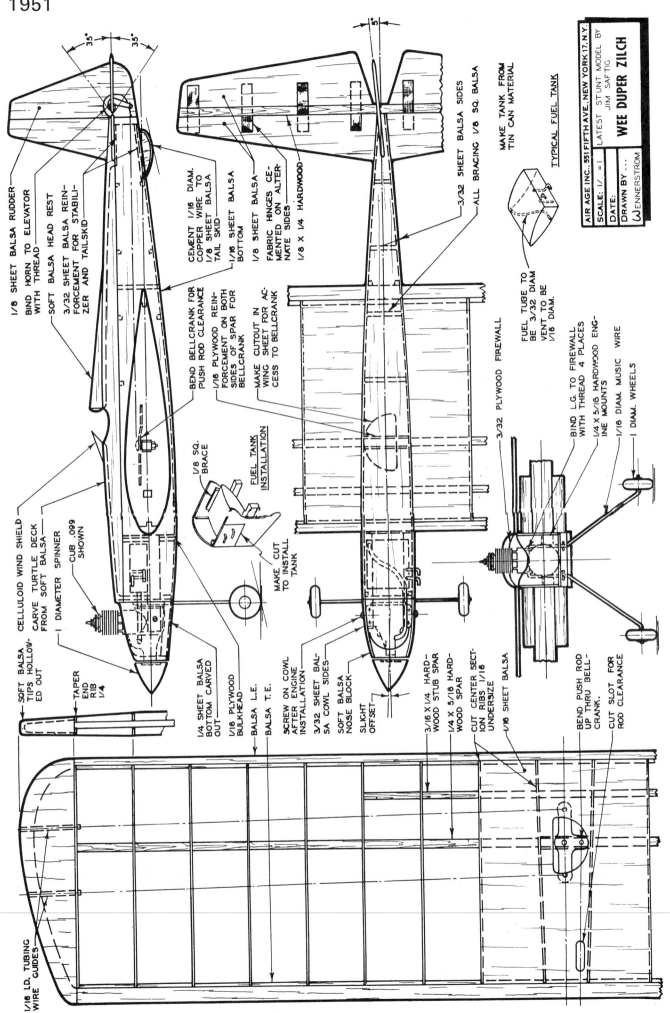

WEE DUPER ZILCH

LATEST STUNT MODEL BY JIM SAFTIG

AIR AGE INC., 551 FIFTH AVE. NEW YORK 17, N.Y.

SCALE: 1/2 = 1
DATE:
DRAWN BY ... WENNERSTROM

MAKE TANK FROM TIN CAN MATERIAL

TYPICAL FUEL TANK

1/8 SHEET BALSA RUDDER

BIND HORN TO ELEVATOR WITH THREAD

SOFT BALSA HEAD REST

3/32 SHEET BALSA REINFORCEMENT FOR STABILIZER AND TAILSKID

CEMENT 1/16 DIAM. COPPER WIRE TO 1/8 SHEET BALSA TAIL SKID

1/16 SHEET BALSA BOTTOM

1/8 SHEET BALSA

FABRIC HINGES CEMENTED ON ALTERNATE SIDES

1/8 X 1/4 HARDWOOD

3/32 SHEET BALSA SIDES

ALL BRACING 1/8 SQ. BALSA

3/32 SHEET BALSA SIDES

FUEL TUBE TO BE 3/32 DIAM VENT TO BE 1/16 DIAM.

BEND BELLCRANK FOR PUSH ROD CLEARANCE

1/16 PLYWOOD REINFORCEMENT ON BOTH SIDES OF SPAR FOR BELLCRANK

MAKE CUTOUT IN WING SHEET FOR ACCESS TO BELLCRANK

FUEL TANK INSTALLATION

1/8 SQ. BRACE

CUT CENTER SECTION RIBS 1/16 UNDERSIZE

MAKE CUT TO INSTALL TANK

3/32 PLYWOOD FIREWALL

BIND L.G. TO FIREWALL WITH THREAD 4 PLACES

1/4 X 5/16 HARDWOOD ENGINE MOUNTS

1/16 DIAM. MUSIC WIRE

1 DIAM. WHEELS

SOFT BALSA CELLULOID WIND SHIELD TIPS HOLLOWED OUT

CARVE TURTLE DECK FROM SOFT BALSA

CUB .099 SHOWN

1 DIAMETER SPINNER

TAPER END RIB 1/4

1/4 SHEET BALSA BOTTOM CARVED OUT

1/16 PLYWOOD BULKHEAD

BALSA L.E.

BALSA T.E.

SCREW ON COWL AFTER ENGINE INSTALLATION

3/32 SHEET BALSA COWL SIDES

SOFT BALSA NOSE BLOCK

SLIGHT OFFSET

3/16 X 1/4 HARDWOOD STUB SPAR

1/4 X 5/16 HARDWOOD SPAR

1/16 SHEET BALSA

BEND PUSH ROD UP THRU BELLCRANK.

CUT SLOT FOR ROD CLEARANCE

1/16 I.D. TUBING WIRE GUIDES

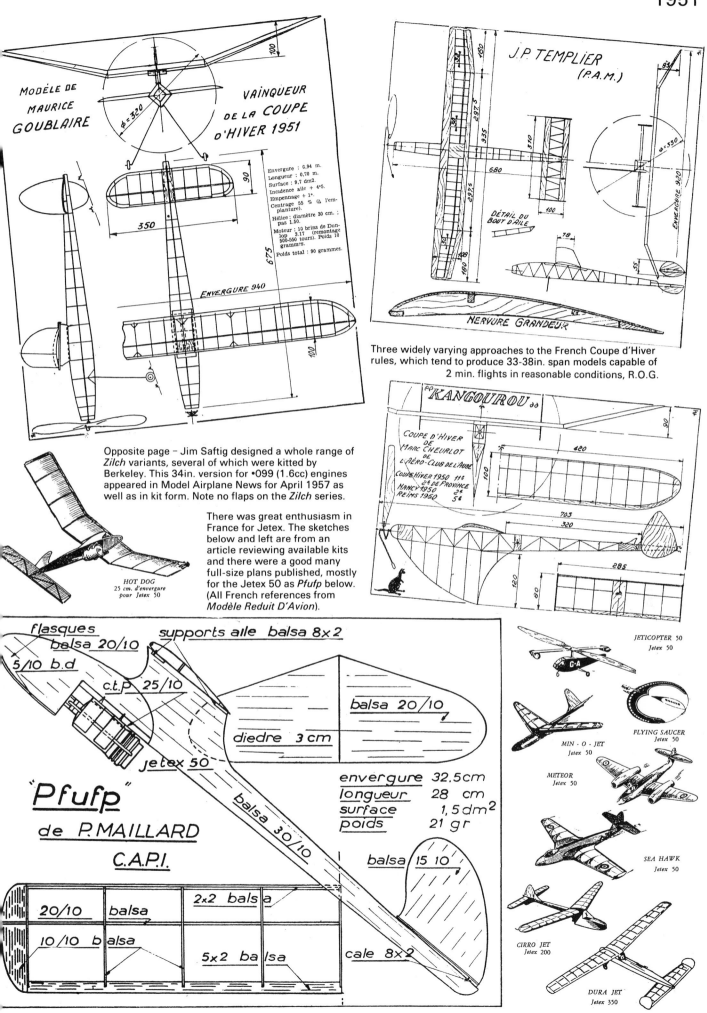

MODÈLE DE MAURICE GOUBLAIRE

VAINQUEUR DE LA COUPE D'HIVER 1951

Envergure : 0,94 m.
Longueur : 0,70 m.
Surface : 9,7 dm2.
Incidence aile + 4°5.
Empennage + 1°.
Centrage 55 % (à l'emplanture).
Hélice : diamètre 30 cm. ; pas 1.50.
Moteur : 10 brins de Dunlop 3.17 (remontage 500-550 tours). Poids 10 grammes.
Poids total : 90 grammes.

ENVERGURE 940

J.P. TEMPLIER (P.A.M.)

DÉTAIL DU BOUT D'AILE

NERVURE GRANDEUR

Three widely varying approaches to the French Coupe d'Hiver rules, which tend to produce 33-38in. span models capable of 2 min. flights in reasonable conditions, R.O.G.

"KANGOUROU"

COUPE D'HIVER DE MARC CHEURLOT DE L'AÉRO-CLUB DE L'AUBE
Coupe Hiver 1950 1ᵉ
2ᵉ de Province
NANCY 1950
REIMS 1950
2ᵉ
5ᵉ

Opposite page – Jim Saftig designed a whole range of *Zilch* variants, several of which were kitted by Berkeley. This 34in. version for •099 (1.6cc) engines appeared in Model Airplane News for April 1957 as well as in kit form. Note no flaps on the *Zilch* series.

There was great enthusiasm in France for Jetex. The sketches below and left are from an article reviewing available kits and there were a good many full-size plans published, mostly for the Jetex 50 as *Pfufp* below. (All French references from *Modèle Reduit D'Avion*).

HOT DOG
25 cm. d'envergure
pour Jetex 50

flasques balsa 20/10

supports aile balsa 8×2

5/10 b.d

c.t.p 25/10

jetex 50

balsa 20/10

diedre 3 cm

envergure 32,5cm
longueur 28 cm
surface 1,5 dm²
poids 21 gr

balsa 30/10

"Pfufp"
de P. MAILLARD
C.A.P.I.

20/10 balsa
10/10 balsa

2×2 balsa

5×2 balsa

balsa 15 10

cale 8×2

JETICOPTER 50
Jetex 50

FLYING SAUCER
Jetex 50

MIN - O - JET
Jetex 50

METEOR
Jetex 50

SEA HAWK
Jetex 50

CIRRO JET
Jetex 200

DURA JET
Jetex 350

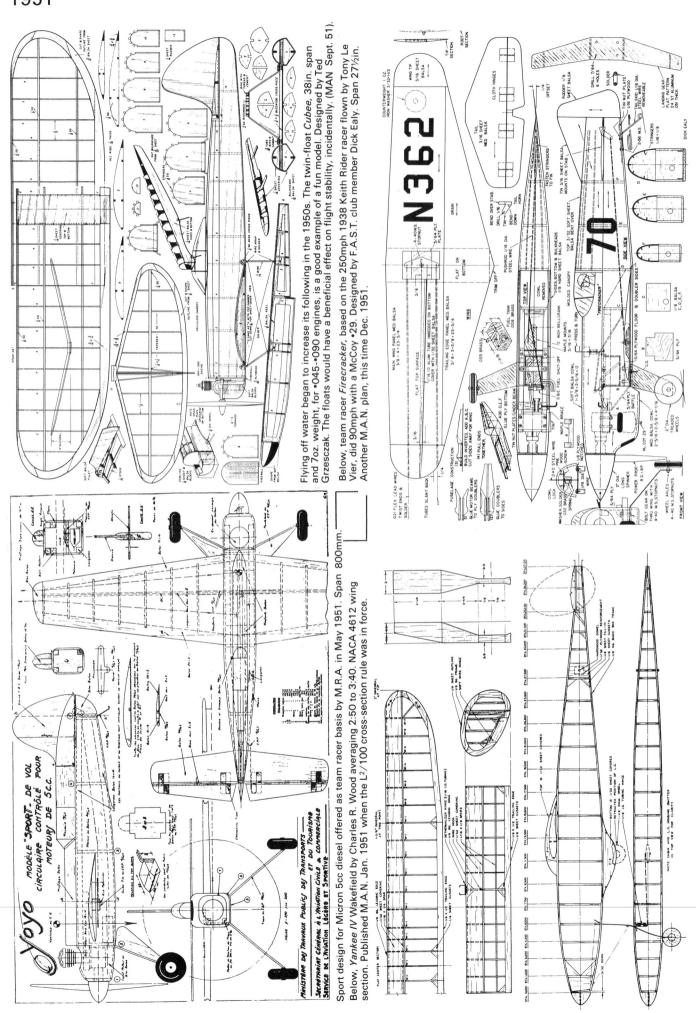

Flying off water began to increase its following in the 1950s. The twin-float *Cubee*, 38in. span and 7oz. weight, for •045-•090 engines, is a good example of a fun model. Designed by Ted Grzeszczak. The floats would have a beneficial effect on flight stability, incidentally. (MAN Sept. 51).

Below, team racer *Firecracker*, based on the 250mph 1938 Keith Rider racer flown by Tony Le Vier, did 90mph with a McCoy •29. Designed by F.A.S.T. club member Dick Ealy. Span 27½in. Another M.A.N. plan, this time Dec. 1951.

Sport design for Micron 5cc diesel offered as team racer basis by M.R.A. in May 1951. Span 800mm. Below, *Yankee IV* Wakefield by Charles R. Wood averaging 2:50 to 3:40. NACA 4612 wing section. Published M.A.N. Jan. 1951 when the L²/100 cross-section rule was in force.

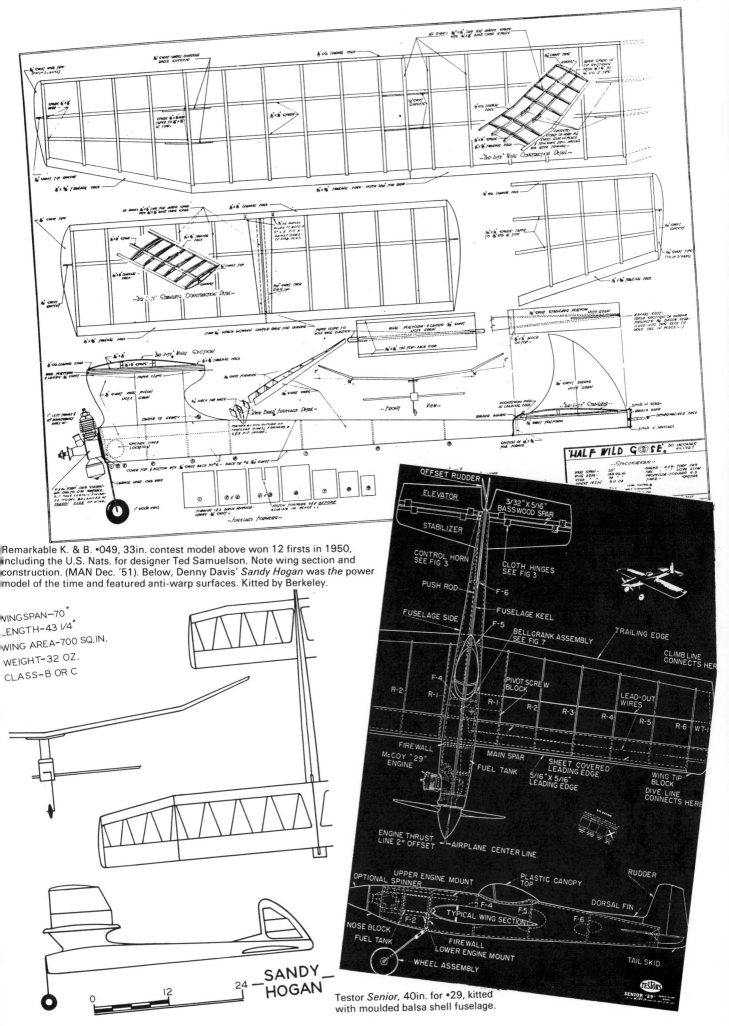

Remarkable K. & B. •049, 33in. contest model above won 12 firsts in 1950, including the U.S. Nats. for designer Ted Samuelson. Note wing section and construction. (MAN Dec. '51). Below, Denny Davis' *Sandy Hogan* was *the* power model of the time and featured anti-warp surfaces. Kitted by Berkeley.

WINGSPAN—70"

LENGTH—43 1/4"

WING AREA—700 SQ.IN.

WEIGHT—32 OZ.

CLASS—B OR C

SANDY HOGAN

Testor *Senior*, 40in. for •29, kitted with moulded balsa shell fuselage.

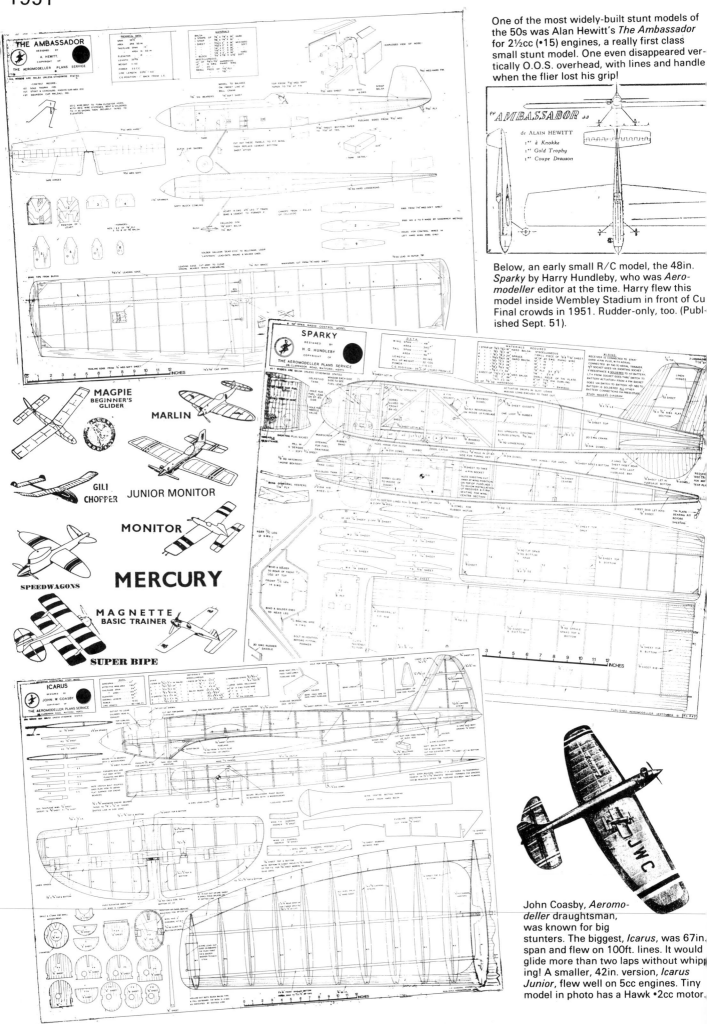

One of the most widely-built stunt models of the 50s was Alan Hewitt's *The Ambassador* for 2½cc (•15) engines, a really first class small stunt model. One even disappeared vertically O.O.S. overhead, with lines and handle when the flier lost his grip!

Below, an early small R/C model, the 48in. *Sparky* by Harry Hundleby, who was *Aeromodeller* editor at the time. Harry flew this model inside Wembley Stadium in front of Cu Final crowds in 1951. Rudder-only, too. (Published Sept. 51).

John Coasby, *Aeromodeller* draughtsman, was known for big stunters. The biggest, *Icarus*, was 67in. span and flew on 100ft. lines. It would glide more than two laps without whipping! A smaller, 42in. version, *Icarus Junior*, flew well on 5cc engines. Tiny model in photo has a Hawk •2cc motor.

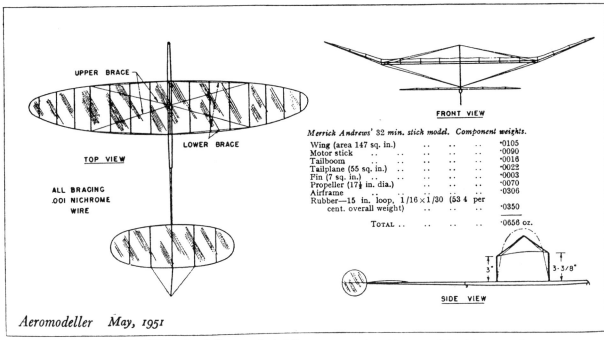

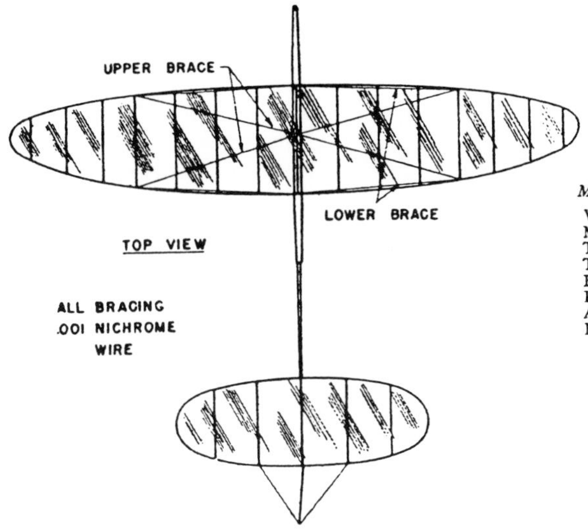
UPPER BRACE
LOWER BRACE
TOP VIEW
ALL BRACING
.001 NICHROME
WIRE

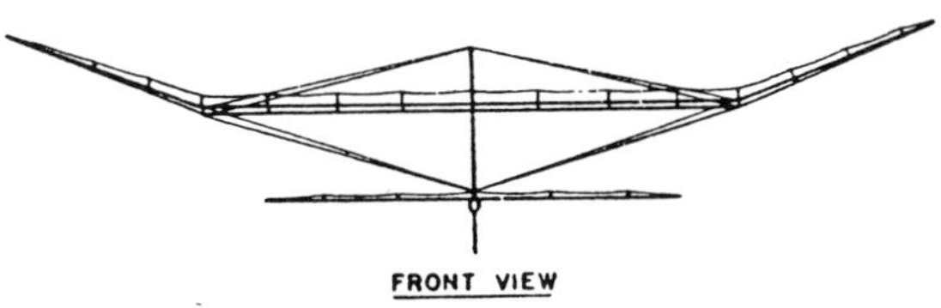
FRONT VIEW

Merrick Andrews' 32 min. stick model. Component weights.

Wing (area 147 sq. in.)	·0105
Motor stick	·0090
Tailboom	·0016
Tailplane (55 sq. in.)	·0022
Fin (7 sq. in.)	·0003
Propeller (17½ in. dia.)	·0070
Airframe	·0306
Rubber—15 in. loop, 1/16 × 1/30 (53 4 per cent. overall weight)	·0350
TOTAL	·0656 oz.

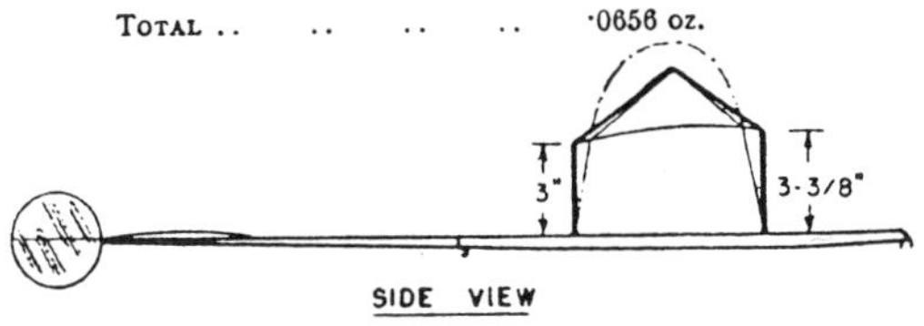
3"
3-3/8"
SIDE VIEW

Aeromodeller May, 1951

A general arrangement diagram of what the U.S.A. acknowledges to be the first "over 30 minute model." Designed and built by Merrick Andrews, the record flight of 32m. 19s. was made in the airship hangar at Lakehurst, New Jersey. Total weight is only ·0656 oz. . . . actually less weight than the dope on many an outdoor model!

Microfilm Formulæ

A good general purpose microfilm solution can be made by adding a teaspoonful of castor oil to two ounces of clear dope or banana oil. The following formulæ have been used to good effect on prewar British models and provide a variety of materials that the film can be made from :—

1. Flexible collodion .. .. .. 1 oz.
   Amyl acetate .. .. .. 16 drops
   Castor oil .. .. 10 drops
2. Plain collodion .. .. .. 1 oz.
   Amyl acetate .. .. .. 16 drops
   Tricresyl phosphate .. .. 16 drops
3. Flexible collodion .. .. .. 1 oz.
   Amyl acetate .. .. .. 16 drops
   Camphorated oil .. .. .. 13 drops
4. Flexible collodion .. .. .. 1 oz.
   Acetone .. .. 18 drops
   Castor oil .. .. 12 drops
   (This is a heavier film).

COMPRESSION—IGNITION ENGINES 1948/51

Type	Class S.M.A.E. F/F	Class S.M.A.E. C/L	Class A.M.A.	Swept Volume c.c.	Bore in.	Stroke in.	Weight oz.	B.H.P. at R.P.M.	Induction System	Type of Mounting	Cut-out
'K' HAWK ...	A	I	½A	.193	.250	.240	1.0	... ...	Shaft R.V.	Beam	No
KALPER	A	I	½A	.324	.251	.400	1.0	.016 at 9500/10000	3-port	Beam	No
ELFIN .49	A	I	½A	.49	N.R.	N.R.	N.R.	... ...	Shaft R.V.	Radial	No
ALLBON DART ...	A	I	½A	.55	.350	.350	1.25	.045+ at 12500/13000	Shaft R.V.	Beam	No
MILLS 75	A	I	½A	.75	.335	.516	1.9	.05 at 10000	3-port	Beam	Optional
E.P.C.	A	I	A	.854	.375	.472	2.0	.04 at 8000	3-port	Beam	No
AMCO 87 Mk. II ...	A	I	A	.854	.375	.472	2.0	.05 at 9000	3-port	Beam	Yes
E.D. Mk.I BEE ...	A	I	A	.984	.437	.400	2.75	.06+ at 9400	Disc R.V.	Beam	No
FROG 100 Mk. II ...	A	I	A	.99	.375	.550	3.25	.07 at 8000	Shaft R.V.	Radial	Extra fitting
MILLS Mk. II (1948)	A	I	A	1.33	.406	.625	3.5	.08 at 8000	3-port	Beam	Yes
MILLS Mk. II (1950)	A	I	A	1.33	.406	.625	3.5	.10+ at 10500	3-port	Beam	Yes
ALLBON JAVELIN	A	I	A	1.49	.525	.420	2.3	.11+ at 11000	Shaft R.V.	Beam	No
ELFIN 1.49	A	I	A	1.49	.503	.466	2.6	.13 at 13500	Shaft R.V.	Beam	No
MITE-DIESEL ...	A	II	A	1.61	.500	.500	2.75	... ...	Shaft R.V.	Beam	Yes
FROG 180	A	II	A	1.66	.485	.550	3.75	.10 at 8000	Shaft R.V.	Radial	Extra fitting
REEVES H.18 ...	A	II	A	1.67	.510	.500	3.25	... ...	Disc R.V.	Beam	No
ELFIN 1.8	A	II	A	1.81	.500	.562	3.5	.13 at 11000	Shaft R.V.	Radial	No
'K' FALCON ...	A	II	A	1.96	.520	.562	4.3	.12 at 9600	Shaft R.V.	Beam or Radial	No
E.D. Mk. II	A	II	A	2.01	.500	.625	6.5	... ...	3-port	Beam	No
E.D. COMP. SPECIAL	A	II	A	2.01	.500	.625	6.0	.11 at 7500	3-port	Beam	No
DEEZIL A	A	II	A	2.05	.473	.708	6.0	.10 at 7000	3-port	Beam	No
MICRO-DIESEL ...	A	II	A	2.13			6.0	.11 at 7000	3-port	Beam	No
MAJESCO "22" ...	A	II	A	2.21	.500	.6875	6.0	... ...	3-port	Beam	No
MILLS 2.4	A	II	A	2.42	.500	.750	5.6	.17 at 10000	Disc R.V.	Beam	Yes
'K' FALCON Mk. II	A	II	A	2.37	.572	.562	4.5	... ...	Shaft R.V.	Beam	No
E.D. 2.46	A	II	A	2.46	.590	.550	N.R.	... ...	Disc R.V.	Beam	No
E.D. Mk. III ...	A	II	A	2.49	.550	.625	6.5	.14 at 8000	Shaft R.V.	Beam	Yes
FROG 250	A	II	A	2.49	.580	.575	5.6	.16 at 10000	Shaft R.V.	Beam or Radial	No
ELFIN 2.49 (1950) ...	A	II	A	2.48	.554	.625	3.5	... ...	Shaft R.V.	Beam	No
ELFIN 2.49 (1949) ...	A	II	A	2.50	.560	.620	3.75	.20+ at 12000	Shaft R.V.	Radial	No
ALLBON 2.8 ...	B	III	A	2.79	.5625	.6875	6.0	.15 at 7000	3-port	Beam	No
REEVES 3.4 ...	B	III	B	3.4			7.0	... ...	Shaft R.V.	Beam	No
AMCO 3.5	B	III	B	3.42	.6875	.5625	4.2	.25+ at 11000	Shaft R.V.	Beam or Radial	No
D.C. 350	B	III	B	3.42	.6875	.5625	5.5	.25+ at 11000	Shaft R.V.	Beam	No
E.D. Mk. IV	B	III	B	3.46	.656	.625	6.5	.25+ at 10500	Disc R.V.	Beam	No
AIR-O DIESEL ...	B	IV	B	4.56	.6875	.750	7.5	... ...	3-port	Beam	No
DRONE	B	IV	B	4.85	.656	.875	9.75	.25 at 7000	Shaft R.V.	Beam	Extra fitting
'K' VULTURE Mk. III	B	IV	B	4.87	.750	.6875	7.5	.25 at 8/9000	Shaft R.V.	Beam	No
MILES SPECIAL 5 c.c.	B	IV	B	4.89	.781	.625	8.5	.40+ at 10/12000	Disc R.V.	Beam	No
ETA "5"	B	IV	B	4.99	.6718	.8593	9.5	.2+ at 6500	3-port	Beam	Yes
D.C. WILDCAT Mk.III	C	V	C	5.32	.6875	.875	9.0	.25 at 8000	3-port	Beam	No

GLOW-PLUG AND SPARK IGNITION ENGINES 1948/51

Type	Class S.M.A.E. F/F	Class S.M.A.E. C/L	Class A.M.A. F/F	Class A.M.A. C/L	Swept Volume cu. in.	Swept Volume c.c.	Bore in.	Stroke in.	Weight oz.	Compression Ratio	B.H.P.	at	R.P.M.	Induction System	Mounting
K. & B. 'Infant-Torpedo' ...	A	I	½A	A	.020	.33	.281	.331	1.0	8 : 1	...	...	...	Shaft R.V.	Radial
K. & B. 'Torpedo-Jr.'	A	I	½A	A	.035	.57	.343	.380	1.2	8 : 1	...	...	...	Shaft R.V.	Radial
Herkimer-'O.K.' Cub .039 ...	A	I	½A	A	.039	.64	.390	.334	1.5	9 : 1	...	...	...	Shaft R.V.	Radial
Anderson 'Baby-Spitfire' ...	A	I	½A	A	.045	.74	.375	.406	1.0	10 : 1	...	...	...	Shaft R.V.	Radial
Anderson 'Spitzy'	A	I	½A	A	.045	.74	.379	.405	1.4	—	.025	at	12000	Shaft R.V.	Radial
K. & B. 'Torpedo-.049'	A	I	½A	A	.049	.80	.406	.380	1.5	—	...	...	...	Shaft R.V.	Radial
McCoy 'Baby-Mac'	A	I	½A	A	.049	.80			1.4	—	...	...	...	Shaft R V.	Radial
Atwood 'Wasp'	A	I	½A	A	.049	.80	.421	.356	1.3	8 : 1	...	...	...	Shaft R.V.	Radial
Herkimer-'O.K.' Cub 049 ...	A	I	½A	A	.049	.80	.390	.415	1.5	—	...	...	...	Shaft R.V.	Radial/Beam
Anderson 'Royal-Spitfire' ...	A	I	A	A	.065	1.06	.436	.437	1.9	6.5 : 1	...	...	...	Shaft R.V.	Beam
Herkimer-'O.K.' Cub 074 ...	A	I	A	A	.074	1.21	.478	.415	1.7	—	...	...	...	Shaft R.V.	Radial/Beam
Frog '150' 'Red-Glow' ...	A	I	A	A	.091	1.48	.500	.460	2.9	8 : 1	...	...	...	Shaft R.V.	Radial
Allbon 'Arrow'	A	I	A	A	.091	1.49	.525	.420	2.2	10 : 1	.08	at	11000	Shaft R.V.	Beam
Elf 'Single' ...	A	II	A	A	.097	1.60	.468	.564	3.0	7 : 1	.08	at	10000	3-port	Radial/Beam
'Glo-Mite' ...	A	II	A	A	.098	1.61	.500	.500	2.7	—	...	...	...	Shaft R.V.	Beam
McCoy '9' ...	A	II	A	A	.098	1.61	.500	.500	2.6	8 : 1	...	...	...	Shaft R.V.	Beam
Herkimer-'O.K.' Cub 099 ...	A	II	A	A	.099	1.62	.515	.480	2.0	9.5 : 1	...	...	...	Shaft R.V.	Beam
Arden 099 ...	A	II	A	A	.099	1.62	.495	.516	2.6	9 : 1	.12+	at	12/13000	Shaft R.V.	Radial
Frog '160' 'Red Glow' ...	A	II	A	A	.101	1.66	.485	.550	3.2	—	.09	at	10000	Shaft R.V.	Radial
'K' Tornado ...	A	II	A	A	.119	1.96	.520	.562	4.2	—	...	...	...	Shaft R.V.	Radial/Beam
E.D. 2.46 ...	A	II	A	A	.150	2.46	.590	.550	5.0	—	2+	at	12000	Disc R.V.	Beam
Elf 'Twin' (2-cyl.)	B	III	A	A	.195	3.20	.468	.564	5.0	7 : 1	.16	at	10000	3-port	Radial
McCoy '19' (1948/49) ...	B	III	A	A	.195	3.20	.625	.630	4.9	9 : 1	.3	at	14000	Disc R.V.	Beam
McCoy '19' (Shaft valve) ...	B	III	A	A	.195	3.20	.625	.630	4.5	—	.28	at	13/14000	Shaft R.V.	Beam
McCoy 'Red-Head 19' ...	B	III	A	A	.195	3.20	.625	.630	5.0	—	.35	at	14000	Disc R.V.	Beam
Ohlsson & Rice 19 (1951) ...	B	III	A	A	.196	3.21	.684	.534	4.8	7 : 1	...	...	...	Shaft R.V.	Radial/Beam
Ohlsson & Rice 19 (3-port) ...	B	III	A	A	.197	3.23	.6875	.531	4.0	6 : 1	.14	at	7000	3-port	Radial/Beam
Arden 199 ...	B	III	A	A	.198	3.25	.635	.625	4.2	9 : 1	.22	at	13000	Shaft R.V.	Radial
Herkimer-'O.K.' 'Bantam' ...	B	III	A	A	.199	3.26	.656	.590	3.5	7 : 1	.20	at	12000	Disc R.V.	Beam
Eta '19' G.P. Series I ...	B	III	A	A	.199	3.27	.640	.620	4.7	8.5 : 1	.35	at	15000	Disc R.V.	Beam
K. & B. '19' ...	B	III	A	A	.199	3.27	.640	.620	6.0	—	...	...	...	Shaft R.V.	Beam
Amco 'Glo .35'	B	III	B	B	.209	3.42	.6875	.5625	4.2	8.5 : 1	.28	at	13000	Shaft R.V.	Radial/Beam
Ohlsson & Rice 23 (1951) ...	B	IV	B	B	.230	3.77	.684	.625	5.0	7 : 1	...	...	...	Shaft R.V.	Radial/Beam
Ohlsson & Rice 23 (3-port) ...	B	IV	B	B	.232	3.80	.6875	.625	4.5	6 : 1	.17	at	7500	3-port	Radial/Beam
K. & B. 'Torpedo-24'	B	IV	B	B	.249	4.08	.662	.724	7.0	7 : 1	...	...	...	Shaft R.V.	Radial/Beam
Campus '29' ...	B	IV	B	B	.278	4.56	.803	.550	—	4 : 1	...	...	...	Shaft R.V.	Beam
McCoy 'Sportsman-29' ...	B	IV	B	B	.293	4.80	.746	.670	6.5	—	.46	at	13/14000	Disc R.V.	Beam
McCoy '29' (Shaft valve) ...	B	IV	B	B	.296	4.85	.750	.670	6.5	—	.4+	at	13/14000	Shaft R.V.	Beam
McCoy 'Red Head 29' (1950) ...	B	IV	B	B	.296	4.85	.750	.670	7.0	8.5 : 1	.6+	at	15000	Disc R.V.	Beam
Forster '29' ...	B	IV	B	B	.297	4.87	.750	.672	6.5	9 : 1	.40	at	13400	Disc R.V.	Beam/Radial
Forster 'G.29' ...	B	IV	B	B	.297	4.87	.750	.672	6.6	10 : 1	.5+	at	14/15000	Disc R.V.	Beam/Radial
Eta 29 Series I (1948/9) ...	B	IV	B	B	.297	4.87	.750	.672	7.0	10 : 1	.54	at	13400	Disc R.V.	Beam

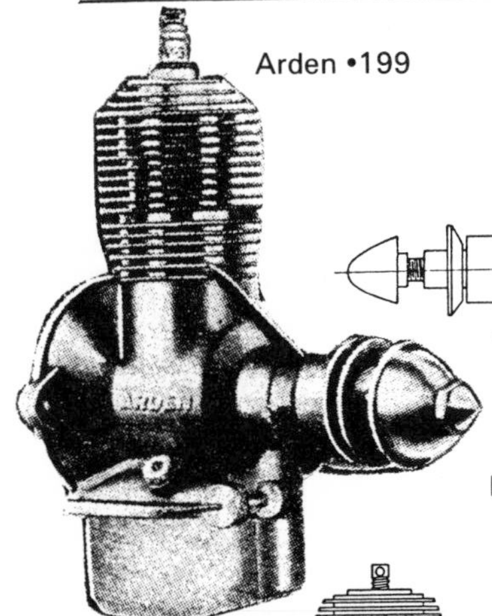
Arden •199

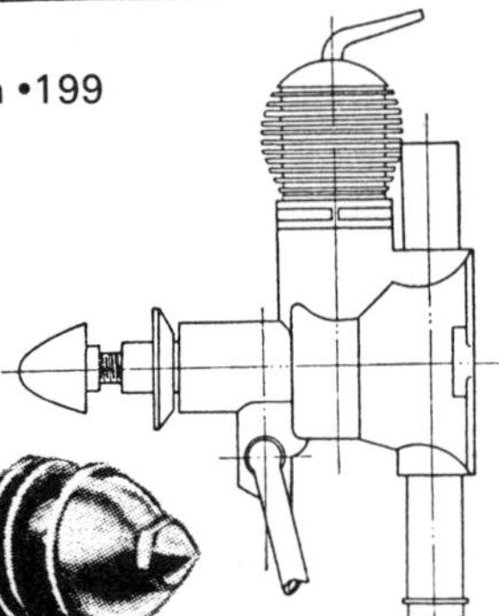
Elfin 1•8

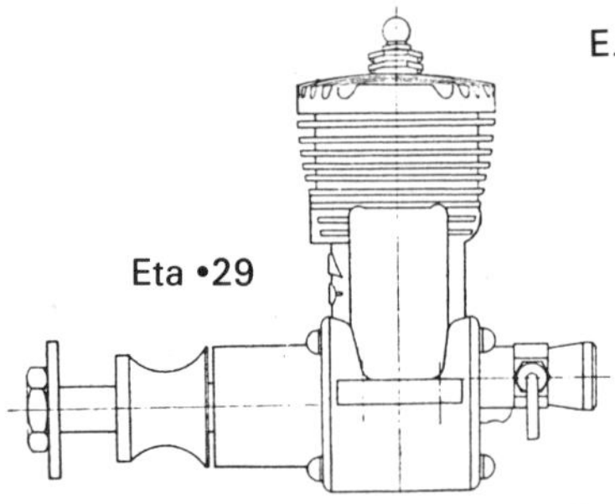
Eta •29

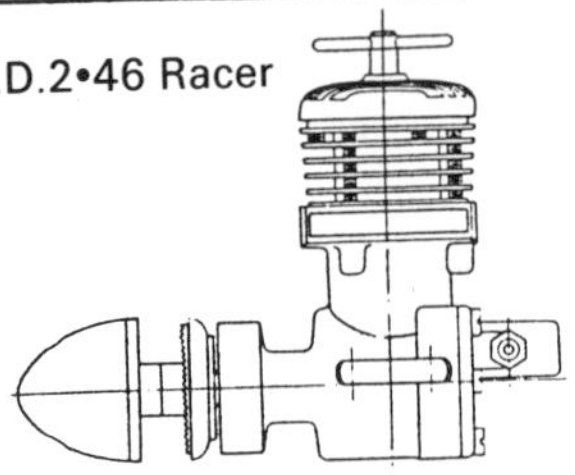
E.D.2•46 Racer

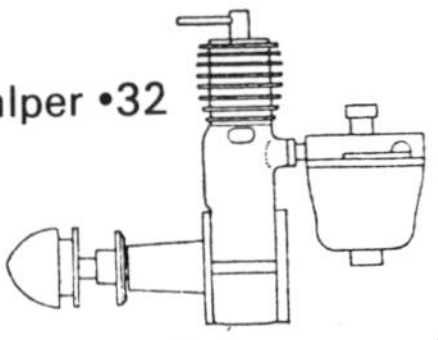
Kalper •32

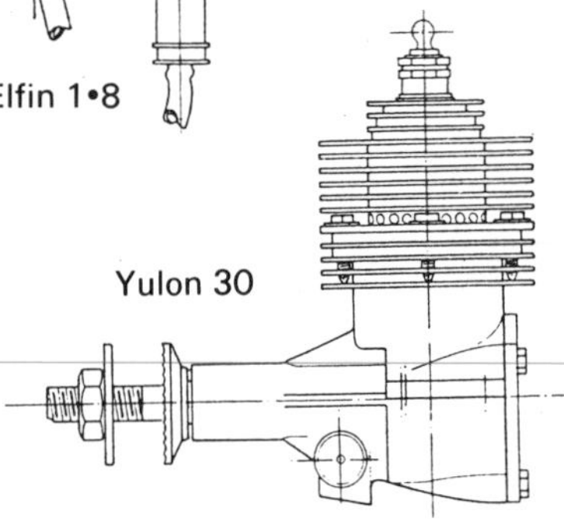
Yulon 30

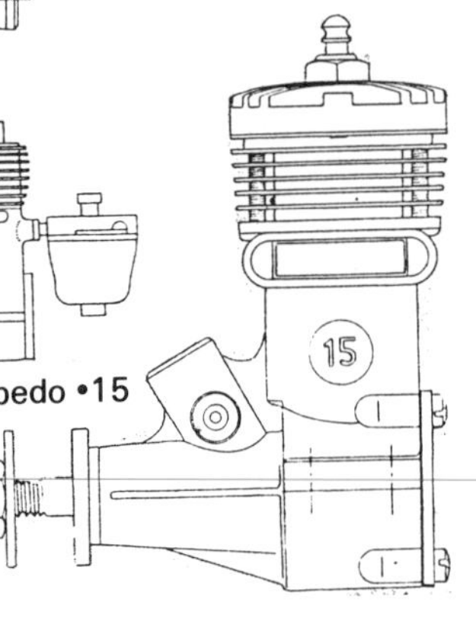

K&B Torpedo •15

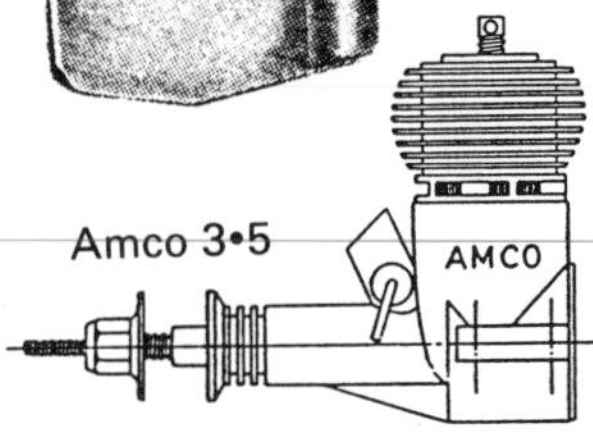

Amco 3•5

The tables of engine data included here were compiled by Ron Warring for *Model Aircraft* in 1951, when Ron was probably at his most prolific. There was some controversy at the time in the matter of engine power output, largely arising from differences in equipment and techniques used by *Model Aircraft*, *Aeromodeller* and various manufacturers themselves to measure output. Figures for b.h.p. in Column 12 are therefore best regarded as a guide.

Ron Warring and Bill Dean both worked for *Aeromodeller* in their 'teens but failed to get on with the then owner, D.A. Russell. Both subsequently contributed regularly to *Model Aircraft* but only occasionally to *Aeromodeller* until 1952, when Russell ceased to be involved in the magazine; shortly after, Warring took over the regular engine tests from Laurence Sparey.

Type	S.M.A.E. F/F	S.M.A.E. C/L	A.M.A. F/F	A.M.A. C/L	Swept Vol. cu. in.	Swept Vol. c.c.	Bore in.	Stroke in.	Weight oz.	Compression Ratio	B.H.P.	at	R.P.M.	Induction System	Mounting
Eta 29 Series I (1949)	B	IV	B	B	.297	4.87	.750	.672	7.0	9 : 1	.54	at	14500	Disc R.V.	Beam
Eta 29 Series II and III	B	IV	B	B	.297	4.87	.750	.672	7.0	8.5 : 1	.6+	at	15/16000	Disc R.V.	Beam
Dooling '29'	B	IV	B	B	.298	4.88	.800	.594	6.8	8.5 : 1	.75	at	17500	Disc R.V.	Beam
Yulon '29'	B	IV	B	B	.298	4.89	.743	.687	5.6	—	.38	at	13000	Shaft R.V.	Beam/Radial
Yulon 'Eagle'	B	IV	B	B	.298	4.89	.743	.687	6.0	—	.4+	at	14000	Shaft R.V.	Beam
K.& B. Torpedo-29	B	IV	B	B	.299	4.90	.725	.724	7.5	6.9 : 1	...	...	...	Shaft R.V.	Beam/Radial
Veco '29'	B	IV	B	B	.299	4.90	.725	.724	7.0	8.5 : 1	.35/.40	at	11/12000	Shaft R.V.	Beam
Herkimer 'O.K.' '29'	B	IV	B	B	.299	4.90	.760	.660	7.5	7 : 1	...	...	...	Shaft R.V.	Beam/Radial
Herkimer 'O.K.' 'Hothead'	B	IV	B	B	.299	4.91	.759	.663	5.4	—	.40	at	10500	Shaft R.V.	Beam/Radial
Ohlsson & Rice '29'	B	IV	B	B	.299	4.90	.738	.700	5.5	7 : 1	.40	at	13000	Shaft R.V.	Beam
Fox '29'	B	IV	B	B	.300	4.92	.748	.680	8.0	10 : 1	...	...	...	Disc R.V.	Beam
De long '30'	B	IV	B	B	.300	4.92	.748	.680			...	...	...	Disc R.V.	Beam
De long '30-Special'	B	IV	B	B	.300	4.92	.748	.680	8.5	9 : 1	.50	at	15000		Beam
Frog '500'	B	IV	C	C	.3005	4.92	.750	.680	7.5	8 : 1	.40	at	12500	Shaft R.V.	Beam/Radial
Yulon '30'	B	IV	C	C	.302	4.95	.746	.691	5.5	—	.37	at	13000	Shaft R.V.	Beam/Radial
Electra 'Pioneer-5'	B	IV	C	C	.303	4.97	.750	.6875	9.0	6 or 10:1	.42	at	12000	Disc R.V.	Beam
1066 'Hawk'	B	IV	C	C	.303	4.97	.750	.6875	9.0	—	...	...	...	Disc R.V.	Beam
'K' Vulture G.P.	B	IV	C	C	.303	4.97	.750	.6875	7.5	—	.25	at	9000	Shaft R.V.	Beam
Forster '305'	B	IV	C	C	.304	4.98	.760	.672	6.5	9 : 1	.40	at	13400	Disc R.V.	Beam/Radial
Forster 'G.31'	B	IV	C	C	.304	4.98	.760	.672	6.6	10 : 1	.5	at	14/15000	Disc R.V.	Beam
Veco '31'	C	V	C	C	.319	5.23	.750	.724	7.0	8.5 : 1	.35/.40	at	11/12000	Shaft R.V.	Beam
K. & B. 'Torpedo 32'	C	V	C	C	.321	5.26	.750	.725	7.5	8.5 : 1	...	...	...	Shaft R.V.	Beam/Radial
Ohlsson & Rice '33'	C	V	C	C	.330	5.41	.759	.729	5.5	7.8 : 1	.40	at	11000	Shaft R.V.	Beam/Radial
Fox '35'	C	V	C	C	.345	5.65	.800	.700	5.7	7 : 1	.5+	at	14000	Shaft R.V.	Beam
McCoy 'Sportsman Jr.'	C	V	C	C	.349	5.72	.809	.670	7.0	8.5 : 1	.41	at	13000	Disc R.V.	Beam
Reeves 6 c.c.	C	V	C	C	.359	5.88	.781	.750	7.9	6 : 1	.17	at	6,500	Shaft R.V.	Beam
Mechanair '5.9'	C	V	C	C	.359	5.88	.781	.750	8.0	—	...	...	...	3-port	Beam
Elf 'Four' (4-cyl.)	C	V	C	C	.389	6.38	.468	.564	9.0	7 : 1	...	...	...	3-port	Beam
Air-O'Mighty Midget	C	V	C	C	.451	7.39	.875	.750	7.5	8 : 1	.60	at	12400	3-port	Beam
Madewell '49'	C	V	C	C	.488	8.00	.891	.783	9.0	5.5 : 1	...	...	...	Shaft R.V.	Beam
Atwood 'Triumph-49'	C	V	C	C	.491	8.05	.890	.790	8.5	7.5 : 1	.75	at	14000	Shaft R.V.	Beam/Radial
McCoy 'Red Head 49'	C	V	C	C	.491	8.05	.890	.790	11.5	9 : 1	.90+	at	15500	Disc R.V.	Beam
Yulon '49'	C	V	C	C	.498	8.16	.960	.688	6.7	—	.55+	at	12000	Shaft R.V.	Beam
Atwood 'Triumph 51'	C	V	C	D	.503	8.24	.900	.790	8.5	7.5 : 1	.75	at	14000	Shaft R.V.	Beam
McCoy 'Sportsman Sr.'	C	VI	C	D	.548	8.98	.940	.790	11.0	9 : 1	.69	at	13800	Disc R.V.	Beam
Fox 59 'Hi-Torque'	C	VI	C	D	.593	9.72	.937	.860	9.5	6 : 1	.80	at	10000	Disc R.V.	Beam
Fox 59 'Hi-Speed'	C	VI	C	D	.593	9.72	.937	.860	9.5	6 : 1	1.12	at	16000	Disc R.V.	Beam
Contestor D.60R	C	VI	C	D	.596	9.77	.945	.850	13.8	6.8 : 1	.61	at	10500	Drum R.V	Beam
Ball BC	C	VI	C	D	.603	9.89	.924	.900	16.0	10 : 1	1.00	at	16000	Shaft R.V.	Beam
Wasp-Twin (2-cyl)	C	VI	C	D	.604	9.90	.740	.702	12.0	7 : 1	.50	at	9000	Shaft R.V.	Beam
Herkimer-'O.K.' 60	C	VI	C	D	.604	9.90	.900	.950	12.0	6 or 8 : 1	.33+	at	8500/9000	Shaft R.V.	Beam
Electra 'Pioneer-10'	C	VI	C	D	.604	9.90	.937	.875	14.0	12 : 1	.62	at	12000	Disc R.V.	Beam
Ohlsson & Rice '60'	C	VI	C	D	.604	9.90	.937	.875	10.0	6 : 1	.5	at	9000	3-port or Shaft	Beam/Radial
1066 Conqueror	C	VI	C	D	.604	9.90	.937	.875	15.0	13 : 1	...	...	...	Disc R.V.	Beam
Hornet	C	VI	C	D	.604	9.90	.937	.875	16.0	10 : 1	1.2	at	18000	Disc R.V.	Beam
Rowell '60'	C	VI	C	D	.604	9.90	.937	.875	19.0	12 : 1	1.0+	at	15000	Disc R.V.	Beam
Anderson Spitfire (1948)	C	VI	C	D	.604	9.90	.937	.875	12.0	6 : 1	.5	at	10000	Shaft R.V.	Beam
Jensen C.I. Special (4-stroke)	C	VI	C	D	.604	9.90	.937	.875	19.5	6.5 : 1	.52	at	10000	O.H.V.	Beam
Super Cyclone	C	VI	C	D	.604	9.90	.906	.937	10.0	5.5 : 1	.55	at	10500	Shaft R.V.	Beam
Nordec R.G.10	C	VI	C	D	.607	9.95	.940	.875	16.3	10 : 1	.63	at	12200	Disc R.V.	Beam
Nordec R.10	C	VI	C	D	.607	9.95	.940	.875	17.0	10 : 1	.74	at	13000	Disc R.V.	Beam
Nordec-Special Series I	C	VI	C	D	.607	9.95	.940	875	16.5	10 : 1	.75	at	13000	Disc R.V.	Beam
Nordec-Special Series II	C	VI	C	D	.607	9.95	.940	.875	16.0	—	1.23	at	15200	Disc R.V.	Beam
McCoy Series 20	C	VI	C	D	.607	9.95	.940	.875	16.0	9.5 : 1	1.4	at	16000	Disc R.V.	Beam
Dooling 61	C	VI	C	D	.607	9.95	1.015	.750	16.0	9.5 : 1	1.5	at	16000	Disc R.V.	Beam
Craftsman-Twin (2-cyl.)	C	VI	C	D	.607	9.95	.750	.6875	15.5	7 : 1	.2+	at	6700	Disc R.V.	Beam
Atwood Champion Type D.R.	C	VI	C	D	.624	10.23	.940	.900	11.5	8 : 1	.90+	at	12500	Dual R.V.	Beam
Super-Wasp (2-cyl)	C	VI	C	D	.645	10.57	.740	.750	12.0	6.5 : 1	.75	at	10000	Shaft R.V.	Radial
Anderson-Spitfire (1949/50)	C	VI	C	D	.647	10.60	.937	.937	12.0	6 : 1	.5+	at	10000	Shaft R.V.	Beam
Orr Tornado-65	C	VI	C	D	.647	10.60	.937	.937	—	12.5 : 1	...	...	...	Disc R.V.	Beam
Hassad 'Blue-streak'	C	VI	C	D	.648	10.62	.940	.934	—	11 : 1	1.0	at	15000	Shaft R.V.	Beam
Burgess M.5 (5-cyl. radial)	—	—	—	—	.920	15.08	.625	.600	22.0	5.5 : 1	.3	at	3500	O.H.V.	Radial
Forster '99'	—	—	—	—	.997	16.34	1.062	1.125	15.0	8 : 1	.62	at	7000	3-port	Beam
Herkimer-'O.K.' Twin (2-cyl)	—	—	—	—	1.208	19.80	.900	.950	23.0	6 : 1	.50	at	6000	3-port	Radial

The above data are prepared as at April 1st, 1951. Weights quoted are actual checked weights wherever possible. Capacities (swept volume) are calculated from makers' bore and stroke measurements. Performance figures are prepared either from manufacturers' information, or from independent test data, or from estimates based thereon. Wherever possible these indicate, in round figures, average production model performance, rather than figures obtained with any one example.

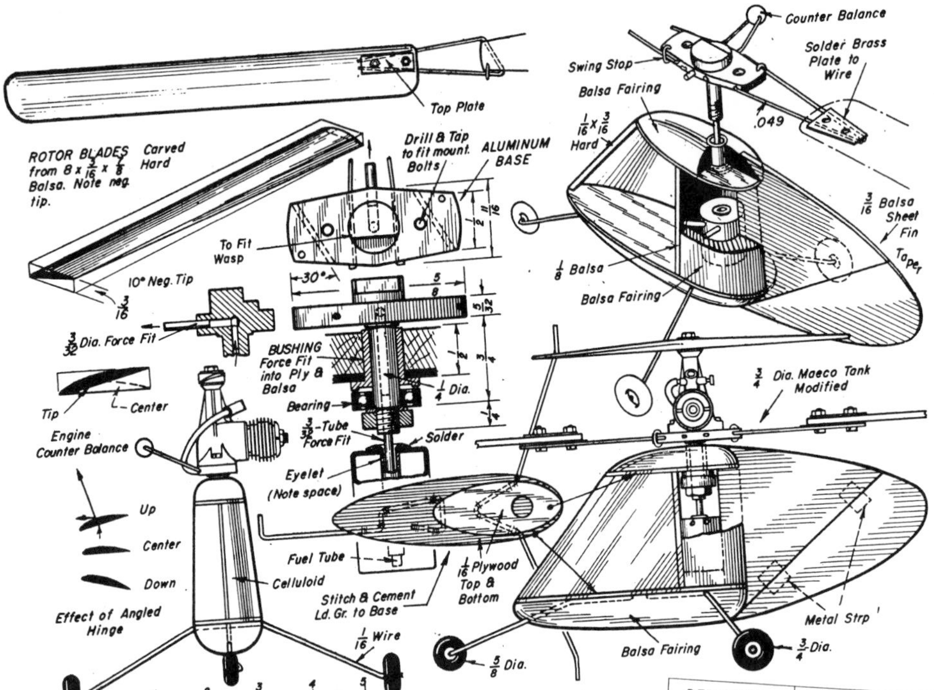

Counter Balance
Solder Brass Plate to Wire
Swing Stop
Balsa Fairing
Top Plate
ROTOR BLADES Carved from 8 x 3/16 x 5/8 Balsa. Note neg. tip.
Hard
Drill & Tap to fit mount. Bolts
ALUMINUM BASE
1/16 x 3/16 Hard
.049
3/16 Balsa Sheet Fin
Taper
To Fit Wasp
10° Neg. Tip
1/8 Balsa
Balsa Fairing
3/32 Dia. Force Fit
BUSHING Force Fit into Ply & Balsa
Bearing
1/4 Dia.
3/4 Dia. Maeco Tank Modified
Tip
Center
Engine Counter Balance
3/32-Tube Force Fit
Solder
Eyelet (Note space)
Up
Center
Down
Fuel Tube
Celluloid
1/16 Plywood Top & Bottom
Stitch & Cement Ld. Gr. to Base
Effect of Angled Hinge
1/16 Wire
Metal Strp
Balsa Fairing
5/8 Dia.
3/4 Dia.

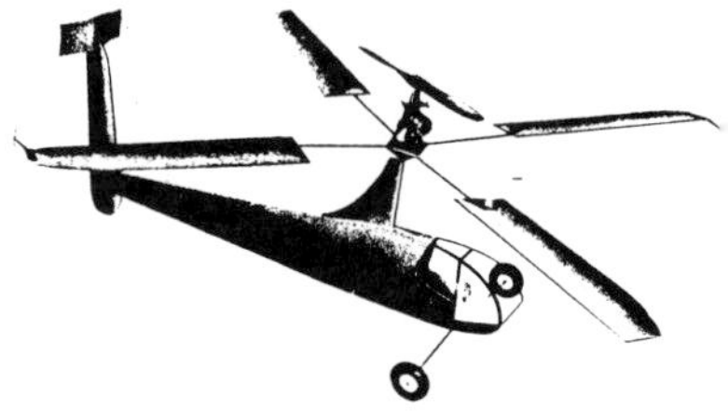

A helicopter design competition run by *Air Tra* had a high entry. Winning design, published F 52 and shown left, was by Paul H. Stahlhuth. Suggestions to improve were much larger van and stiffer hinges. Above and below, kitted by Berkeley in '53 were *Cloud-copter D* and *TR*, t latter having an adjustable tail rotor. Diameter and 25in. respectively.

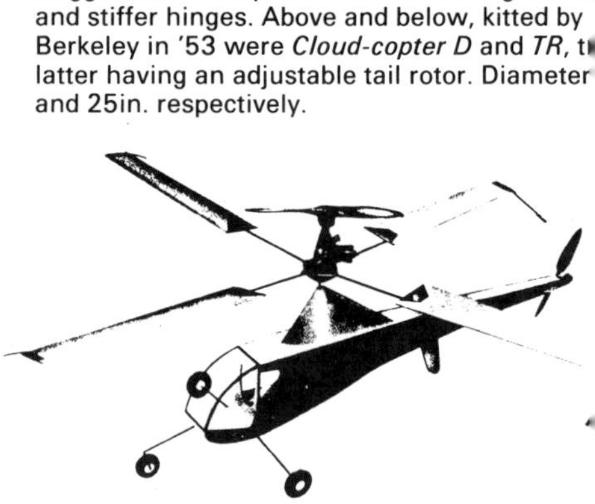

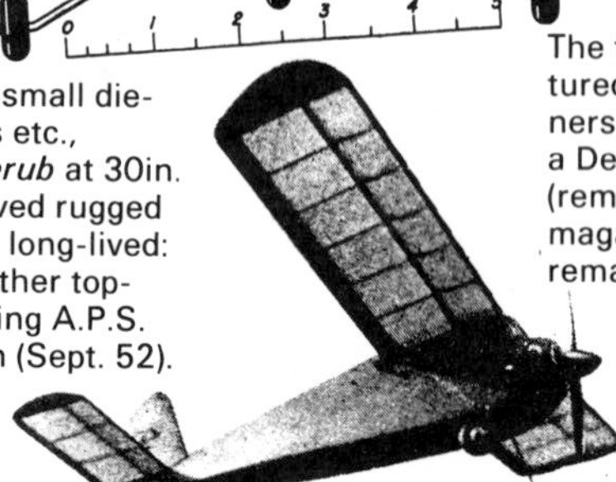

For small diesels etc., *Cherub* at 30in. proved rugged and long-lived: another top-selling A.P.S. plan (Sept. 52).

The third power model featured in the 1949-52 beginners' series, *Debutante* was a December give-away plan (remaining parts on a magazine page) but has remained a "top 20" plan for 36 years.

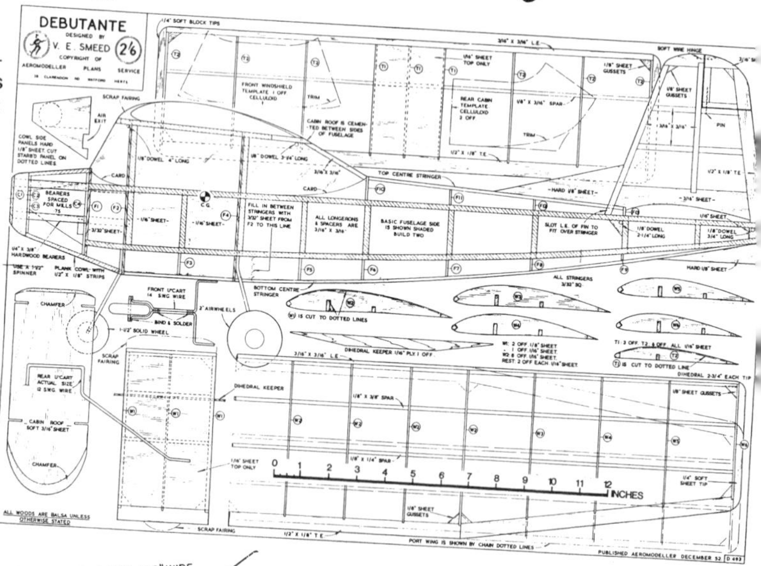

DEBUTANTE
DESIGNED BY V. E. SMEED
2/6
AEROMODELLER PLANS SERVICE
INCHES
ALL WOODS ARE BALSA UNLESS OTHERWISE STATED
PUBLISHED AEROMODELLER DECEMBER 52

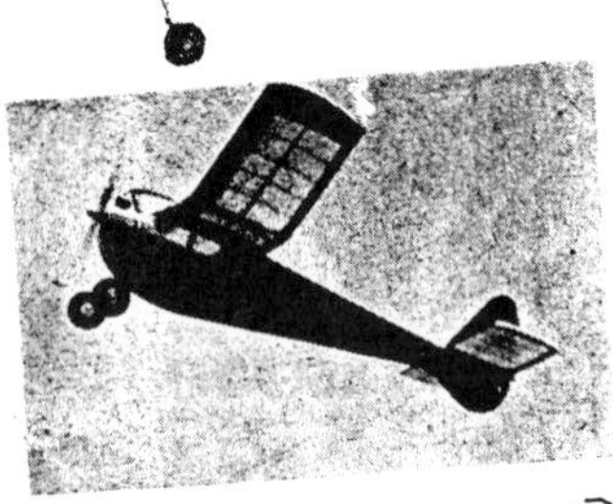

Designed to a specification by Fr. F. Callon, who wrote much of the "Especially for the Beginner" series, *Madcap* came as a cabin or profile high performance design, both on one plan in April 52 and both still built today.

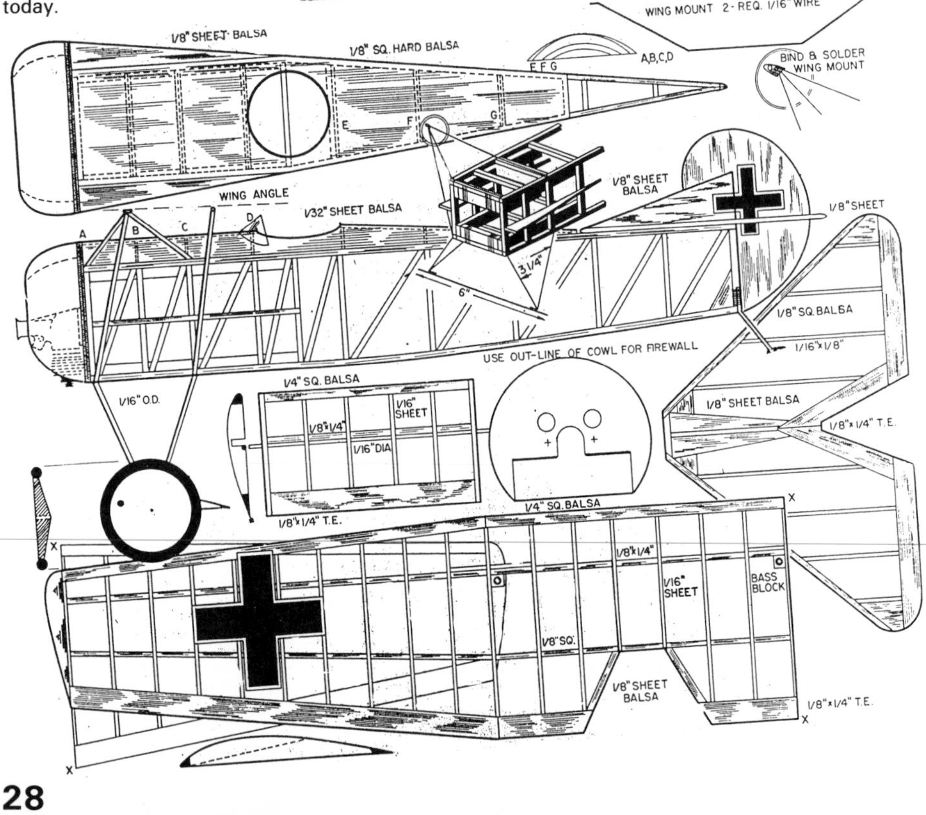

WING MOUNT 2- REQ. 1/16" WIRE
1/8" SHEET BALSA
1/8" SQ. HARD BALSA
A,B,C,D
E F G
BIND & SOLDER WING MOUNT
WING ANGLE
1/32" SHEET BALSA
1/8" SHEET BALSA
1/8" SHEET
3 1/4"
6"
1/8" SQ.BALSA
1/16"x1/8"
USE OUT-LINE OF COWL FOR FIREWALL
1/4" SQ. BALSA
1/16" SHEET
1/8"x1/4"
1/16"DIA
1/16" O.D.
1/8" SHEET BALSA
1/8"x 1/4" T.E.
1/8"x1/4" T.E.
1/4" SQ. BALSA
1/8"x1/4"
1/16" SHEET
BASS BLOCK
1/8"SQ.
1/8" SHEET BALSA
1/8"x1/4" T.E.

The Fokker D8, known in the U.S.A. as the "Fl ing Razor," has always been a popular prototy because of its parasol wing and generous tail areas. This version, by Ted Grzeszak, appeared *MAN* Jan. 52 and was a large, light model (38½in. span, 7oz. weight) for ½A engines. No that trailing edges should be ⅛×¾in., not as shown, and that 1¼in. of dihedral was used under each tip.

Unknown to today's modellers, the English k firm Halfax produced (to bottom) *Spartan* (5ft., £1•18•6!), *Hermes, Sabr* and *Rapier* amon a range of goo models.

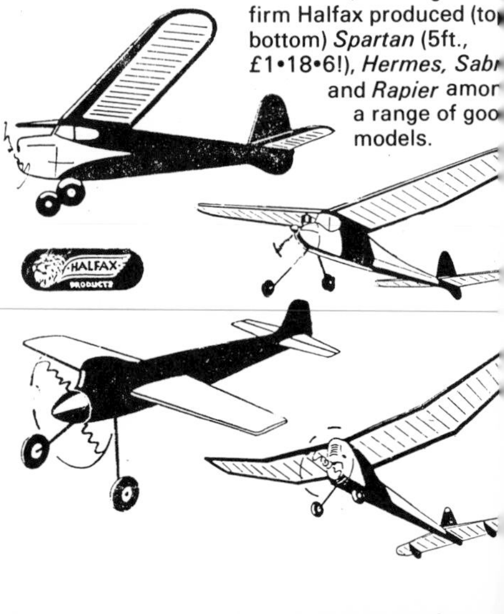

HALFAX PRODUCTS

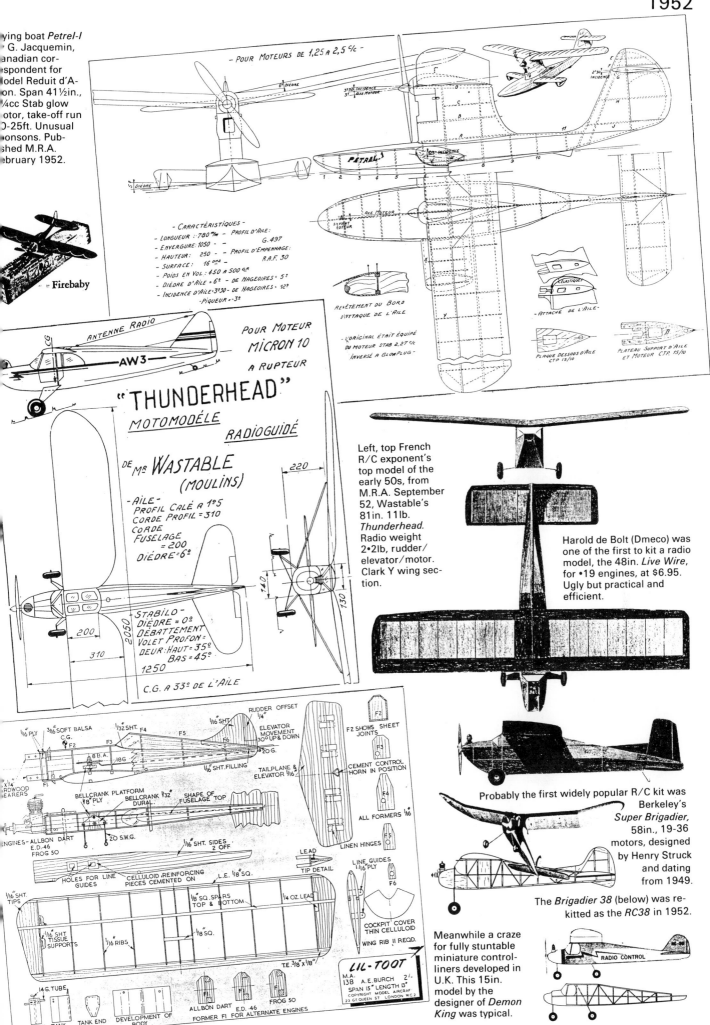

ying boat *Petrel-I*
G. Jacquemin,
anadian cor-
spondent for
odel Reduit d'A-
on. Span 41½in.,
¼cc Stab glow
otor, take-off run
0-25ft. Unusual
onsons. Pub-
shed M.R.A.
bruary 1952.

Firebaby

Left, top French
R/C exponent's
top model of the
early 50s, from
M.R.A. September
52, Wastable's
81in. 11lb.
Thunderhead.
Radio weight
2•2lb, rudder/
elevator/motor.
Clark Y wing sec-
tion.

Harold de Bolt (Dmeco) was
one of the first to kit a radio
model, the 48in. *Live Wire*,
for •19 engines, at $6.95.
Ugly but practical and
efficient.

Probably the first widely popular R/C kit was
Berkeley's *Super Brigadier*,
58in., 19-36
motors, designed
by Henry Struck
and dating
from 1949.

The *Brigadier 38* (below) was re-
kitted as the *RC38* in 1952.

Meanwhile a craze
for fully stuntable
miniature control-
liners developed in
U.K. This 15in.
model by the
designer of *Demon
King* was typical.

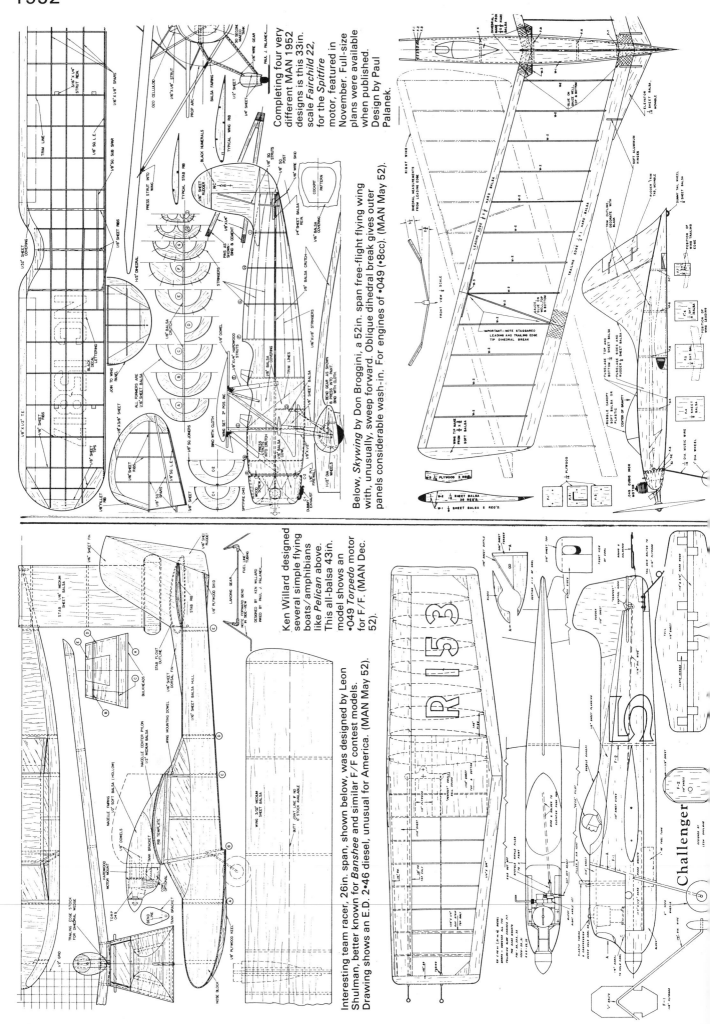

Completing four very different MAN 1952 designs is this 33in. scale *Fairchild 22*, featured in November. Full-size plans were available when published. Design by Paul Palanek.

Below, *Skywing* by Don Broggini, a 52in. span free-flight flying wing with, unusually, sweep forward. Oblique dihedral break gives outer panels considerable wash-in. For engines of •049 (•8cc). (MAN May 52).

Interesting team racer, 26in. span, shown below, was designed by Leon Shulman, better known for *Banshee* and similar F/F contest models. Drawing shows an E.D. 2•46 diesel, unusual for America. (MAN May 52).

Ken Willard designed several simple flying boats/amphibians like *Pelican* above. This all-balsa 43in. model shows an •049 *Torpedo* motor for F/F. (MAN Dec. 52).

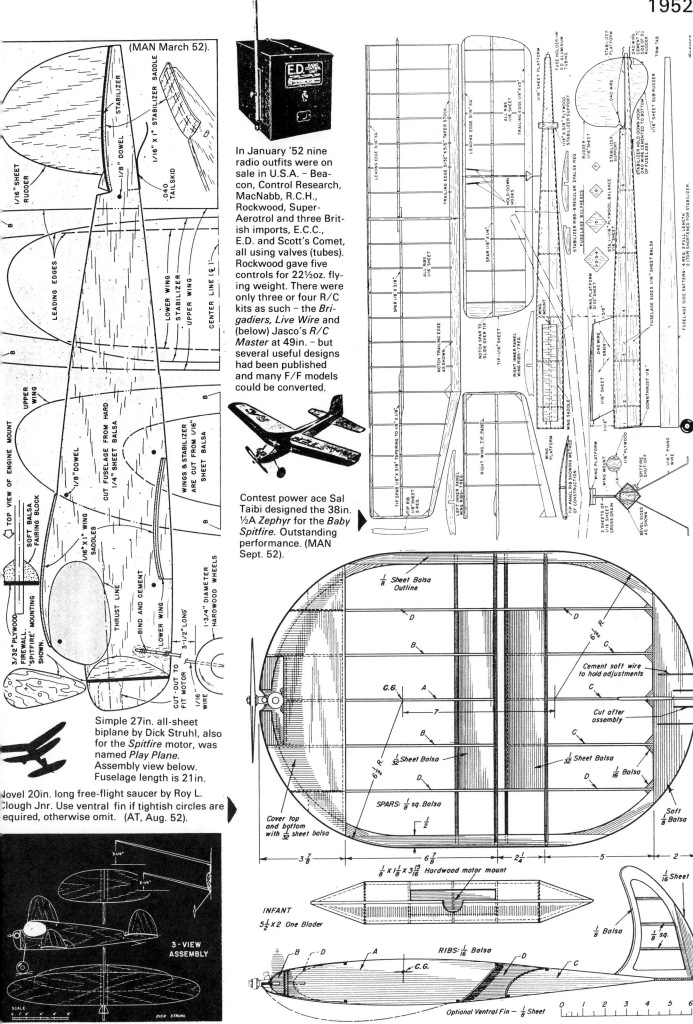

(MAN March 52).

1/16" SHEET RUDDER

STABILIZER

1/8" DOWEL

1/16" x 1" STABILIZER SADDLE

.040 TAILSKID

UPPER WING

LOWER WING

STABILIZER

UPPER WING

LEADING EDGES

CENTER LINE (℄)

TOP VIEW OF ENGINE MOUNT

SOFT BALSA FAIRING BLOCK

3/32" PLYWOOD FIREWALL 'SPITFIRE' MOUNTING SHOWN.

1/8" DOWEL

CUT FUSELAGE FROM HARD 1/4" SHEET BALSA

WINGS & STABILIZER ARE CUT FROM 1/16" SHEET BALSA

1/16" x 1" WING SADDLES

THRUST LINE

BIND AND CEMENT

LOWER WING

CUT-OUT TO FIT MOTOR

3-1/2" LONG

1/16" WIRE

1-3/4" DIAMETER HARDWOOD WHEELS

Simple 27in. all-sheet biplane by Dick Struhl, also for the *Spitfire* motor, was named *Play Plane*. Assembly view below. Fuselage length is 21in.

Novel 20in. long free-flight saucer by Roy L. Clough Jnr. Use ventral fin if tightish circles are required, otherwise omit. (AT, Aug. 52).

In January '52 nine radio outfits were on sale in U.S.A. – Beacon, Control Research, MacNabb, R.C.H., Rockwood, Super-Aerotrol and three British imports, E.C.C., E.D. and Scott's Comet, all using valves (tubes). Rockwood gave five controls for 22½oz. flying weight. There were only three or four R/C kits as such – the *Brigadiers*, *Live Wire* and (below) Jasco's *R/C Master* at 49in. – but several useful designs had been published and many F/F models could be converted.

Contest power ace Sal Taibi designed the 38in. ½A *Zephyr* for the *Baby Spitfire*. Outstanding performance. (MAN Sept. 52).

LEADING EDGE 1/16" SQ.

TRAILING EDGE 3/32" X 5/8" TAPER STOCK

LEADING EDGE 3/16" SQ.

ALL RIBS 1/16 SHEET

TRAILING EDGE 1/8" X 1/2"

SPAR 1/8" X 3/8"

ALL RIBS 1/16 SHEET

SPAR 1/8" X 3/8"

WING MOUNT

NOTCH TRAILING EDGE AS SHOWN

NOTCH SPAR TO SLIDE OVER TIP

TIP-1/16" SHEET

RIGHT INNER PANEL WING RIBS-7 REQ.

RIGHT WING TIP PANEL

WING PLATFORM

WING PLATFORM 3/32 SHEET

WING PLATFORM

WING MOUNT

TIP SPAR 1/8" X 3/8" TAPERING TO 1/8" X 1/4"

TIP RIB 2 REQ.

LEFT INNER PANEL WING RIBS-7 REQ.

TIP PANEL SHOWING METHOD OF CONSTRUCTION

TIP PANEL RIB

1/16" x 3/8" PLYWOOD STABILIZER SUPPORT

RUDDER 1/16 SHEET

STA. 1-1/16" PLYWOOD BALANCE STA. 1/8" X 1/4"

040 WIRE GRAIN

1/16" SHEET

2 SHEETS OF 1/16 SHEET CROSS GRAIN

1/16" PLYWOOD

WING MOUNT

SPITFIRE SHUT-OFF

STABILIZER PLATFORM

FUSE HOLDER 1/4" O.D. ALUMINUM TUBING

HOLD-DOWN HOOKS

FUSELAGE BULK-HEADS

STABILIZER RIBS-9 REGULAR 2 FALSE REQ

040 WIRE

STABILIZER PLATFORM

STABILIZER SUPPORT

.040 WIRE HOLD DOWN HOOK CEMENT TO BOTTOM OF FUSELAGE

STABILIZER HOLD-DOWN HOOK .040 WIRE CEMENTED TO BOTTOM OF STABILIZER

STABILIZER PLATFORM

.040 WIRE ON SIDE OF SUB RUDDER

TRIM TAB

FUSELAGE SIDES 1/16" SHEET BALSA

FUSELAGE SIDE PATTERN- 4 REQ 2 FULL LENGTH 2 (TOP) SHORTENED FOR STABILIZER

1/16" SHEET BALSA

DOWNTHRUST 1/8"

BEVEL SIDES AS SHOWN

1/16" PIANO WIRE

1/8 Sheet Balsa Outline

D

D

B

6½" R.

Cement soft wire to hold adjustments

C.G.

A

7

B

Cut after assembly

C

6½" R.

1/32 Sheet Balsa

1/32 Sheet Balsa

1/16 Balsa

D

SPARS: 1/8 sq. Balsa

D

Soft 1/8 Balsa

Cover top and bottom with 1/32 sheet balsa

1/2

3 7/8

6 7/8

2 1/4

5

2

1/8 x 1 1/8 x 3 15/16 Hardwood motor mount

INFANT
5½ x 2 One Blader

1/16 Sheet

1/8 Balsa

1/8 sq.

B

D

A

C.G.

RIBS: 1/16 Balsa

D

C

Optional Ventral Fin – 1/8 Sheet

0 1 2 3 4 5 6

3-1/4"

2-1/4"

3-VIEW ASSEMBLY

SCALE

DICK STRUHL

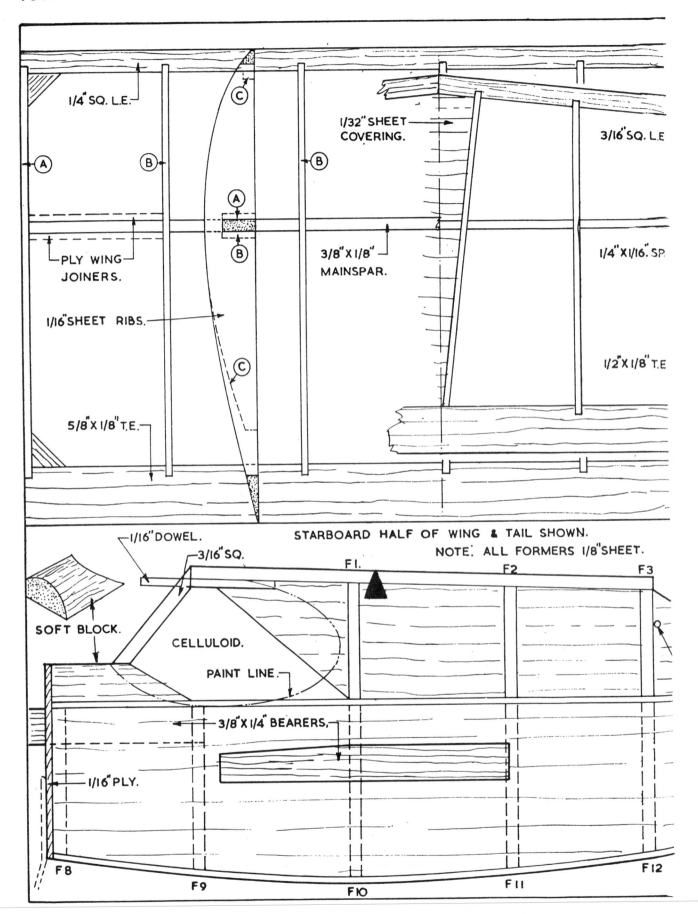

1/4" SQ. L.E.

1/32" SHEET COVERING.

3/16"SQ. L.E

Ⓐ   Ⓒ

Ⓐ

Ⓑ   Ⓑ

PLY WING JOINERS.

Ⓐ

Ⓑ

3/8" X 1/8" MAINSPAR.

1/4" X 1/16". SP.

1/16" SHEET RIBS.

Ⓒ

1/2" X 1/8" T.E

5/8" X 1/8" T.E.

1/16" DOWEL.

STARBOARD HALF OF WING & TAIL SHOWN.

3/16" SQ.

NOTE: ALL FORMERS 1/8" SHEET.

F1.   F2   F3

SOFT BLOCK.

CELLULOID.

PAINT LINE.

3/8" X 1/4" BEARERS.

1/16" PLY.

F 8   F 12

F 9   F 10   F 11

Titch was a 29in. design for up to •5cc engines by the late Ron Warring which appeared full-size in *Aeromodeller* in July 1952. Draw a centre-line on a piece of 1/16in. sheet 1⅜ × 18½in. and cement centrally formers 8-16. Cut two sides and cement to the formers, fit engine bearers, sand and sheet bottom. Trim excess from crutch. Cut vertical keel and cement in place, then add formers 1-7 and cabin top. Bend undercarriage and bind to ply firewall, cement to F8 and add soft block. Sand all over, fit dowels, rear ply saddle, hook and underfin and tissue cover. Wing and tail are conventional, fin is cemented to tailplane after

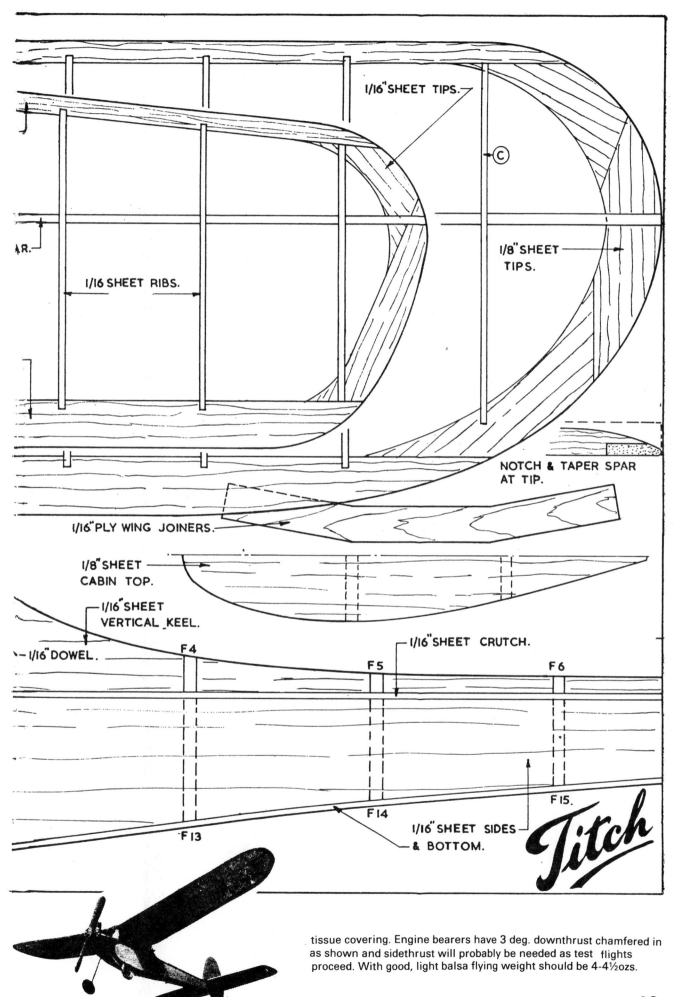

1/16" SHEET TIPS.

C

1/16 SHEET RIBS.

1/8" SHEET TIPS.

NOTCH & TAPER SPAR AT TIP.

1/16" PLY WING JOINERS.

1/8" SHEET CABIN TOP.

1/16" SHEET VERTICAL KEEL.

1/16" DOWEL.

F4

F5

1/16" SHEET CRUTCH.

F6

F13

F14

F15

1/16" SHEET SIDES & BOTTOM.

Titch

tissue covering. Engine bearers have 3 deg. downthrust chamfered in as shown and sidethrust will probably be needed as test flights proceed. With good, light balsa flying weight should be 4-4½ozs.

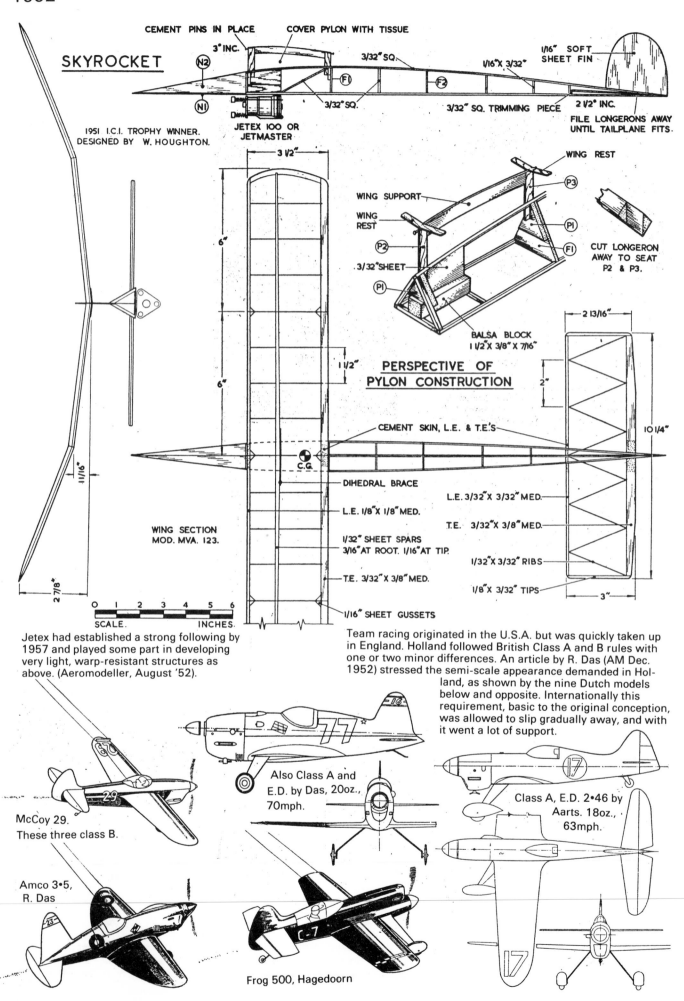

SKYROCKET

1951 I.C.I. TROPHY WINNER.
DESIGNED BY W. HOUGHTON.

CEMENT PINS IN PLACE
COVER PYLON WITH TISSUE
3° INC.
N2
F1
3/32" SQ.
F2
1/16"X 3/32"
1/16" SOFT SHEET FIN
3/32" SQ.
N1
3/32" SQ. TRIMMING PIECE
2 1/2° INC.
JETEX 100 OR JETMASTER
FILE LONGERONS AWAY UNTIL TAILPLANE FITS.

WING REST
WING SUPPORT
WING REST
P3
P1
P2
F1
CUT LONGERON AWAY TO SEAT P2 & P3.
.3/32" SHEET
P1
BALSA BLOCK 1 1/2" X 3/8" X 7/16"

PERSPECTIVE OF PYLON CONSTRUCTION

3 1/2"
6"
6"
1 1/2"
2 13/16"
2"
10 1/4"
CEMENT SKIN, L.E. & T.E'S
C.G.
DIHEDRAL BRACE
L.E. 1/8" X 1/8" MED.
1/32" SHEET SPARS 3/16" AT ROOT. 1/16" AT TIP.
T.E. 3/32" X 3/8" MED.
WING SECTION MOD. MVA. 123.
1/16" SHEET GUSSETS
L.E. 3/32" X 3/32" MED.
T.E. 3/32" X 3/8" MED.
1/32" X 3/32" RIBS
1/8" X 3/32" TIPS
3"

11/16"
2 7/8"

0 1 2 3 4 5 6
SCALE. INCHES.

Jetex had established a strong following by 1957 and played some part in developing very light, warp-resistant structures as above. (Aeromodeller, August '52).

Team racing originated in the U.S.A. but was quickly taken up in England. Holland followed British Class A and B rules with one or two minor differences. An article by R. Das (AM Dec. 1952) stressed the semi-scale appearance demanded in Holland, as shown by the nine Dutch models below and opposite. Internationally this requirement, basic to the original conception, was allowed to slip gradually away, and with it went a lot of support.

McCoy 29. These three class B.

Also Class A and E.D. by Das, 20oz., 70mph.

Class A, E.D. 2•46 by Aarts. 18oz., 63mph.

Amco 3•5, R. Das

Frog 500, Hagedoorn

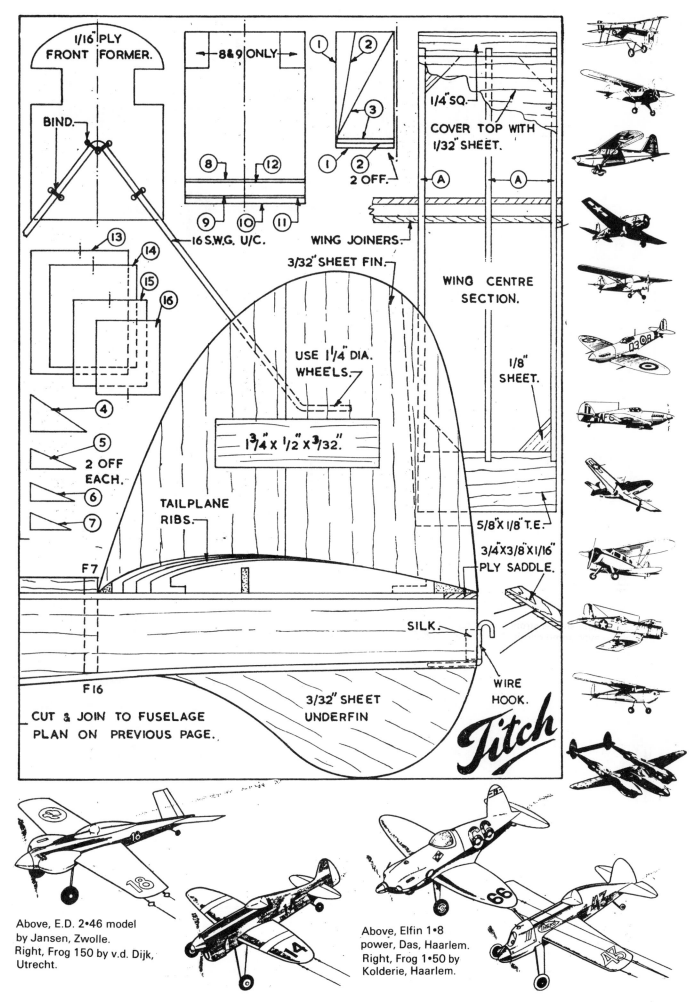

1/16" PLY FRONT FORMER.

BIND.

8&9 ONLY

① ② ③ ① ②
2 OFF.

⑧ ⑫
⑨ ⑩ ⑪

16 S.W.G. U/C.

1/4" SQ.

COVER TOP WITH 1/32" SHEET.

Ⓐ Ⓐ

WING JOINERS.

WING CENTRE SECTION.

3/32" SHEET FIN.

⑬ ⑭ ⑮ ⑯

USE 1 1/4" DIA. WHEELS.

1/8" SHEET.

④
⑤
2 OFF EACH.
⑥
⑦

1 3/4" X 1/2" X 3/32".

TAILPLANE RIBS.

F7

5/8"X1/8" T.E.

3/4"X3/8"X1/16" PLY SADDLE.

SILK.

F16

WIRE HOOK.

CUT & JOIN TO FUSELAGE PLAN ON PREVIOUS PAGE.

3/32" SHEET UNDERFIN

Titch

Above, E.D. 2•46 model by Jansen, Zwolle. Right, Frog 150 by v.d. Dijk, Utrecht.

Above, Elfin 1•8 power, Das, Haarlem. Right, Frog 1•50 by Kolderie, Haarlem.

1952

One result of the quite radical changes to the Wakefield rules in 1951 was the emergence of the long-fuselage Wake. Joe Bilgri and Joe Foster were leading exponents and both produced remarkable results, but limitations on rubber weight introduced in 1953 killed off the 5ft. long fuselage approach.

The elliptical surfac[es?] point to a Carl Gold[-]berg design and his 36in. Comet *Clippe[r] Jnr.,* kitted in the 1930s, was still go[ing] strong in 1952, tho[...]

½A motors were [mak-]ing inroads on rub[ber] power interest.

Responsible for man[y] kit designs for KeilKr[aft] and other makers, Albert Hatfull also pr[o-]duced a number of scale-type jet design[s] for the Jetex 50 of which this F9F-2 *Panther* is typical.

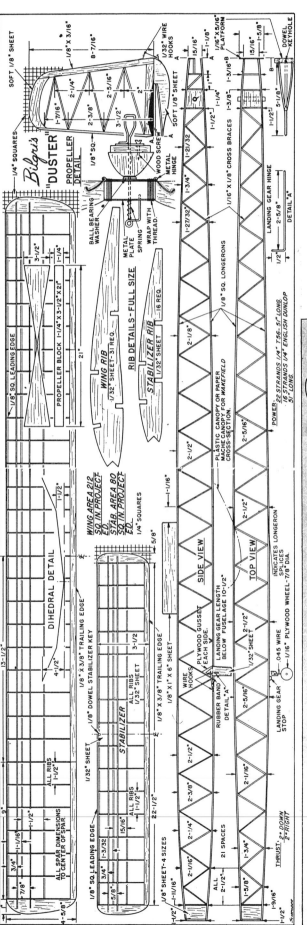

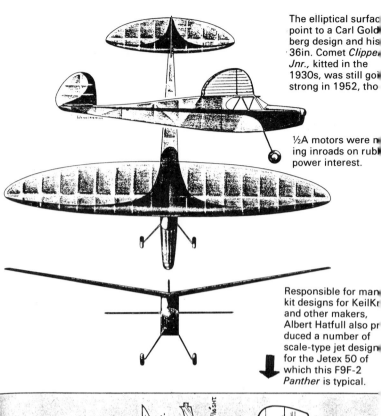

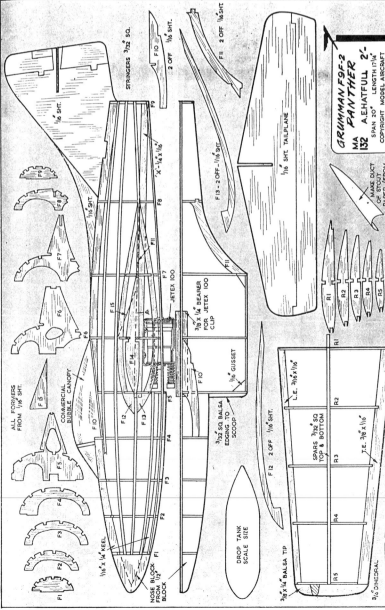

1952

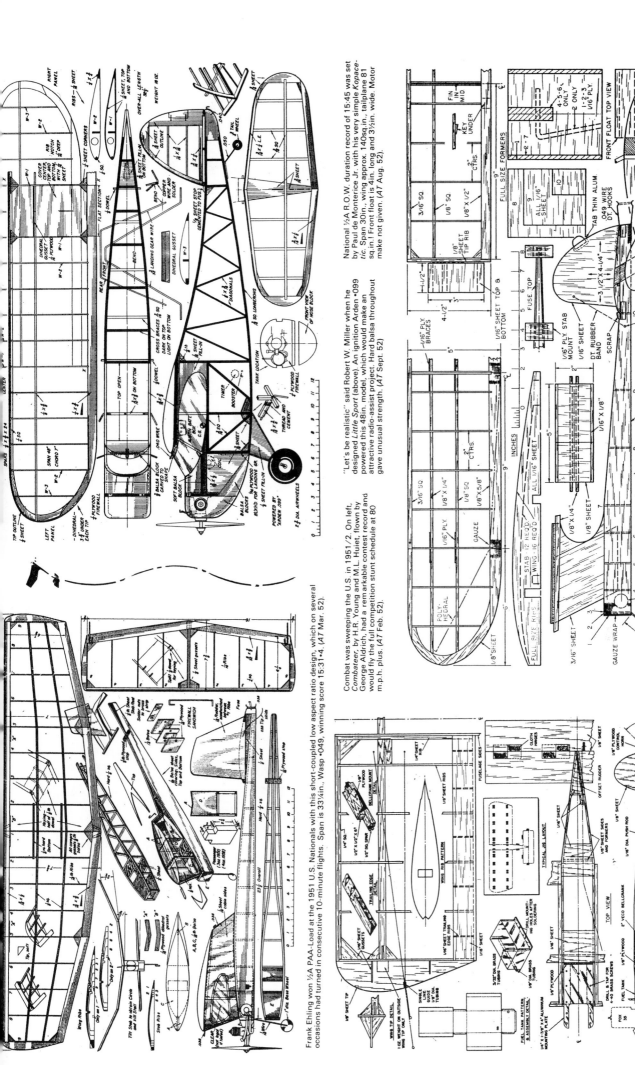

Frank Ehling won ½A PAA-Load at the 1951 U.S. Nationals with this short-coupled low aspect ratio design, which on several occasions had turned in consecutive 10-minute flights. Span is 33¾in., Wasp ·049, winning score 15:31·4. (AT Mar. 52).

Combat was sweeping the U.S. in 1951/2. On left, *Combateer*, by H.R. Young and M.L. Huiet, flown by George Aldrich, had a remarkable contest record and would fly the full competition stunt schedule at 80 m.p.h. plus. (AT Feb. 52)

"Let's be realistic," said Robert W. Miller when he designed *Little Sport* (above). An ignition Arden ·099 powered this 48in. model, which would make an attractive radio-assist project. Hard balsa throughout gave unusual strength. (AT Sept. 52)

National ½A R.O.W. duration record of 15:45 was set by Paul de Monterice Jr. with his very simple *Kopace-tic*. Span 30in., wing approx. 140sq.in., tailplane 81 sq.in.! Front float is 4in. long and 3½in. wide. Motor make not given. (AT Aug. 52).

37

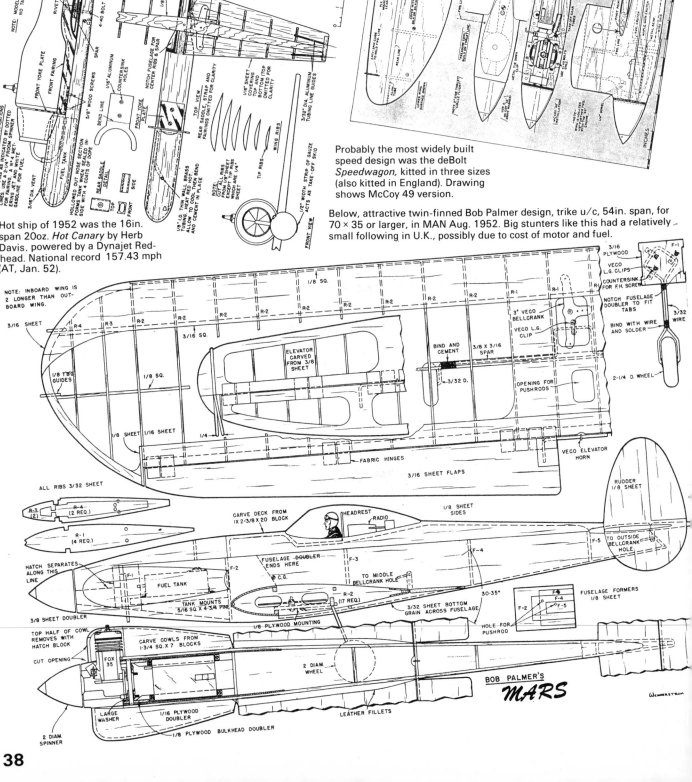

Probably the most widely built speed design was the deBolt *Speedwagon,* kitted in three sizes (also kitted in England). Drawing shows McCoy 49 version.

Below, attractive twin-finned Bob Palmer design, trike u/c, 54in. span, for 70 × 35 or larger, in MAN Aug. 1952. Big stunters like this had a relatively small following in U.K., possibly due to cost of motor and fuel.

Hot ship of 1952 was the 16in. span 20oz. *Hot Canary* by Herb Davis, powered by a Dynajet Red-head. National record 157.43 mph (AT, Jan. 52).

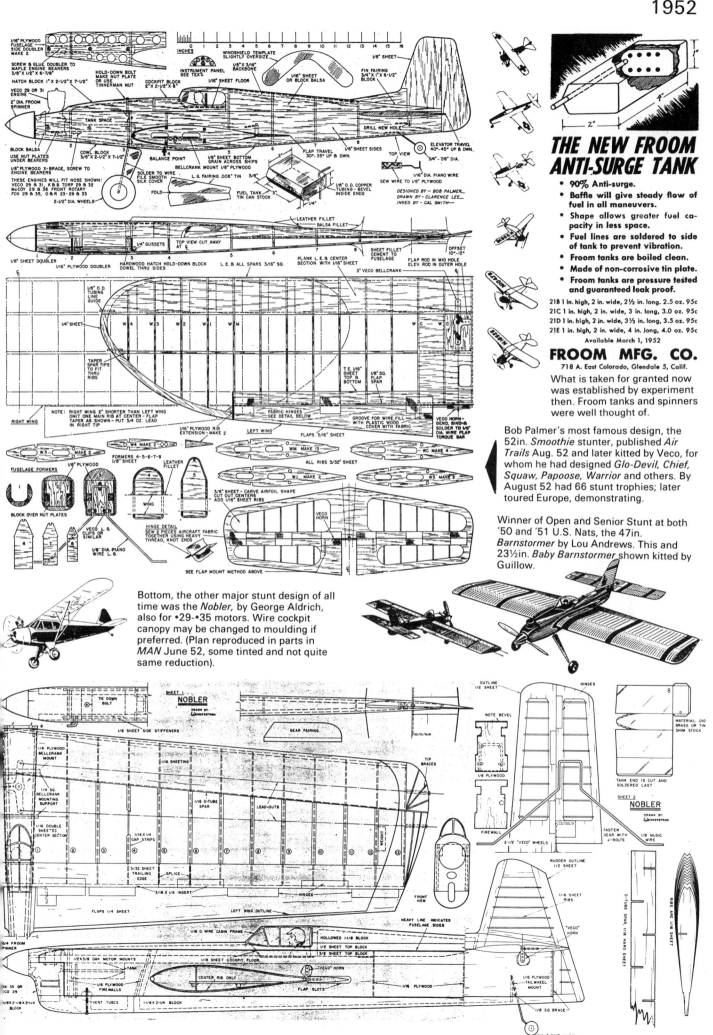

THE NEW FROOM ANTI-SURGE TANK

What is taken for granted now was established by experiment then. Froom tanks and spinners were well thought of.

Bob Palmer's most famous design, the 52in. *Smoothie* stunter, published *Air Trails* Aug. 52 and later kitted by Veco, for whom he had designed *Glo-Devil, Chief, Squaw, Papoose, Warrior* and others. By August 52 had 66 stunt trophies; later toured Europe, demonstrating.

Winner of Open and Senior Stunt at both '50 and '51 U.S. Nats, the 47in. *Barnstormer* by Lou Andrews. This and 23½in. *Baby Barnstormer* shown kitted by Guillow.

Bottom, the other major stunt design of all time was the *Nobler*, by George Aldrich, also for •29-•35 motors. Wire cockpit canopy may be changed to moulding if preferred. (Plan reproduced in parts in *MAN* June 52, some tinted and not quite same reduction).

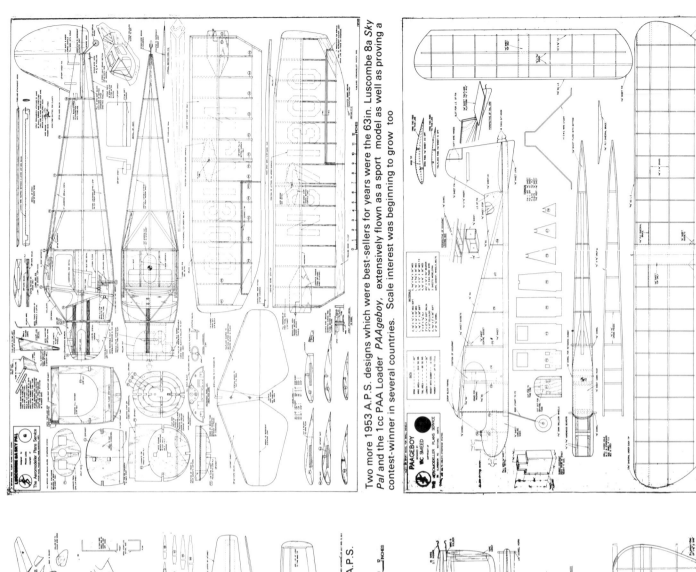

Two more 1953 A.P.S. designs which were best-sellers for years were the 63in. Luscombe 8a *Sky Pal* and the 1cc PAA Loader *PAAgeboy*, extensively flown as a sport model as well as proving a contest-winner in several countries. Scale interest was beginning to grow too

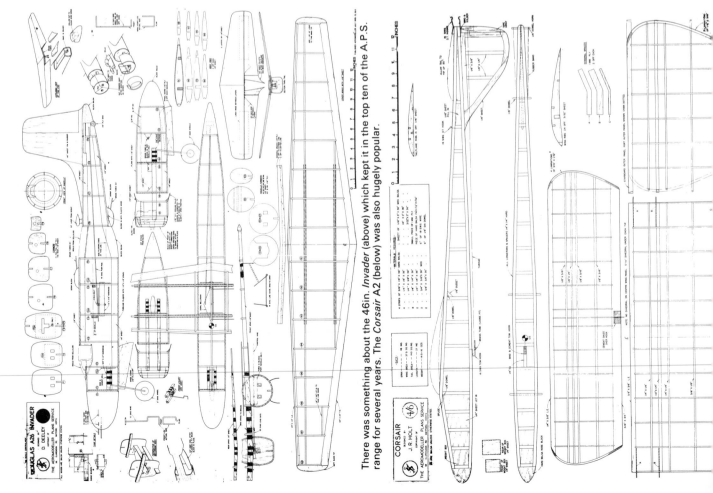

There was something about the 46in. *Invader* (above) which kept it in the top ten of the A.P.S. range for several years. The *Corsair* A2 (below) was also hugely popular.

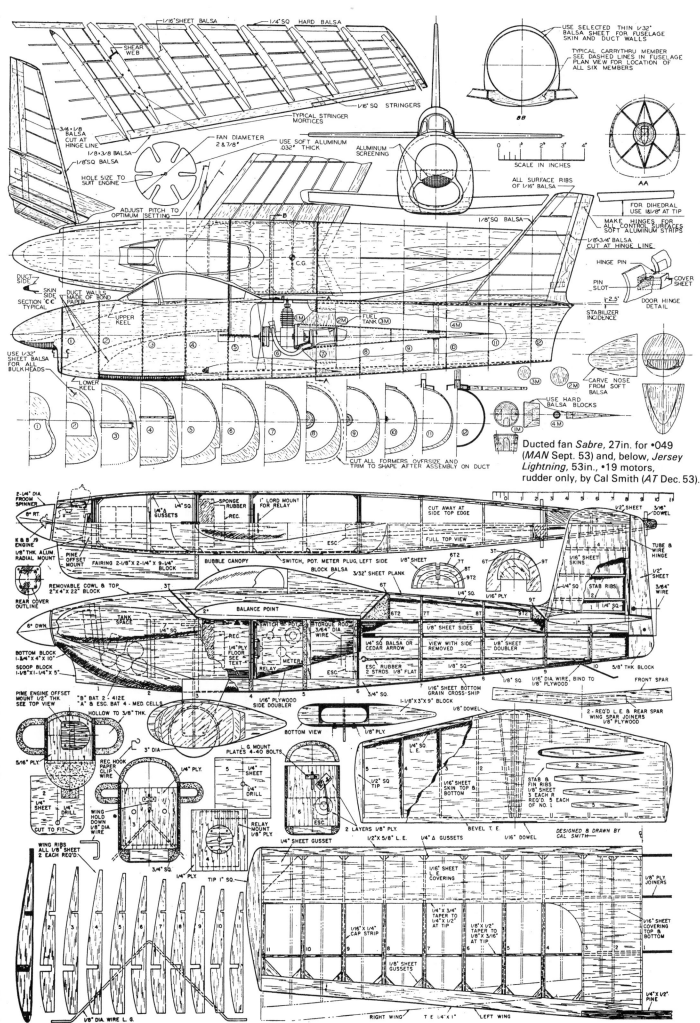

1953

Ducted fan *Sabre*, 27in. for •049 (*MAN* Sept. 53) and, below, *Jersey Lightning*, 53in., •19 motors, rudder only, by Cal Smith (*AT* Dec. 53).

THE GNAT
TEAM RACER
by Ron Moulton

Two versions of this model can be built to suit any of the 1/2A Team Race rules. 35 or 50 sq. ins. for 1 c.c. or 1·5 c.c.

Team racing in smaller sizes enjoyed a vogue towards the mid-50s. Ron Moulton's "gnatty" design appeared as full-size plans in Oct. 53 *Aeromodeller*. American approach by Granger Williams (below) was scale-like racer for •049 motors in *MAN* May 53.

One of the top English C/L speed fliers was/is Pete Wright, who held numerous world records in the early 50s. His *Gook* clocked 104mph (165·7 km/h) using an E.D. 2•46 Racer converted to glow and a 6×10 Stant prop.

Fair play for American readers! List below is of Sig balsa prices, as we have English prices later. Sig's were always a little over average due to their selectivity, but what quality!

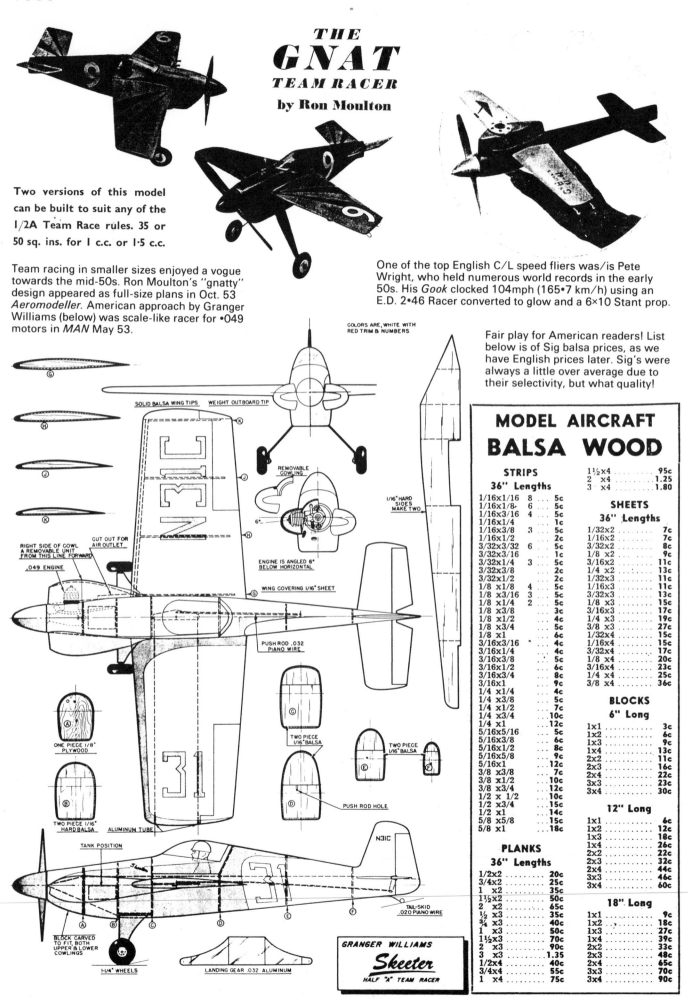

COLORS ARE WHITE WITH RED TRIM & NUMBERS

SOLID BALSA WING TIPS · WEIGHT OUTBOARD TIP

REMOVABLE COWLING

1/16" HARD SIDES MAKE TWO

ENGINE IS ANGLED 6° BELOW HORIZONTAL

WING COVERING 1/16" SHEET

RIGHT SIDE OF COWL A REMOVABLE UNIT FROM THIS LINE FORWARD

CUT OUT FOR AIR OUTLET

.049 ENGINE

PUSH ROD .032 PIANO WIRE

ONE PIECE 1/8" PLYWOOD

TWO PIECE 1/16" BALSA

TWO PIECE 1/16" BALSA

PUSH ROD HOLE

TWO PIECE 1/16" HARD BALSA

ALUMINUM TUBE

N31C

TANK POSITION

TAIL-SKID .020 PIANO WIRE

BLOCK CARVED TO FIT, BOTH UPPER & LOWER COWLINGS

1-1/4" WHEELS

LANDING GEAR .032 ALUMINUM

GRANGER WILLIAMS
Skeeter
HALF "A" TEAM RACER

MODEL AIRCRAFT
BALSA WOOD

STRIPS
36" Lengths

1/16x1/16	8	5c
1/16x1/8	6	5c
1/16x3/16	4	5c
1/16x1/4		1c
1/16x3/8	3	5c
1/16x1/2		2c
3/32x3/32	6	5c
3/32x3/16		1c
3/32x1/4	3	5c
3/32x3/8		2c
3/32x1/2		2c
1/8 x1/8	4	5c
1/8 x3/16	3	5c
1/8 x1/4	2	5c
1/8 x3/8		3c
1/8 x1/2		4c
1/8 x3/4		5c
1/8 x1		6c
3/16x3/16		4c
3/16x1/4		4c
3/16x3/8		5c
3/16x1/2		6c
3/16x3/4		8c
3/16x1		9c
1/4 x1/4		4c
1/4 x3/8		5c
1/4 x1/2		7c
1/4 x3/4		10c
1/4 x1		12c
5/16x5/16		5c
5/16x3/8		6c
5/16x1/2		8c
5/16x5/8		9c
5/16x1		12c
3/8 x3/8		7c
3/8 x1/2		10c
3/8 x3/4		12c
1/2 x 1/2		10c
1/2 x3/4		15c
1/2 x1		14c
5/8 x5/8		15c
5/8 x1		18c

PLANKS
36" Lengths

1/2x2	20c
3/4x2	25c
1 x2	35c
1½x2	50c
2 x2	65c
½ x3	35c
¾ x3	40c
1 x3	50c
1½x3	70c
2 x3	90c
3 x3	1.35
1/2x4	40c
3/4x4	55c
1 x4	75c

1½x4	95c
2 x4	1.25
3 x4	1.80

SHEETS
36" Lengths

1/32x2	7c
1/16x2	7c
3/32x2	8c
1/8 x2	9c
3/16x2	11c
1/4 x2	13c
1/32x3	11c
1/16x3	11c
3/32x3	13c
1/8 x3	15c
3/16x3	17c
1/4 x3	19c
3/8 x3	27c
1/32x4	15c
1/16x4	15c
3/32x4	17c
1/8 x4	20c
3/16x4	23c
1/4 x4	25c
3/8 x4	36c

BLOCKS
6" Long

1x1	3c
1x2	6c
1x3	9c
1x4	13c
2x2	11c
2x3	16c
2x4	22c
3x3	23c
3x4	30c

12" Long

1x1	6c
1x2	12c
1x3	18c
1x4	26c
2x2	22c
2x3	32c
2x4	44c
3x3	46c
3x4	60c

18" Long

1x1	9c
1x2	18c
1x3	27c
1x4	39c
2x2	33c
2x3	48c
2x4	65c
3x3	70c
3x4	90c

Sid Allen, a familiar figure at 1950s events, and his 60in. D.H. *Gipsy Moth*, a popular plan of the time.

George Fuller with his 1½cc *Stomper* which, with *Dixielander*, became among the most popular contest power models ever.

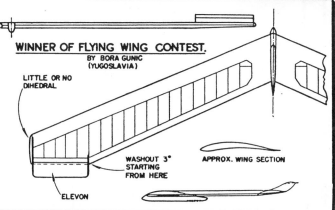

WINNER OF FLYING WING CONTEST.
BY BORA GUNIC (YUGOSLAVIA)

LITTLE OR NO DIHEDRAL
WASHOUT 3° STARTING FROM HERE
APPROX. WING SECTION
ELEVON

A classic which still attracts builders of big models is *Mercury IV*, by Mick Smith, still available as a plan. (*AM* Mar. 53).

Below, an early Jedelsky wing, though not then known by that name. Model by Helbert Jansa (Austria), 9ft. span, 6½in. chord, 18oz. weight, seen at an international tailless competition in Germany.

Three-flight total of 527•4 secs. won tailless glider contest. "Garden-seat" position of model's elevons is interesting, otherwise structure etc. is quite conventional

Below, another hot-shot contest model of the time was Barry Wheeler's *Eliminator,* available both as an *Aeromodeller* plan and a kit.

John Lamble designed this 32in. F/F Dart *Kitten* with pendulum rudder, enjoying a brief vogue in 1952-55.

AM Oct. 1953

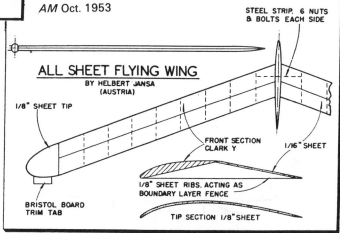

ALL SHEET FLYING WING
BY HELBERT JANSA (AUSTRIA)

STEEL STRIP. 6 NUTS & BOLTS EACH SIDE
1/8" SHEET TIP
FRONT SECTION CLARK Y
1/16" SHEET
1/8" SHEET RIBS. ACTING AS BOUNDARY LAYER FENCE
BRISTOL BOARD TRIM TAB
TIP SECTION 1/8" SHEET

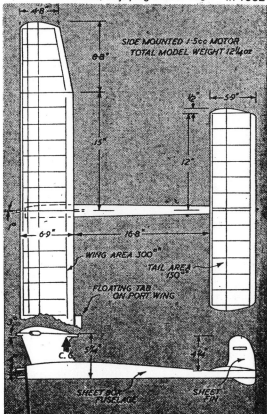

SIDE MOUNTED 1.5cc MOTOR TOTAL MODEL WEIGHT 12¼oz
WING AREA 300□"
TAIL AREA 150□"
FLOATING TAB ON PORT WING
SHEET FUSELAGE
SHEET FIN

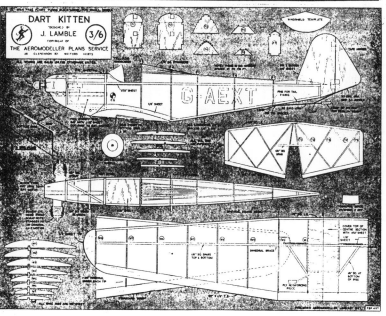

DART KITTEN
DESIGNED BY J. LAMBLE 3/6
COPYRIGHT OF THE AEROMODELLER PLANS SERVICE

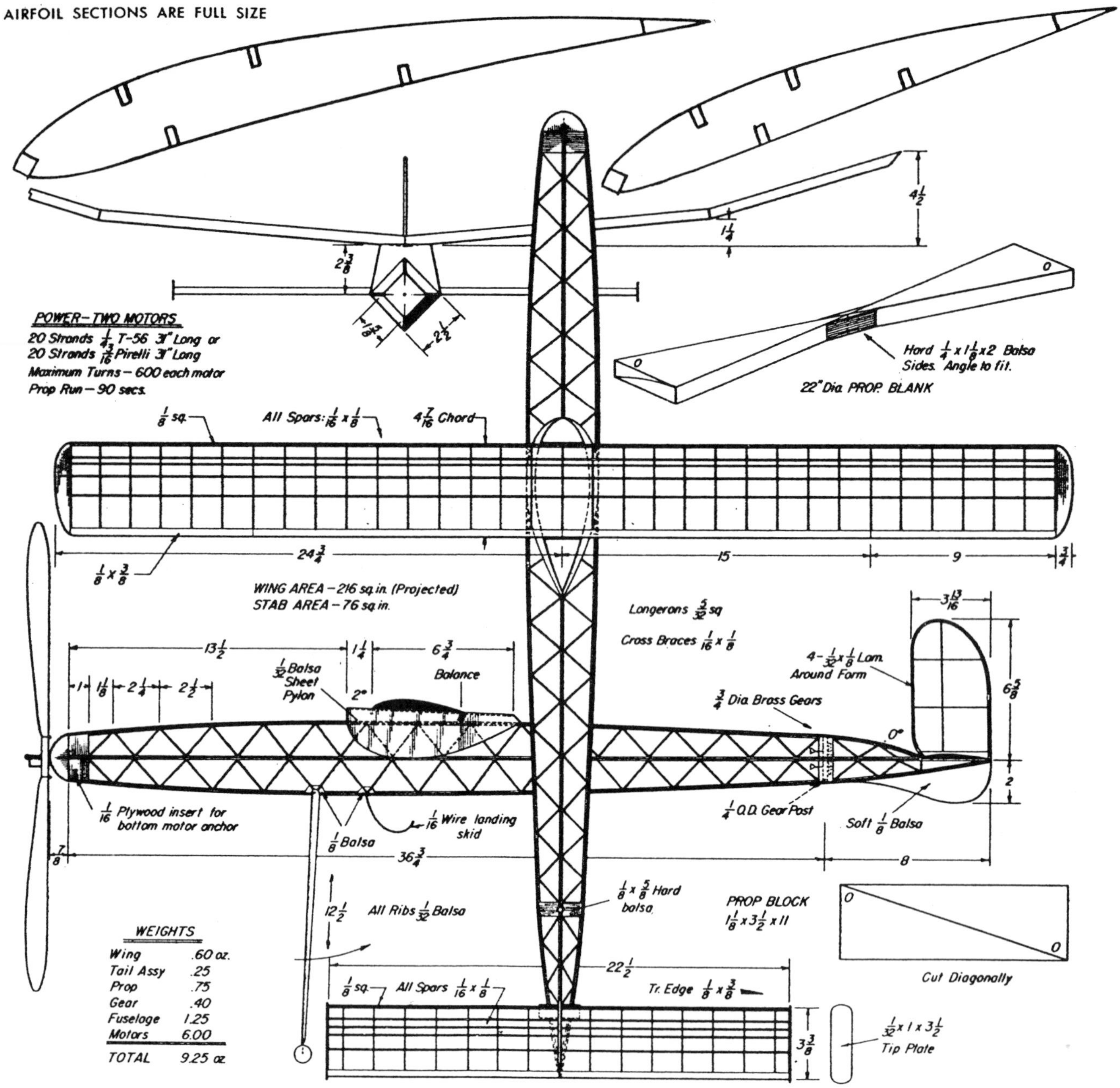
AIRFOIL SECTIONS ARE FULL SIZE
POWER–TWO MOTORS
20 Strands 1/4 T-56 31" Long or
20 Strands 1/16 Pirelli 31" Long
Maximum Turns – 600 each motor
Prop Run – 90 secs.
Hard 1/4 x 1 1/8 x 2 Balsa Sides. Angle to fit.
22" Dia. PROP. BLANK
1/8 sq.
All Spars: 1/16 x 1/8
4 7/16 Chord
1/8 x 3/8
24 3/4
15
9
3/4
WING AREA – 216 sq. in. (Projected)
STAB AREA – 76 sq. in.
Longerons 5/32 sq.
Cross Braces 1/16 x 1/8
3 13/16
4 - 1/32 x 1/8 Lam. Around Form
13 1/2
1 1/4
6 3/4
Balance
1/32 Balsa Sheet Pylon
2°
3/4 Dia. Brass Gears
6 5/8
0°
1/16 Plywood insert for bottom motor anchor
1/16 Wire landing skid
1/4 O.D. Gear Post
Soft 1/8 Balsa
1/8 Balsa
36 3/4
8
1/8 x 5/8 Hard balsa
PROP BLOCK
1 1/8 x 3 1/2 x 11
Cut Diagonally
12 1/2
All Ribs 1/32 Balsa
WEIGHTS
Wing .60 oz.
Tail Assy .25
Prop .75
Gear .40
Fuselage 1.25
Motors 6.00
TOTAL 9.25 oz.
22 1/2
1/8 sq.
All Spars 1/16 x 1/8
Tr. Edge 1/8 x 3/8
3 3/8
1/32 x 1 x 3 1/2
Tip Plate

Built in late '51 by Joe Bilgri after reports of Scandinavian conditions from Joe Foster and Manny Andrade, *The Drifter* was designed to cope with windy conditions. Was in the U.S. Wakefield team in 1952 in Sweden but was lost in the first round with 40 secs. more than any other model. Lowest official contest time overall 4:07. Gears gave 90 sec. motor run. Rearward balance point and low-pitch prop were most important features, says designer (*AT* Feb. 53).

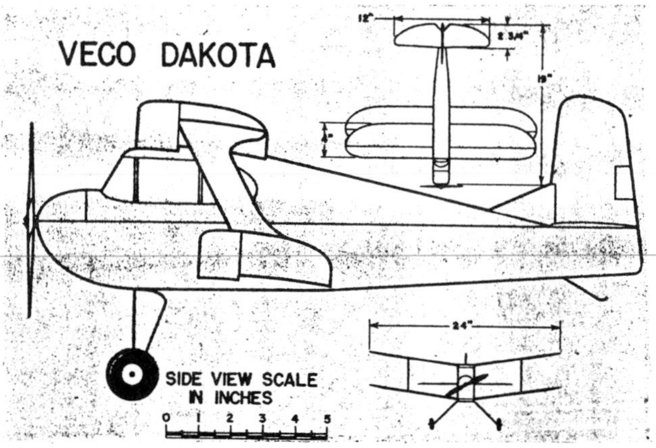
VECO DAKOTA
12"
2 3/4"
19"
24"
SIDE VIEW SCALE
IN INCHES
0 1 2 3 4 5

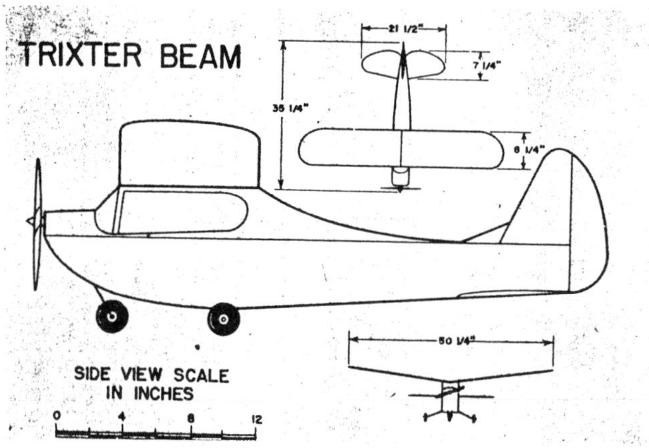
TRIXTER BEAM
21 1/2"
7 1/4"
35 1/4"
8 1/4"
50 1/4"
SIDE VIEW SCALE
IN INCHES
0 4 8 12

The small-engine revolution which started with the K&B Infant •020 (•33cc) in 1950 led to the introduction of scores of small power models in kit form, of which the 24in. span Veco *Dakota* is a good example for fun flying.

One of the early radio control kits which had a long run of popularity was the Trixter *Beam,* 50¼in. span for •09-•14 engines, 35-50ozs., designed by Lou Andrews and kitted by Paul K. Guillow, better known for C/L stunt kits.

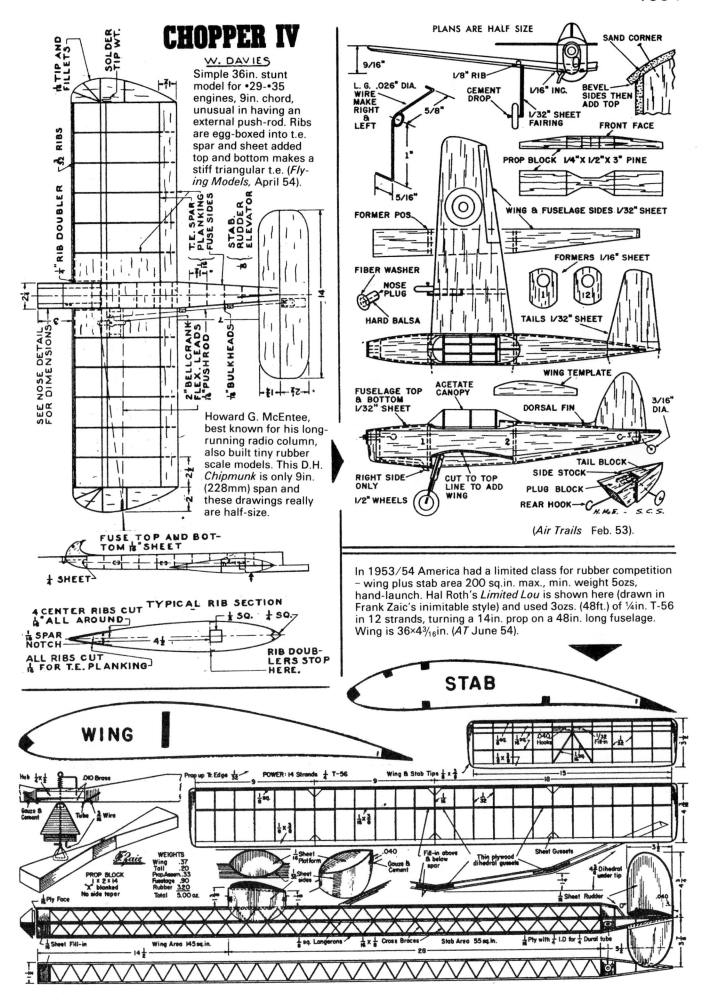

CHOPPER IV
W. DAVIES

Simple 36in. stunt model for •29-•35 engines, 9in. chord, unusual in having an external push-rod. Ribs are egg-boxed into t.e. spar and sheet added top and bottom makes a stiff triangular t.e. (*Flying Models,* April 54).

PLANS ARE HALF SIZE

9/16"

L. G. .026" DIA. WIRE MAKE RIGHT & LEFT

5/8"

1"

5/16"

1/8" RIB

CEMENT DROP

1/16" INC.

1/32" SHEET FAIRING

SAND CORNER

BEVEL SIDES THEN ADD TOP

FRONT FACE

PROP BLOCK 1/4"X 1/2"X 3" PINE

WING & FUSELAGE SIDES 1/32" SHEET

FORMERS 1/16" SHEET

TAILS 1/32" SHEET

FORMER POS.

FIBER WASHER

NOSE PLUG

HARD BALSA

FUSELAGE TOP & BOTTOM 1/32" SHEET

RIGHT SIDE ONLY

1/2" WHEELS

ACETATE CANOPY

CUT TO TOP LINE TO ADD WING

WING TEMPLATE

DORSAL FIN

3/16" DIA.

TAIL BLOCK

SIDE STOCK

PLUG BLOCK

REAR HOOK

H. M̄.E. - S.C.S.

Howard G. McEntee, best known for his long-running radio column, also built tiny rubber scale models. This D.H. *Chipmunk* is only 9in. (228mm) span and these drawings really are half-size.

(*Air Trails* Feb. 53).

1/16" TIP AND FILLETS

SOLDER TIP WT.

1/16" RIB DOUBLER

3/32 RIBS

1/4" RIB DOUBLER

T.E. SPAR PLANKING FUSE SIDES

STAB. RUDDER ELEVATOR

2" BELLCRANK FLEX. LEADS PUSHROD

1/16" BULKHEADS

SEE NOSE DETAIL FOR DIMENSIONS

FUSE TOP AND BOTTOM 1/16" SHEET

1/16" SHEET

4 CENTER RIBS CUT 1/16" ALL AROUND

TYPICAL RIB SECTION

1/16" SPAR NOTCH

1/8 SQ.   1/8 SQ.

4 1/2

ALL RIBS CUT 1/16 FOR T.E. PLANKING

RIB DOUBLERS STOP HERE.

In 1953/54 America had a limited class for rubber competition – wing plus stab area 200 sq.in. max., min. weight 5ozs, hand-launch. Hal Roth's *Limited Lou* is shown here (drawn in Frank Zaic's inimitable style) and used 3ozs. (48ft.) of ¼in. T-56 in 12 strands, turning a 14in. prop on a 48in. long fuselage. Wing is 36×4³⁄₁₆in. (*AT* June 54).

STAB

.040 Hooks

1/32 Fill-in

WING

Hub 1/4x1/2

.010 Brass

Gauze & Cement

Tube   1/16 Wire

Prop up Tr. Edge 1/32

POWER: 14 Strands 1/4 T-56

Wing & Stab Tips 1/8 x 1/4

1/8 sq.

1/8 x 1/4

.040

1/16 Sheet Platform

1/32 Sheet sides

Gauze & Cement

Fill-in above & below spar

Thin plywood dihedral gussets

Sheet Gussets

4 1/2 Dihedral under tip

Sheet Rudder

.040

Zaic

WEIGHTS
Wing .37
Tail .20
Prop.Assem. .33
Fuselage .90
Rubber .320
Total 5.00 oz.

PROP BLOCK
1 x 2 x 14
"X" blanked
No side taper

Ply Face

1/8 Sheet Fill-in

14 1/2

Wing Area 145 sq.in.

1/8 sq. Longerons

1/16 X 1/8 Cross Braces

Stab Area 55 sq.in.

28

1/8 Ply with 1/4 I.D. for Dural tube

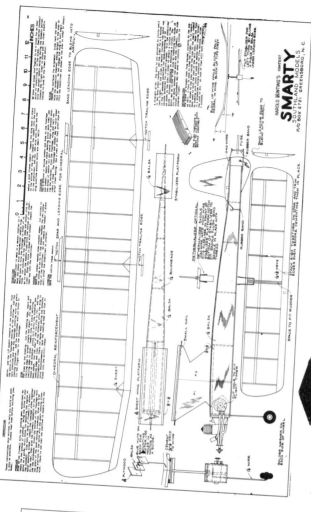

A lesser-known U.S. kit firm, Southland Models, produced the 30in. *Smarty* for Wasp and similar •049 motors. Simple, but would get high and just sit there till the D/T popped.

Slightly different from the usual constant-chord stunter was the 36in. *Stuntster*, for •19 motors, which appeared in *Flying Models* Feb. 1954.

Eric Fearnley's *Luton Minor* at 43in. for motors around •5cc was a free full-size plan in *Aeromodeller* Christmas 1953 issue and tempted a lot of people into scale modelling.

Adhesive manufacturers UHU in Germany and, on a smaller scale, Soude-Gres in France sponsored many model plans. This A1, *Der Kleine UHU*, was built in thousands.

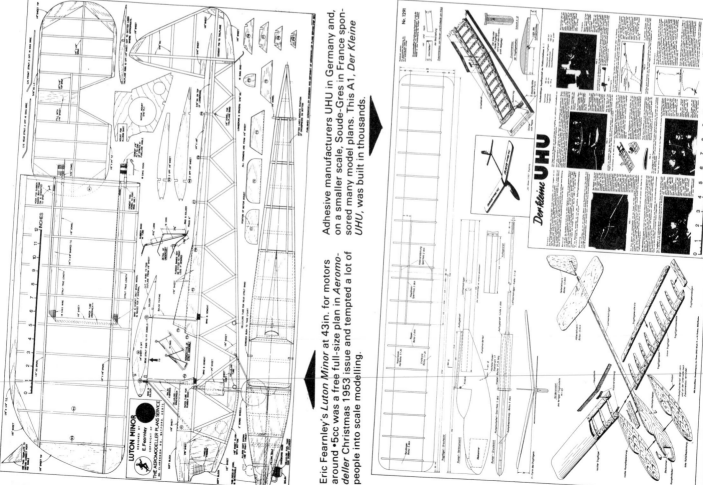

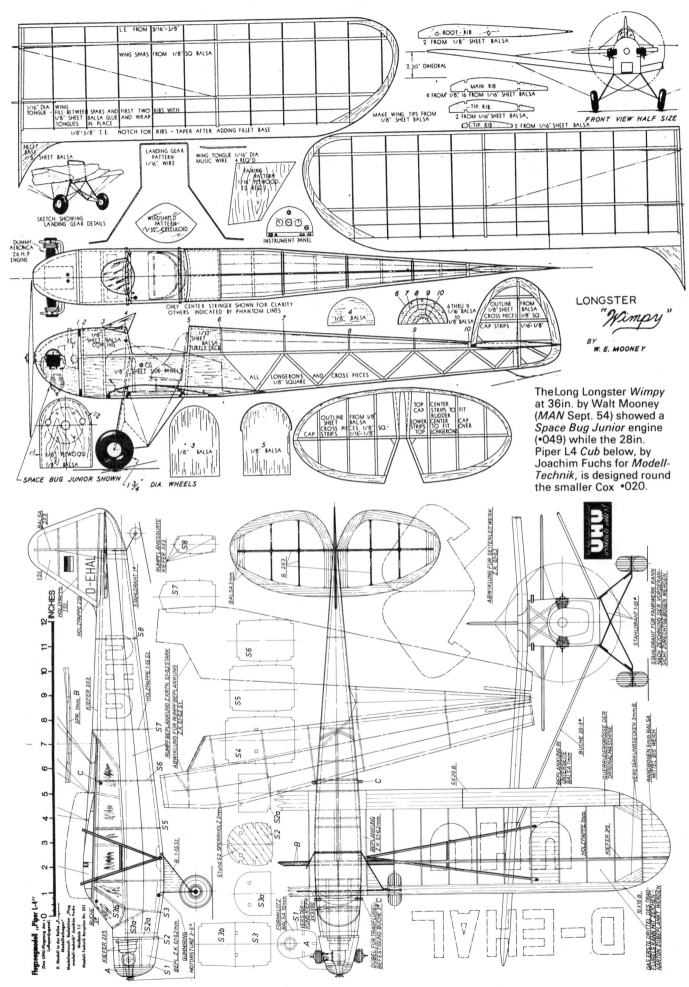

L.E. FROM 3/16 • 3/8

WING SPARS FROM 1/8" SQ. BALSA

1/16" DIA. WING TONGUE - FILL BETWEEN SPARS AND FIRST TWO RIBS WITH 1/8" SHEET BALSA GLUE AND WRAP TONGUES IN PLACE

1/8" • 3/8" T.E. NOTCH FOR RIBS - TAPER AFTER ADDING FILLET BASE

FILLET BASE 1/8" SHEET BALSA

SKETCH SHOWING LANDING GEAR DETAILS

LANDING GEAR PATTERN 1/16" WIRE

WING TONGUE 1/16" DIA MUSIC WIRE 4 REQ'D

FAIRING PATTERN 1/16" PLYWOOD X2 REQ'D

WINDSHIELD PATTERN 1/32" CELLULOID

INSTRUMENT PANEL

DUMMY AERONCA 26 H.P. ENGINE

ONLY CENTER STRINGER SHOWN FOR CLARITY OTHERS INDICATED BY PHANTOM LINES

1/8" SHEET BALSA COWLING

1/32" SHEET BALSA TURTLE DECK

1/8" SHEET SIDE PANELS

CG

ALL LONGERONS AND CROSS PIECES 1/8" SQUARE

SPACE BUG JUNIOR SHOWN

1 3/4" DIA. WHEELS

1/8" PLYWOOD BALSA

#3 1/8" BALSA

#5 1/8" BALSA

6 7 8 9 10

#4 1/8" BALSA

6 THRU 9 1/16" BALSA 10 1/8" BALSA

OUTLINE 1/8" SHEET CROSS PIECES 1/8" SQ. CAP STRIPS 1/16" 1/8"

0 ROOT RIB 0
2 FROM 1/8" SHEET BALSA

2.30° DIHEDRAL

MAIN RIB
4 FROM 1/8", 16 FROM 1/16" SHEET BALSA

TIP RIB
2 FROM 1/16" SHEET BALSA

MAKE WING TIPS FROM 1/8" SHEET BALSA

TIP RIB 2 FROM 1/16" SHEET BALSA

FRONT VIEW HALF SIZE

OUTLINE SHEET CROSS PIECES 1/8" SQ. CAP STRIPS FROM 1/8 BALSA

LOWER STRIPS TOP

TOP CAP CENTER STRIPS TO FIT RUDDER CAP OVER CENTER TO FIT LONGERON

LONGSTER "Wimpy"

BY

W. E. MOONEY

The Long Longster *Wimpy* at 36in. by Walt Mooney (*MAN* Sept. 54) showed a *Space Bug Junior* engine (•049) while the 28in. Piper L4 *Cub* below, by Joachim Fuchs for *Modell-Technik*, is designed round the smaller Cox •020.

Flugzeugmodell „Piper L-4"

(Das UHU-Flugzeug der Reihe „J" Luftsportgerät)

Modellflugzeugen

Modell-techik" Baugplan Nr. 351

Maßstab 1:1

UHU

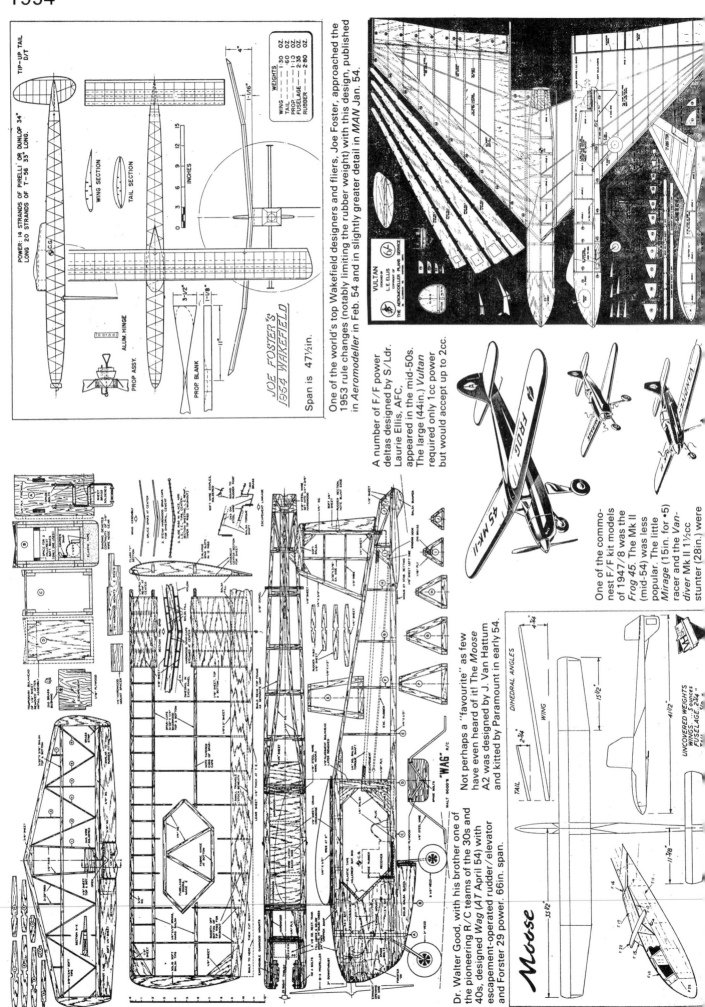

JOE FOSTER'S 1954 WAKEFIELD

Span is 47½in.

One of the world's top Wakefield designers and fliers, Joe Foster, approached the 1953 rule changes (notably limiting the rubber weight) with this design, published in *Aeromodeller* in Feb. 54 and in slightly greater detail in *MAN* Jan. 54.

A number of F/F power deltas designed by S/Ldr. Laurie Ellis, AFC, appeared in the mid-50s. The large (44in.) *Vultan* required only 1cc power but would accept up to 2cc.

One of the commonest F/F kit models of 1947/8 was the *Frog 45*. The Mk II (mid-54) was less popular. The little *Mirage* (15in. for •5) racer and the *Van-diver Mk II* 1½cc stunter (28in.) were

Dr. Walter Good, with his brother one of the pioneering R/C teams of the 30s and 40s, designed *Wag* (*AT* April 54) with escapement-operated rudder/elevator and Forster 29 power. 66in. span.

Not perhaps a "favourite" as few have even heard of it! The *Moose* A2 was designed by J. Van Hattum and kitted by Paramount in early 54.

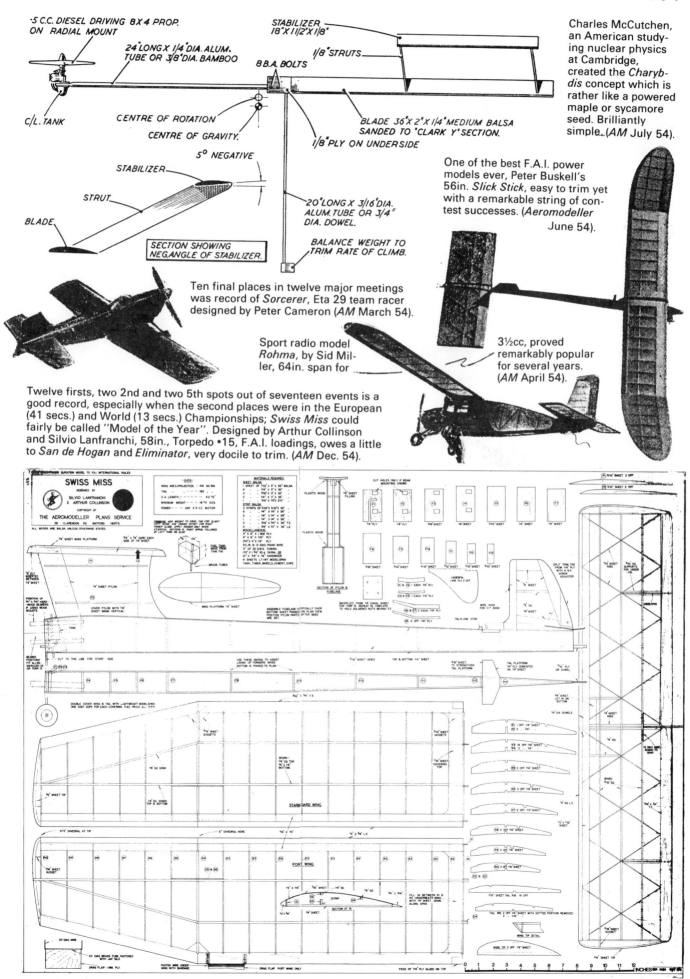

·5 C.C. DIESEL DRIVING 8 X 4 PROP.
ON RADIAL MOUNT

24"LONG X 1/4"DIA. ALUM.
TUBE OR 3/8"DIA. BAMBOO

STABILIZER
18"X 11/2"X 1/8"

1/8"STRUTS

8 B.A. BOLTS

C/L. TANK

CENTRE OF ROTATION

CENTRE OF GRAVITY.

BLADE 36"X 2"X 1/4"MEDIUM BALSA
SANDED TO "CLARK Y" SECTION.

1/8"PLY ON UNDERSIDE

5° NEGATIVE

STABILIZER

STRUT

BLADE

SECTION SHOWING
NEG. ANGLE OF STABILIZER.

20"LONG X 3/16"DIA.
ALUM.TUBE OR 3/4"
DIA. DOWEL

BALANCE WEIGHT TO
TRIM RATE OF CLIMB.

Charles McCutchen, an American study-ing nuclear physics at Cambridge, created the *Charybdis* concept which is rather like a powered maple or sycamore seed. Brilliantly simple. (*AM July 54*).

One of the best F.A.I. power models ever, Peter Buskell's 56in. *Slick Stick*, easy to trim yet with a remarkable string of con-test successes. (*Aeromodeller June 54*).

Ten final places in twelve major meetings was record of *Sorcerer*, Eta 29 team racer designed by Peter Cameron (*AM March 54*).

Sport radio model *Rohma*, by Sid Mil-ler, 64in. span for

3½cc, proved remarkably popular for several years. (*AM April 54*).

Twelve firsts, two 2nd and two 5th spots out of seventeen events is a good record, especially when the second places were in the European (41 secs.) and World (13 secs.) Championships; *Swiss Miss* could fairly be called "Model of the Year". Designed by Arthur Collinson and Silvio Lanfranchi, 58in., Torpedo •15, F.A.I. loadings, owes a little to *San de Hogan* and *Eliminator*, very docile to trim. (*AM Dec. 54*).

AMAZON "400"

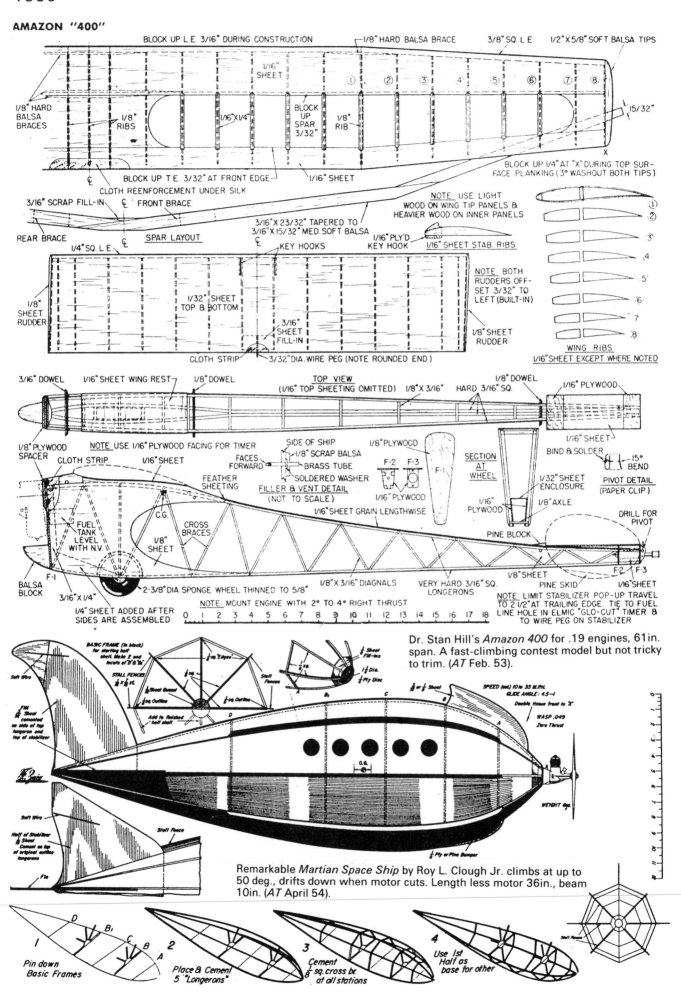

BLOCK UP L.E. 3/16" DURING CONSTRUCTION — 1/8" HARD BALSA BRACE — 3/8" SQ. L.E. — 1/2" X 5/8" SOFT BALSA TIPS

1/8" HARD BALSA BRACES
1/8" RIBS
1/16" X 1/4"
1/16" SHEET
BLOCK UP SPAR 3/32"
1/8" RIB
15/32"
X
BLOCK UP T.E. 3/32" AT FRONT EDGE
1/16" SHEET
BLOCK UP 1/4" AT "X" DURING TOP SURFACE PLANKING (3° WASHOUT BOTH TIPS)
CLOTH REENFORCEMENT UNDER SILK
3/16" SCRAP FILL-IN
FRONT BRACE
REAR BRACE
SPAR LAYOUT
3/16" X 23/32" TAPERED TO 3/16" X 15/32" MED. SOFT BALSA
NOTE USE LIGHT WOOD ON WING TIP PANELS & HEAVIER WOOD ON INNER PANELS
1/16" PLY'D KEY HOOK
1/16" SHEET STAB. RIBS
KEY HOOKS
1/4" SQ. L.E.
1/8" SHEET RUDDER
1/32" SHEET TOP & BOTTOM
3/16" SHEET FILL-IN
NOTE: BOTH RUDDERS OFFSET 3/32" TO LEFT (BUILT-IN)
1/8" SHEET RUDDER
CLOTH STRIP
3/32" DIA. WIRE PEG (NOTE ROUNDED END)
WING RIBS 1/16" SHEET EXCEPT WHERE NOTED

3/16" DOWEL
1/16" SHEET WING REST
1/8" DOWEL
TOP VIEW (1/16" TOP SHEETING OMITTED)
1/8" X 3/16"
1/8" DOWEL HARD 3/16" SQ.
1/16" PLYWOOD
1/8" PLYWOOD SPACER
NOTE: USE 1/16" PLYWOOD FACING FOR TIMER
1/16" SHEET
SIDE OF SHIP
1/8" PLYWOOD
SECTION AT WHEEL
1/16" SHEET
BIND & SOLDER
15° BEND
CLOTH STRIP
1/16" SHEET
FACES FORWARD
1/8" SCRAP BALSA
BRASS TUBE
SOLDERED WASHER
FILLER & VENT DETAIL (NOT TO SCALE)
F-2 F-3
F-1
1/32" SHEET ENCLOSURE
PIVOT DETAIL (PAPER CLIP)
FEATHER SHEETING
C.G.
1/8" SHEET
1/16" PLYWOOD
1/16" SHEET GRAIN LENGTHWISE
1/16" PLYWOOD
1/8" AXLE
DRILL FOR PIVOT
FUEL TANK LEVEL WITH N.V.
CROSS BRACES
PINE BLOCK
BALSA BLOCK
F-1
3/16" X 1/4"
2-3/8" DIA. SPONGE WHEEL THINNED TO 5/8"
1/4" SHEET ADDED AFTER SIDES ARE ASSEMBLED
1/8" X 3/16" DIAGNALS
VERY HARD 3/16" SQ. LONGERONS
PINE SKID
1/8" SHEET
F-2 F-3
1/16" SHEET
NOTE: MOUNT ENGINE WITH 2° TO 4° RIGHT THRUST
0 1 2 3 4 5 6 7 8 9 10 11 12 13 14 15 16 17 18
NOTE: LIMIT STABILIZER POP-UP TRAVEL TO 2-1/2" AT TRAILING EDGE. TIE TO FUEL LINE HOLE IN ELMIC "GLO-CUT" TIMER & TO WIRE PEG ON STABILIZER

Dr. Stan Hill's *Amazon 400* for .19 engines, 61 in. span. A fast-climbing contest model but not tricky to trim. (*AT* Feb. 53).

BASIC FRAME (in block) for starting half shell. Make 2 and locate at 'D' & 'A'
STALL FENCES
SPEED (est.) 10 to 35 M.P.H.
GLIDE ANGLE: 4.5→1
Double Tissue front to "X"
WASP .049 Zero Thrust
Soft Wire
WEIGHT 6 oz.
Half of Stabilizer
Stall Fence
Fin

Remarkable *Martian Space Ship* by Roy L. Clough Jr. climbs at up to 50 deg., drifts down when motor cuts. Length less motor 36 in., beam 10 in. (*AT* April 54).

1 Pin down Basic Frames
2 Place & Cement 5 "Longerons"
3 Cement sq. cross br. at all stations
4 Use 1st Half as base for other

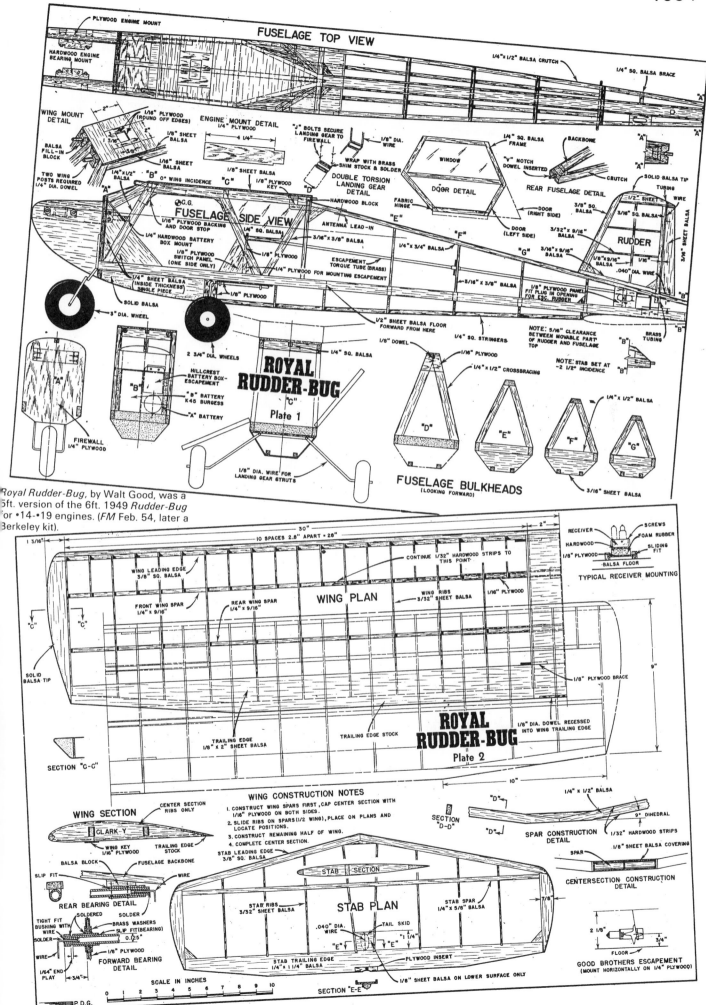

Royal Rudder-Bug, by Walt Good, was a 5ft. version of the 6ft. 1949 *Rudder-Bug* for •14-•19 engines. (*FM* Feb. 54, later a Berkeley kit).

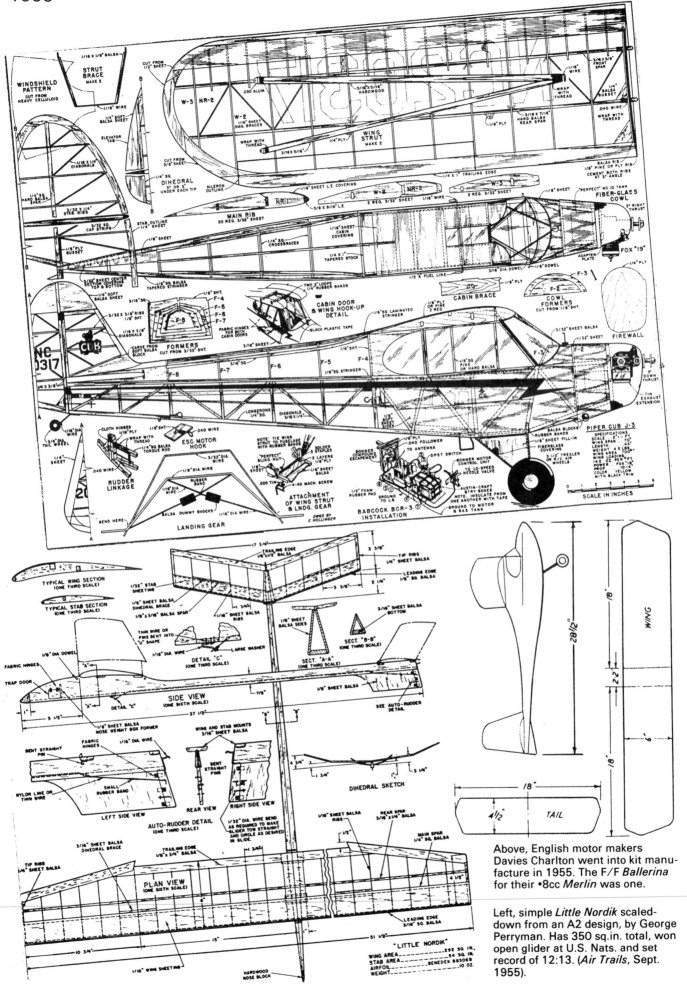

Above, English motor makers Davies Charlton went into kit manufacture in 1955. The F/F *Ballerina* for their •8cc *Merlin* was one.

Left, simple *Little Nordik* scaled-down from an A2 design, by George Perryman. Has 350 sq.in. total, won open glider at U.S. Nats. and set record of 12:13. (*Air Trails*, Sept. 1955).

Opposite page the ever-popular *Cub J3*, here at 70in. span for Babcock radio, designed by Chuck Hollinger and featured in January 1955 *Air Trails*. Uses a •19 size motor and has a flying weight of 4½lbs.

World Class A C/L speed record model by Prati Amato of Bologna, Italy, used a Super Tigre G205 2½cc engine to return 190•470 km/h or nearly 120 mph. By 1955 cast aluminium ''speed pans'' (lower fuselage halves) were becoming the norm. (*AT* Sept. 55).

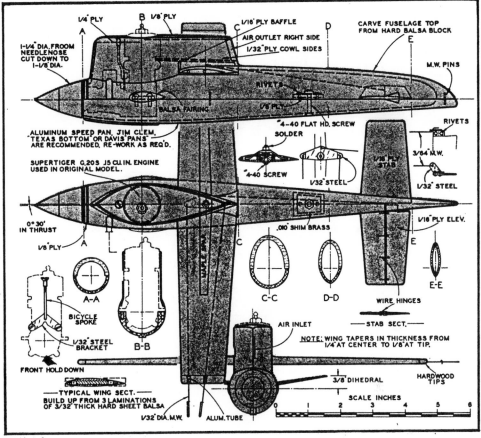

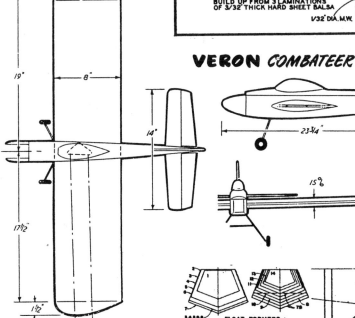

VERON *COMBATEER*

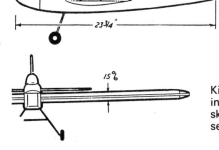

Kit reviews in *Model Aircraft* often included three-view dimensioned sketches. Combat flying was first seen officially in Belgium in 1950.

Floats for the *Cub* opposite, or similar size models, were featured in Feb. 55 *AT*. These particular ones were developed over a period by Chuck Hollinger. Scale to 40% span for other models was the suggestion.

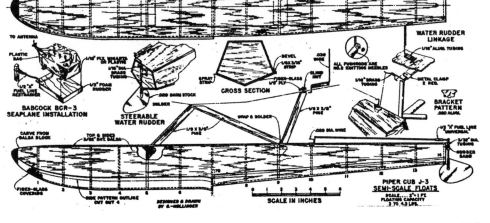

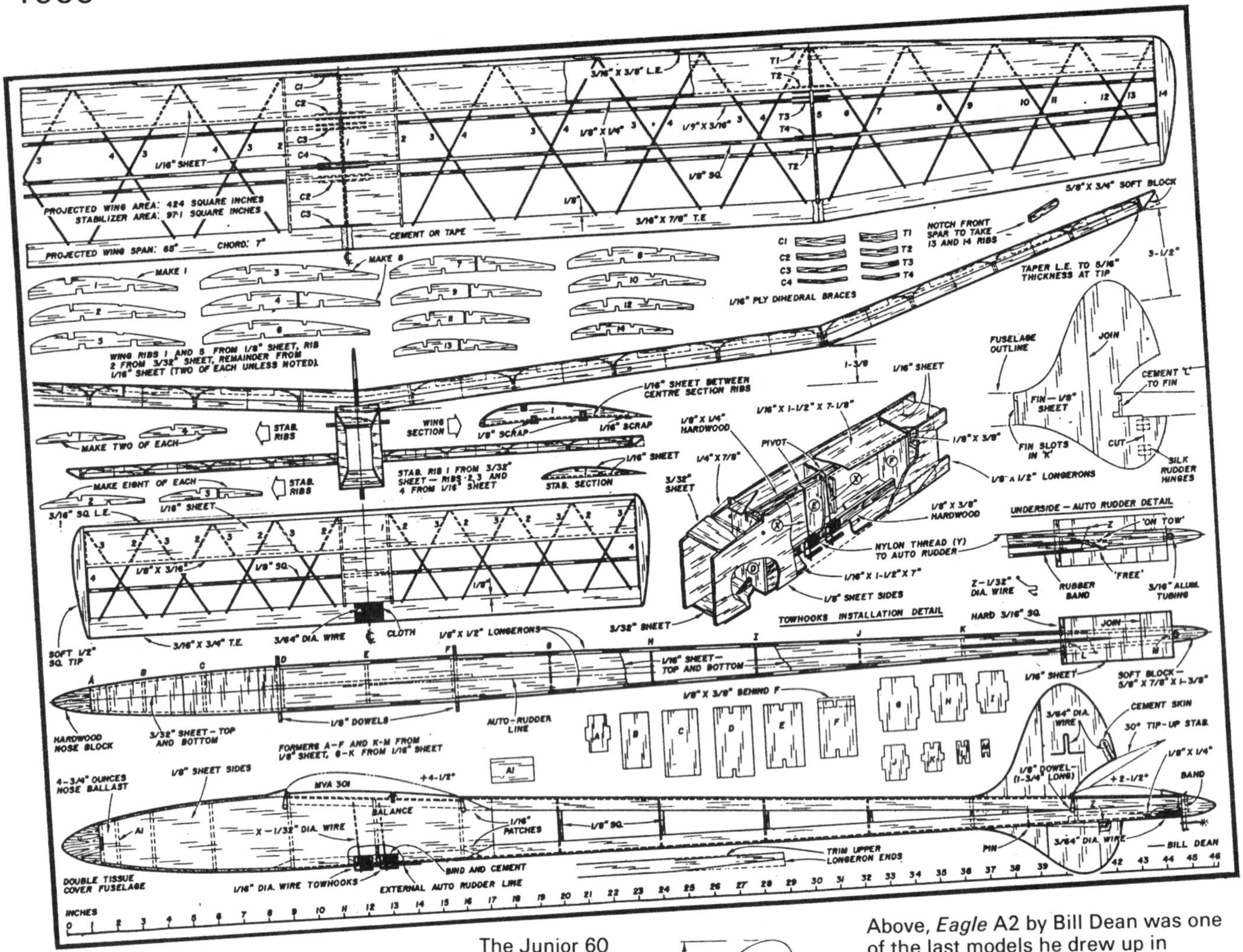
PROJECTED WING AREA: 424 SQUARE INCHES
STABILIZER AREA: 97·1 SQUARE INCHES
PROJECTED WING SPAN: 68"
CHORD: 7"
CEMENT OR TAPE
3/16" X 7/8" T.E.
5/8" X 3/4" SOFT BLOCK
NOTCH FRONT SPAR TO TAKE 13 AND 14 RIBS
TAPER L.E. TO 5/16" THICKNESS AT TIP
1/16" PLY DIHEDRAL BRACES
WING RIBS 1 AND 5 FROM 1/8" SHEET, RIB 2 FROM 3/32" SHEET, REMAINDER FROM 1/16" SHEET (TWO OF EACH UNLESS NOTED)
STAB. RIB 1 FROM 3/32" SHEET — RIBS 2,3 AND 4 FROM 1/16" SHEET
TOWHOOKS INSTALLATION DETAIL
UNDERSIDE — AUTO RUDDER DETAIL
DOUBLE TISSUE COVER FUSELAGE
1/16" DIA. WIRE TOWHOOKS
EXTERNAL AUTO RUDDER LINE
BILL DEAN
INCHES

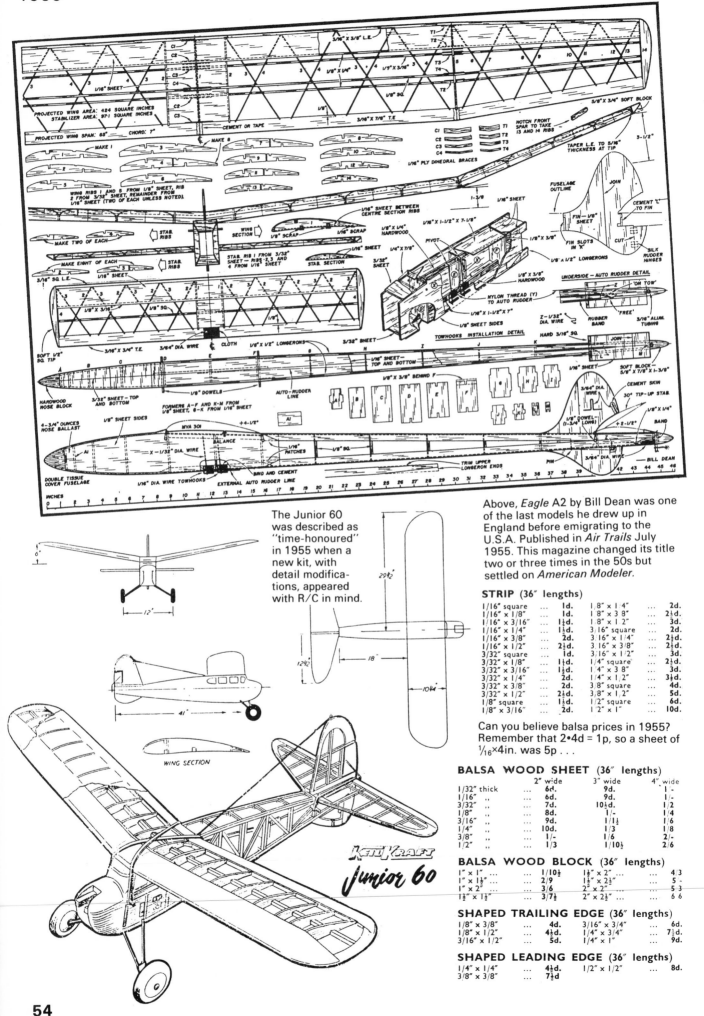

The Junior 60 was described as "time-honoured" in 1955 when a new kit, with detail modifications, appeared with R/C in mind.

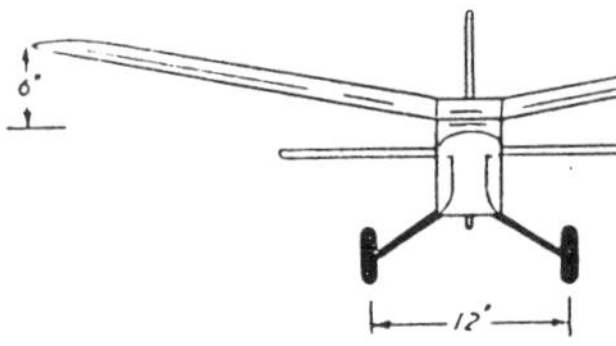
6"
12"

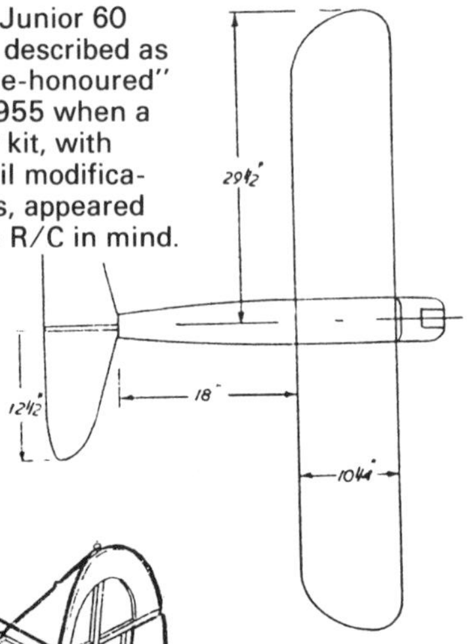
29½"
12½"
18"
10¼"

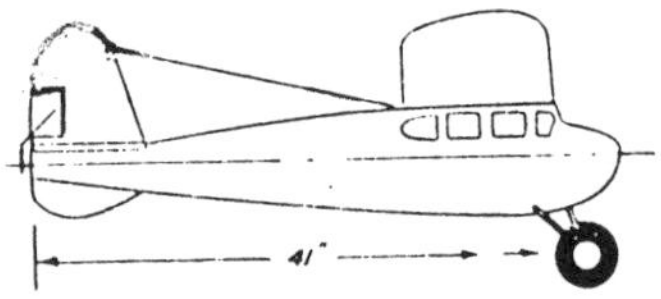
41"

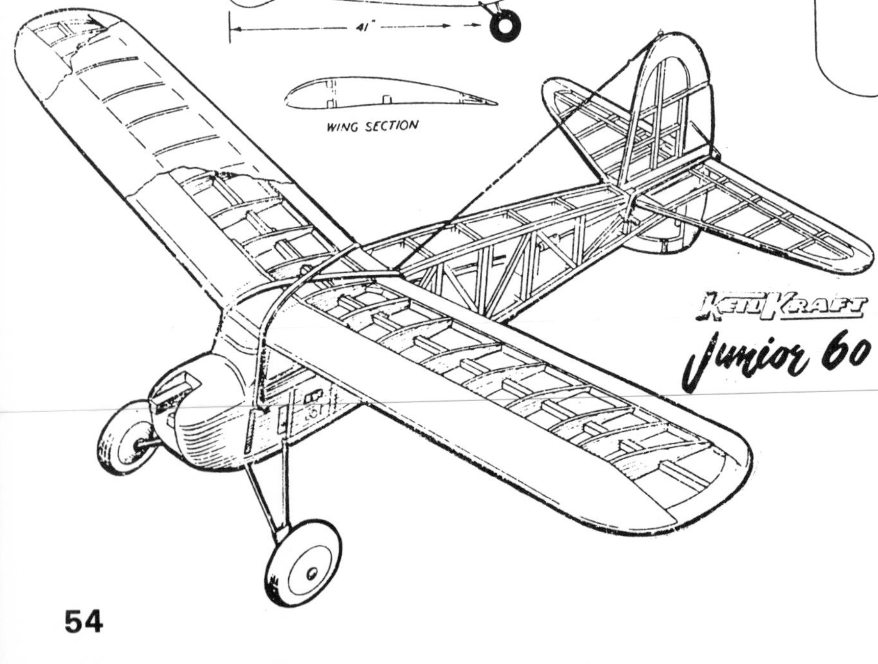
WING SECTION
Junior 60

Above, *Eagle* A2 by Bill Dean was one of the last models he drew up in England before emigrating to the U.S.A. Published in *Air Trails* July 1955. This magazine changed its title two or three times in the 50s but settled on *American Modeler*.

STRIP (36″ lengths)

1/16″ square	... 1d.	1/8″ × 1/4″	... 2d.		
1/16″ × 1/8″	... 1d.	1/8″ × 3/8″	... 2½d.		
1/16″ × 3/16″	... 1½d.	1/8″ × 1/2″	... 3d.		
1/16″ × 1/4″	... 1½d.	3/16″ square	... 2d.		
1/16″ × 3/8″	... 2d.	3/16″ × 1/4″	... 2½d.		
1/16″ × 1/2″	... 2½d.	3/16″ × 3/8″	... 2½d.		
3/32″ square	... 1d.	3/16″ × 1/2″	... 3d.		
3/32″ × 1/8″	... 1½d.	1/4″ square	... 2½d.		
3/32″ × 3/16″	... 1½d.	1/4″ × 3/8″	... 3d.		
3/32″ × 1/4″	... 2d.	1/4″ × 1/2″	... 3½d.		
3/32″ × 3/8″	... 2d.	3/8″ square	... 4d.		
3/32″ × 1/2″	... 2½d.	3/8″ × 1/2″	... 5d.		
1/8″ square	... 1½d.	1/2″ square	... 6d.		
1/8″ × 3/16″	... 2d.	1/2″ × 1″	... 10d.		

Can you believe balsa prices in 1955? Remember that 2•4d = 1p, so a sheet of 1/16×4in. was 5p . . .

BALSA WOOD SHEET (36″ lengths)

	2″ wide	3″ wide	4″ wide
1/32″ thick	... 6d.	9d.	1/-
1/16″ ,,	... 6d.	9d.	1/-
3/32″ ,,	... 7d.	10½d.	1/2
1/8″ ,,	... 8d.	1/-	1/4
3/16″ ,,	... 9d.	1/1½	1/6
1/4″ ,,	... 10d.	1/3	1/8
3/8″ ,,	... 1/-	1/6	2/-
1/2″ ,,	... 1/3	1/10½	2/6

BALSA WOOD BLOCK (36″ lengths)

1″ × 1″ ...	... 1/10½	1½″ × 2″ ...	... 4/3
1″ × 1½″ ...	... 2/9	1½″ × 2½″ ...	... 5/-
1″ × 2″ ...	... 3/6	2″ × 2″ ...	... 5/3
1½″ × 1½″	... 3/7½	2″ × 2½″ ...	... 6/6

SHAPED TRAILING EDGE (36″ lengths)

1/8″ × 3/8″	... 4d.	3/16″ × 3/4″	... 6d.
1/8″ × 1/2″	... 4½d.	1/4″ × 3/4″	... 7½d.
3/16″ × 1/2″	... 5d.	1/4″ × 1″	... 9d.

SHAPED LEADING EDGE (36″ lengths)

1/4″ × 1/4″	... 4½d.	1/2″ × 1/2″	... 8d.
3/8″ × 3/8″	... 7½d		

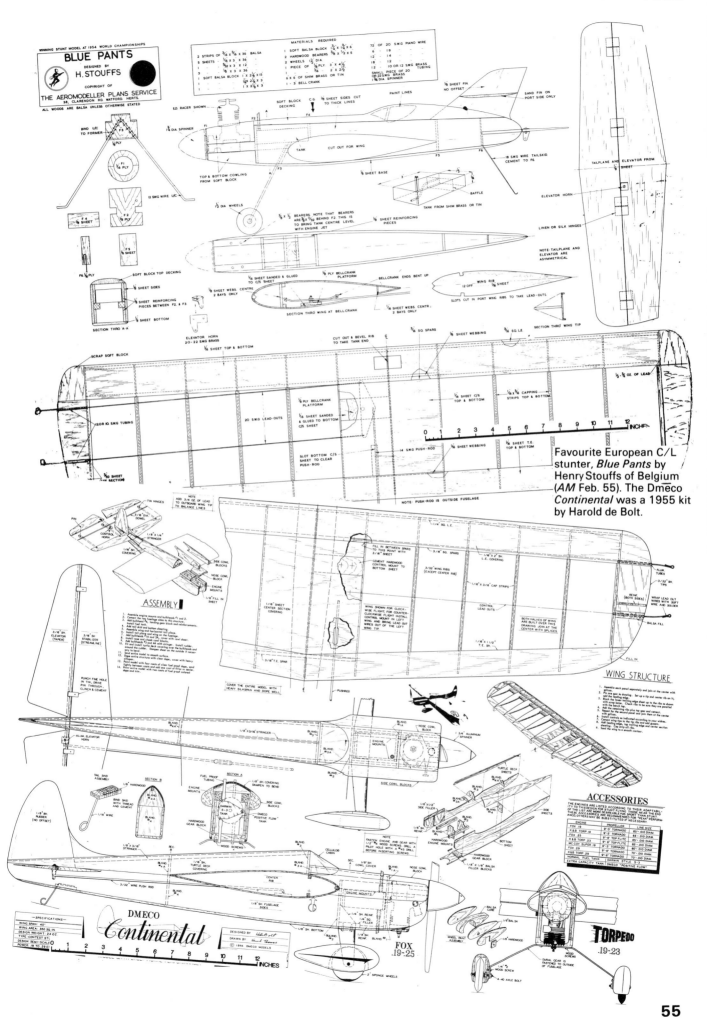

Favourite European C/L stunter, *Blue Pants* by Henry Stouffs of Belgium (*AM* Feb. 55). The Dmeco *Continental* was a 1955 kit by Harold de Bolt.

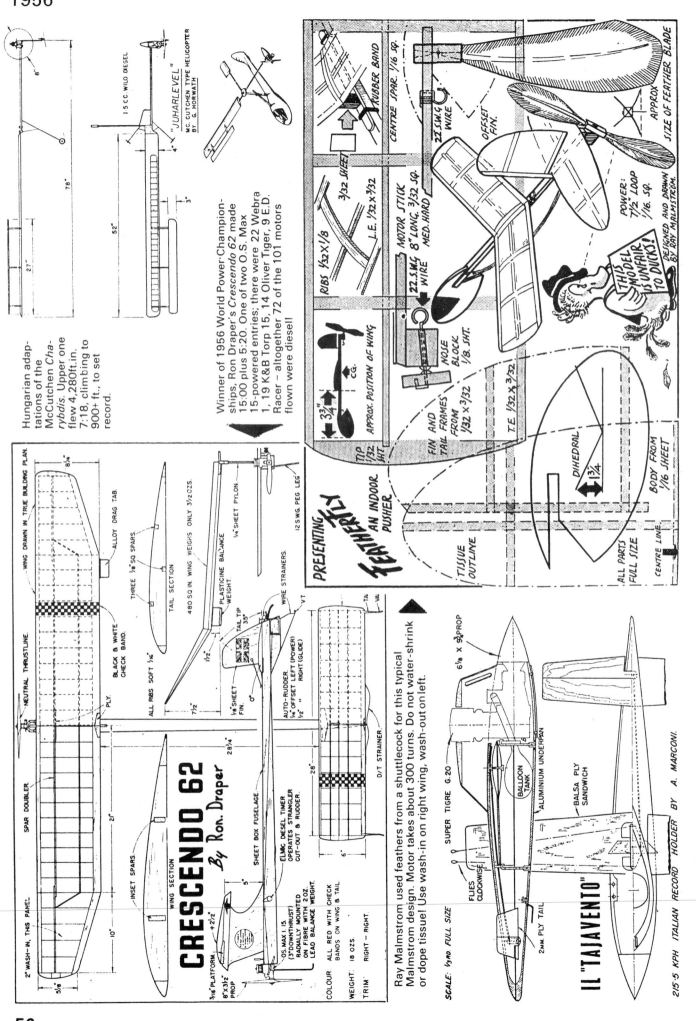

"JUHARLEVEL"
MC. CUTCHEN TYPE HELICOPTER
BY. G. HORWATH

1·5 C.C. WILD DIESEL

Hungarian adaptations of the McCutchen Charybdis. Upper one flew 4,280ft.in. 7:18, climbing to 900+ ft., to set record.

Winner of 1956 World Power-Championships, Ron Draper's Crescendo 62 made 15:00 plus 5:20. One of two O.S. Max 15-powered entries; there were 22 Webra 1, 19 K&B Torp 15, 14 Oliver Tiger, 9 E.D. Racer – altogether 72 of the 101 motors flown were diesel!

RUBBER BAND

CENTRE SPAR. 1/16 SQ.

OFFSET FIN.

22 S.W.G WIRE

APPROX SIZE OF FEATHER BLADE

POWER: 7½″ LOOP 1/16. SQ.

Designed and drawn BY RAY MALMSTROM.

THIS MODEL IS UNFAIR TO DUCKS!

3/32 SHEET

L.E. 1/32 X 3/32

RIBS 1/32 X 1/8

22 S.W.G. WIRE

MOTOR STICK 8″ LONG. 3/32 SQ. MED. HARD

NOSE BLOCK 1/8 SHT.

APPROX. POSITION OF WING

C.G.

FIN AND TAIL FRAMES FROM 1/32 X 3/32

T.E. 1/32 X 3/32

TIP 1/32 SHT.

TISSUE OUTLINE

DIHEDRAL 1¾

BODY FROM 1/16 SHEET

CENTRE LINE

ALL PARTS FULL SIZE

PRESENTING FEATHERFLY AN INDOOR PUSHER

3¾″

WING SECTION

WING DRAWN IN TRUE BUILDING PLAN.

8¼

ALLOY DRAG TAB.

THREE 1/8 SQ SPARS.

TAIL SECTION

ALL RIBS SOFT 1/16

PLASTICINE BALANCE WEIGHT.

1/4″ SHEET PYLON

WIRE STRAINERS.

480 SQ IN. WING WEIGHS ONLY 3½ OZS.

12 S.W.G. PEG LEG

TAIL TIP 35°

1/2″

7/2″

1/4″ SHEET FIN.

0°

AUTO-RUDDER ¼″ OFFSET LEFT (POWER) ½″ ″ RIGHT (GLIDE)

V.T

D/T STRAINER.

2″ WASH-IN, THIS PANEL.

NEUTRAL THRUSTLINE.

SPAR DOUBLER

INSET SPARS.

BLACK & WHITE CHECK BAND.

PLY.

+2½″

21″

28¼″

28″

6″

5/16

10″

5

3/16 PLATFORM.

8″X3½″ PROP

CRESCENDO 62
By Ron. Draper

SHEET BOX FUSELAGE.

ELMIC DIESEL TIMER OPERATES STRANGLER CUT-OUT & RUDDER.

O.S. MAX I 15. (3°DOWNTHRUST) RADIALLY MOUNTED ON FIBRE WITH 2 OZ. LEAD BALANCE WEIGHT.

COLOUR   ALL RED WITH CHECK BANDS ON WING & TAIL

WEIGHT.   18 OZS.

TRIM   RIGHT – RIGHT.

Ray Malmstrom used feathers from a shuttlecock for this typical Malmstrom design. Motor takes about 300 turns. Do not water-shrink or dope tissue Use wash-in on right wing, wash-out on left.

SCALE: ⅓rd FULL SIZE

6⅛ x 3¾ PROP

SUPER TIGRE G.20

BALLOON TANK

ALUMINIUM UNDERPAN

BALSA PLY SANDWICH

FLIES CLOCKWISE

2MM PLY TAIL

IL "TAJAVENTO"

215·5 KPH ITALIAN RECORD HOLDER BY A. MARCONI.

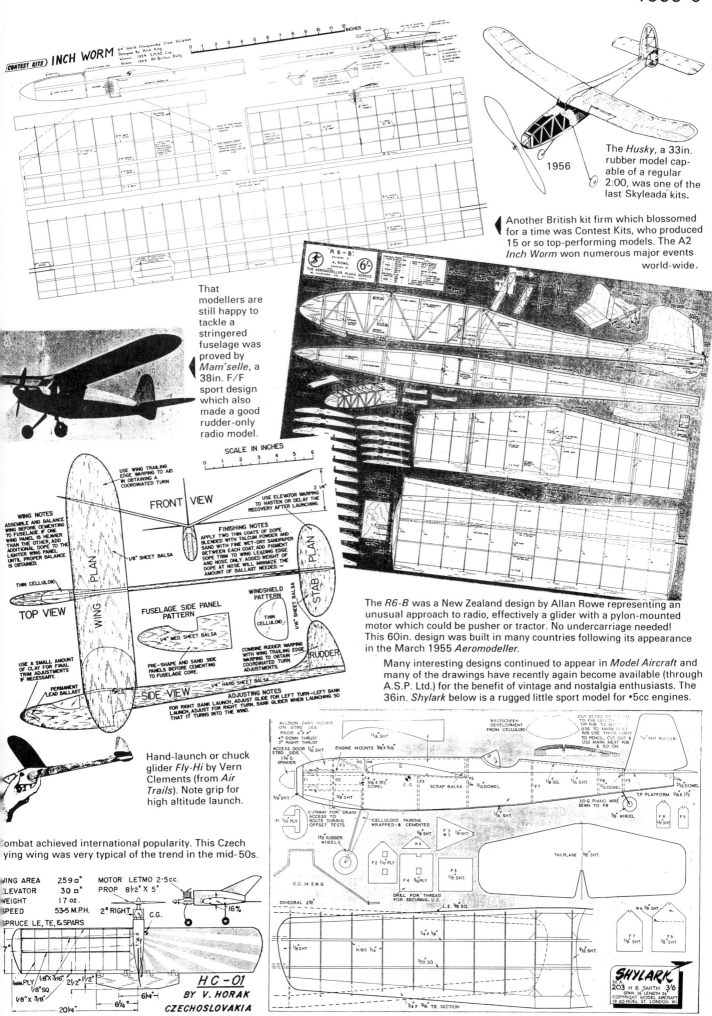

CONTEST KITS INCH WORM

64" World Championship Class Sailplane
Designed By Mick King
Winner 1954 S.M.A.E. Cup
Winner 1954 All Britain Rally

The *Husky*, a 33in. rubber model capable of a regular 2:00, was one of the last Skyleada kits.

Another British kit firm which blossomed for a time was Contest Kits, who produced 15 or so top-performing models. The A2 *Inch Worm* won numerous major events world-wide.

That modellers are still happy to tackle a stringered fuselage was proved by *Mam'selle*, a 38in. F/F sport design which also made a good rudder-only radio model.

FRONT VIEW

USE WING TRAILING EDGE WARPING TO AID IN OBTAINING A COORDINATED TURN.

USE ELEVATOR WARPING TO HASTEN OR DELAY THE RECOVERY AFTER LAUNCHING

FINISHING NOTES
APPLY TWO THIN COATS OF DOPE BLENDED WITH TALCUM POWDER AND SAND WITH FINE WET-DRY SANDPAPER BETWEEN EACH COAT. ADD PIGMENT DOPE TRIM TO WING LEADING EDGE AND NOSE ONLY. ADDED WEIGHT OF DOPE AT NOSE WILL MINIMIZE THE AMOUNT OF BALLAST NEEDED.

WING NOTES
ASSEMBLE AND BALANCE WING BEFORE CEMENTING TO FUSELAGE. IF ONE WING PANEL IS HEAVIER THAN THE OTHER, ADD ADDITIONAL DOPE TO THE LIGHTER WING PANEL UNTIL PROPER BALANCE IS OBTAINED.

1/8" SHEET BALSA

THIN CELLULOID

TOP VIEW

WINDSHIELD PATTERN

THIN CELLULOID

FUSELAGE SIDE PANEL PATTERN

1/4" MED. SHEET BALSA

PRE-SHAPE AND SAND SIDE PANELS BEFORE CEMENTING TO FUSELAGE CORE.

COMBINE RUDDER WARPING WITH WING TRAILING EDGE WARPING TO OBTAIN COORDINATED TURN ADJUSTMENTS.

USE A SMALL AMOUNT OF CLAY FOR FINAL TRIM ADJUSTMENTS IF NECESSARY.

PERMANENT LEAD BALLAST

SIDE VIEW   1/4" HARD SHEET BALSA

ADJUSTING NOTES
FOR RIGHT BANK LAUNCH, ADJUST GLIDE FOR LEFT TURN-LEFT BANK LAUNCH, ADJUST FOR RIGHT TURN. BANK GLIDER WHEN LAUNCHING SO THAT IT TURNS INTO THE WIND.

Hand-launch or chuck glider *Fly-Hi* by Vern Clements (from *Air Trails*). Note grip for high altitude launch.

The *R6-B* was a New Zealand design by Allan Rowe representing an unusual approach to radio, effectively a glider with a pylon-mounted motor which could be pusher or tractor. No undercarriage needed! This 60in. design was built in many countries following its appearance in the March 1955 *Aeromodeller*.

Many interesting designs continued to appear in *Model Aircraft* and many of the drawings have recently again become available (through A.S.P. Ltd.) for the benefit of vintage and nostalgia enthusiasts. The 36in. *Shylark* below is a rugged little sport model for •5cc engines.

Combat achieved international popularity. This Czech flying wing was very typical of the trend in the mid-50s.

WING AREA   259 ▫"
ELEVATOR   30 ▫"
WEIGHT   17 oz.
SPEED   53·5 M.P.H.
SPRUCE LE, TE, & SPARS

MOTOR LETMO 2·5cc.
PROP 8½" X 5"

HC-01
BY V. HORAK
CZECHOSLOVAKIA

SHYLARK
MA 203 H B SMITH
SPAN 36" LENGTH 26
COPYRIGHT MODEL AIRCRAFT
19 20 NOEL ST. LONDON W1

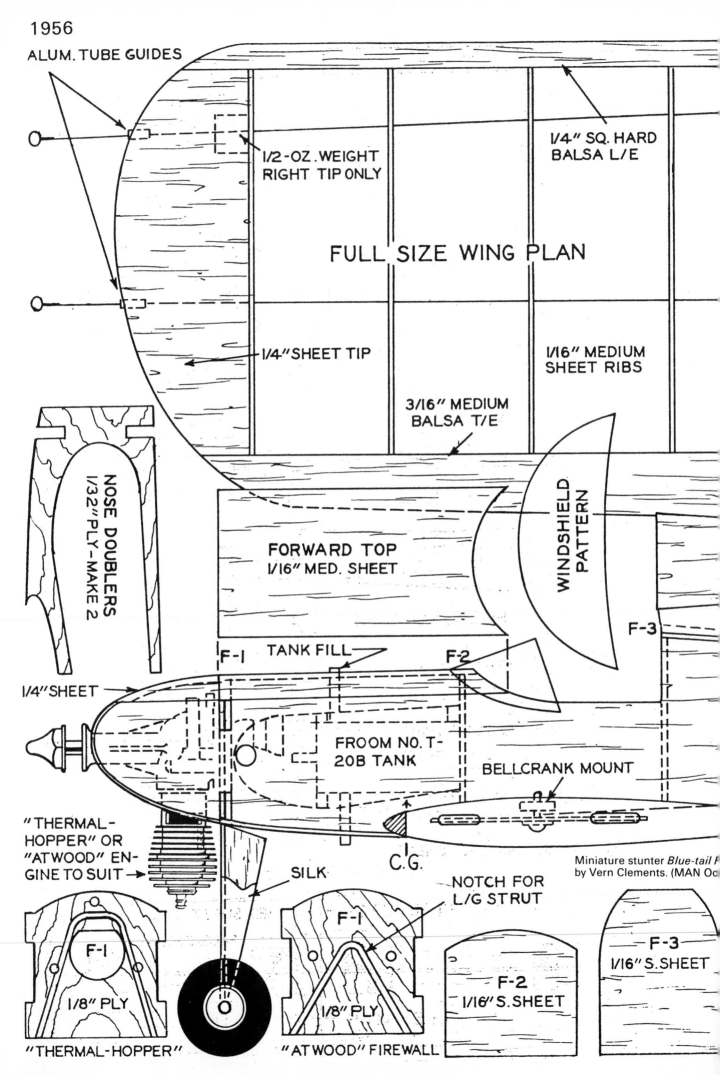

1956

ALUM. TUBE GUIDES

1/2-OZ. WEIGHT RIGHT TIP ONLY

1/4" SQ. HARD BALSA L/E

FULL SIZE WING PLAN

1/4" SHEET TIP

1/16" MEDIUM SHEET RIBS

3/16" MEDIUM BALSA T/E

NOSE DOUBLERS 1/32" PLY—MAKE 2

WINDSHIELD PATTERN

FORWARD TOP 1/16" MED. SHEET

F-3

F-1

TANK FILL

F-2

1/4" SHEET

FROOM NO. T-20B TANK

BELLCRANK MOUNT

"THERMAL-HOPPER" OR "ATWOOD" ENGINE TO SUIT →

C.G.

Miniature stunter *Blue-tail F* by Vern Clements. (MAN Oc

SILK

NOTCH FOR L/G STRUT

F-1

1/8" PLY

F-1

1/8" PLY

F-2 1/16" S. SHEET

F-3 1/16" S. SHEET

"THERMAL-HOPPER"

"ATWOOD" FIREWALL

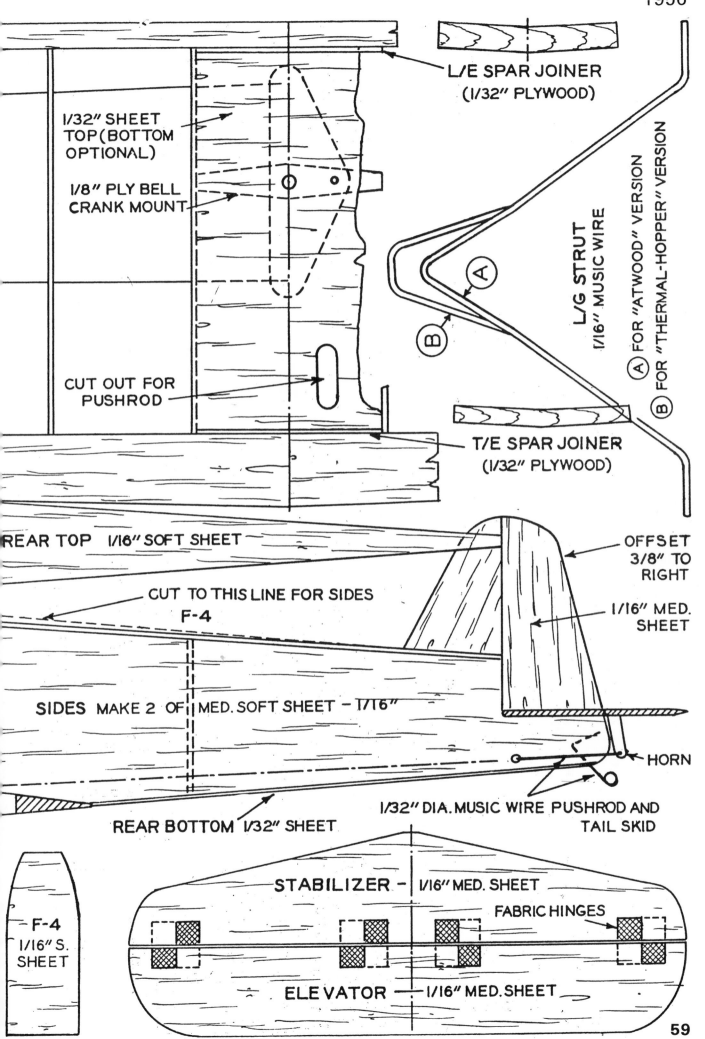

L/E SPAR JOINER
(1/32" PLYWOOD)

1/32" SHEET TOP (BOTTOM OPTIONAL)

1/8" PLY BELL CRANK MOUNT

CUT OUT FOR PUSHROD

L/G STRUT
1/16" MUSIC WIRE

Ⓐ FOR "ATWOOD" VERSION
Ⓑ FOR "THERMAL-HOPPER" VERSION

T/E SPAR JOINER
(1/32" PLYWOOD)

REAR TOP 1/16" SOFT SHEET

CUT TO THIS LINE FOR SIDES F-4

OFFSET 3/8" TO RIGHT

1/16" MED. SHEET

SIDES MAKE 2 OF MED. SOFT SHEET – 1/16"

HORN

1/32" DIA. MUSIC WIRE PUSHROD AND TAIL SKID

REAR BOTTOM 1/32" SHEET

F-4
1/16" S. SHEET

STABILIZER – 1/16" MED. SHEET

FABRIC HINGES

ELEVATOR – 1/16" MED. SHEET

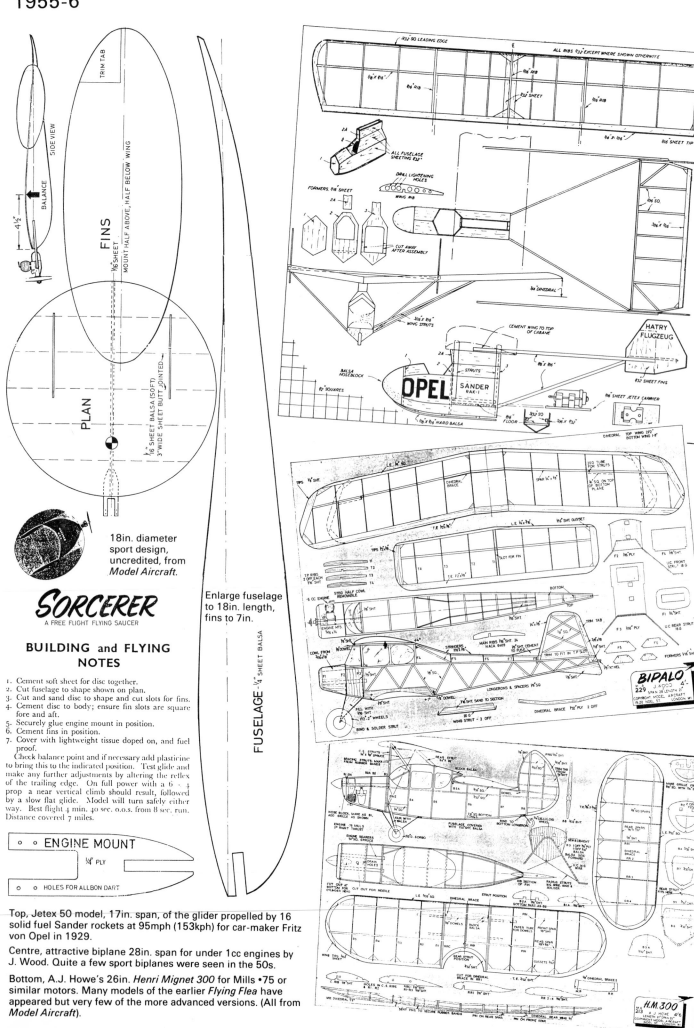

SIDE VIEW

TRIM TAB

FINS
1/16" SHEET
MOUNT HALF ABOVE, HALF BELOW WING

BALANCE

4½"

PLAN

1/16" SHEET BALSA (SOFT)
3" WIDE SHEET BUTT JOINTED

18in. diameter sport design, uncredited, from *Model Aircraft*.

SORCERER
A FREE FLIGHT FLYING SAUCER

BUILDING and FLYING NOTES

1. Cement soft sheet for disc together.
2. Cut fuselage to shape shown on plan.
3. Cut and sand disc to shape and cut slots for fins.
4. Cement disc to body; ensure fin slots are square fore and aft.
5. Securely glue engine mount in position.
6. Cement fins in position.
7. Cover with lightweight tissue doped on, and fuel proof.

Check balance point and if necessary add plasticine to bring this to the indicated position. Test glide and make any further adjustments by altering the reflex of the trailing edge. On full power with a 6 · 4 prop a near vertical climb should result, followed by a slow flat glide. Model will turn safely either way. Best flight 4 min. 40 sec. o.o.s. from 8 sec. run. Distance covered 7 miles.

ENGINE MOUNT
1/4" PLY
○ ○ HOLES FOR ALLBON DART

Enlarge fuselage to 18in. length, fins to 7in.

FUSELAGE 1/4" SHEET BALSA

Top, Jetex 50 model, 17in. span, of the glider propelled by 16 solid fuel Sander rockets at 95mph (153kph) for car-maker Fritz von Opel in 1929.

Centre, attractive biplane 28in. span for under 1cc engines by J. Wood. Quite a few sport biplanes were seen in the 50s.

Bottom, A.J. Howe's 26in. *Henri Mignet 300* for Mills •75 or similar motors. Many models of the earlier *Flying Flea* have appeared but very few of the more advanced versions. (All from *Model Aircraft*).

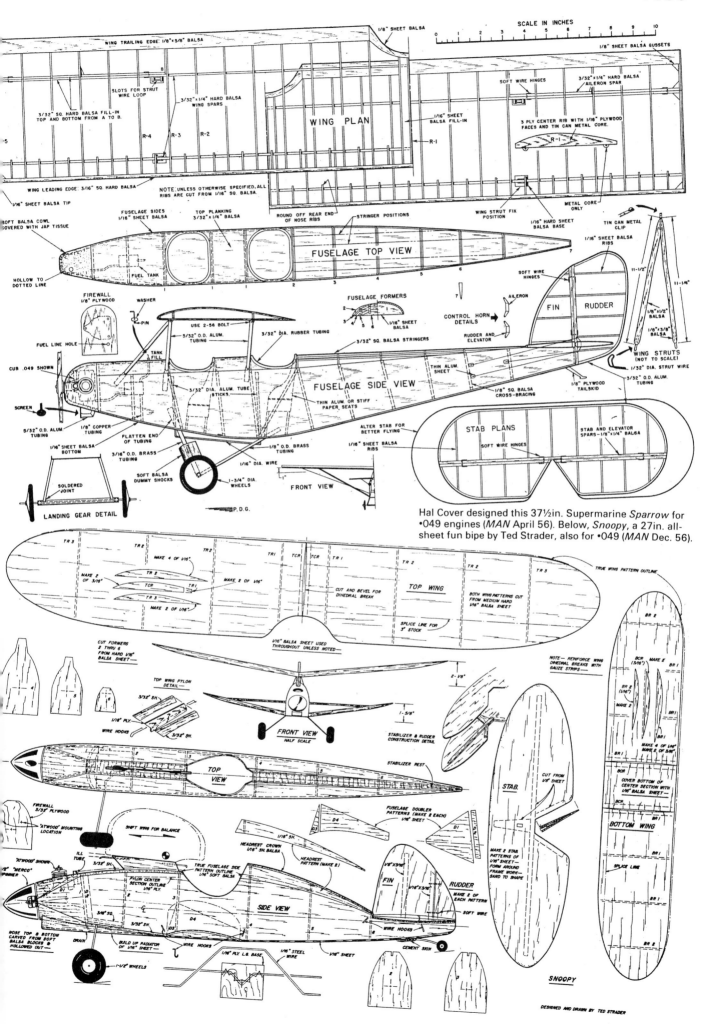

Hal Cover designed this 37½in. Supermarine *Sparrow* for •049 engines (*MAN* April 56). Below, *Snoopy*, a 27in. all-sheet fun bipe by Ted Strader, also for •049 (*MAN* Dec. 56).

SNOOPY

DESIGNED AND DRAWN BY TED STRADER

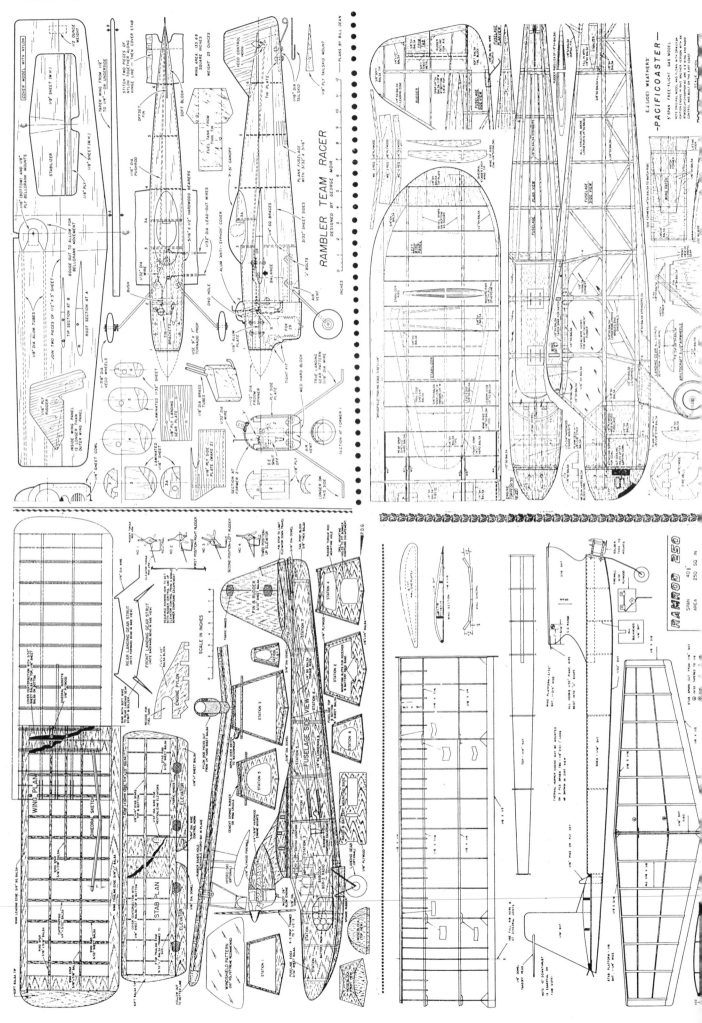

RAMBLER TEAM RACER

DESIGNED BY GEORGE MOIR

— PLANS BY BILL DEAN —

E. J. (JOE) WEATHERS'
—PACIFICOASTER—
5' SPAN FREE-FLIGHT GAS MODEL

RAMROD 250

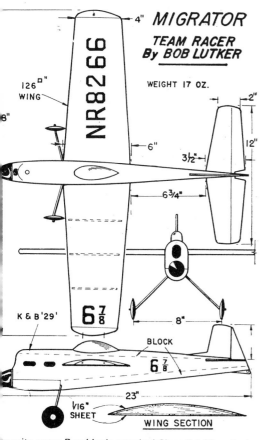

MIGRATOR
TEAM RACER
By BOB LUTKER

NR8266

126□" WING

WEIGHT 17 OZ.

4"
2"
6"
3½"
12"
6¾"
8"
23"

K & B '29'

BLOCK

6⅞
6⅞

1/16" SHEET

WING SECTION

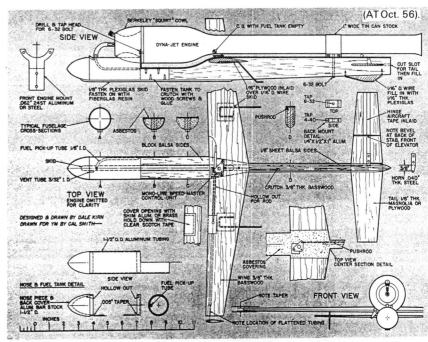

(AT Oct. 56).

DESIGNED & DRAWN BY DALE KIRN
DRAWN FOR YM BY CAL SMITH

Team racer *Migrator*, published *Aeromodeller* Dec. 56, was descended from winner of 1951 U.S. Nats. Torpedo •29, 8×9in. prop, terrific acceleration to 85-90mph.

Dynajet powered *Shock Wave* set new mark of 166•6 mph for Clem/Beasley/Kirm team at 1956 King Orange meet.

Below, Mercury *Thunderbird* racer notched up an official 105mph on 5cc for designer Sid McGoun. KK *Joker* was stunter for half-cc motors and kit, at 11s.5d (57p or almost exactly $1) was fully die-cut and included cement, tissue paste, finished wedge tank, bell-crank and a lot more . . . Radio circuit is the famous Hill 2-valve receiver, probably built by more modellers than any other. (AM June 1956).

pposite page: *Rambler* is a typical Class B (•29 or 5cc)
am racer of the mid-50s. This design by George Moir
peared in *MAN* March 1955. Span 28in.

nother of Ken Willard's amphibians, this one 50in.
an for •09 (1½cc) engines and radio; latter used a
nner compound escapement for rudder and elevator.
T April 55).

bert Weathers designed *Pacificoaster* in 1945 but its
itability for R/C led to publication in Nov. 56 *MAN*.
is version 5ft. span but 6ft. wing also used. 10cc (•60)

p F/F contest design of 1955 was *Ramrod*, by Ron St.
an. This one 40½in. span, 250sq.in., •09 power,
hers 53½, 432, •15, 63, 600, •19-•23 and 70, 750,
9-•35 (*MAN* June 56).

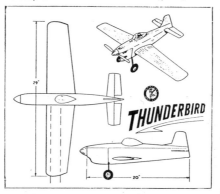

THUNDERBIRD

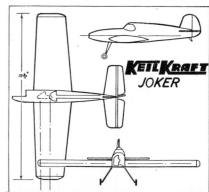

KEILKRAFT JOKER

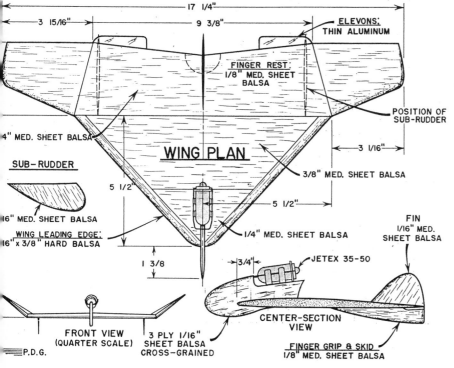

17 1/4"
3 15/16"
9 3/8"

ELEVONS:
THIN ALUMINUM

FINGER REST:
1/8" MED. SHEET
BALSA

POSITION OF
SUB-RUDDER

4" MED. SHEET BALSA

WING PLAN

3 1/16"

SUB-RUDDER

3/8" MED. SHEET BALSA

5 1/2"

5 1/2"

6" MED. SHEET BALSA

WING LEADING EDGE:
6" x 3/8" HARD BALSA

1 3/8

1/4" MED. SHEET BALSA

JETEX 35-50

3/4"

FIN
1/16" MED.
SHEET BALSA

FRONT VIEW
(QUARTER SCALE)

P.D.G.

3 PLY 1/16"
SHEET BALSA
CROSS-GRAINED

CENTER-SECTION
VIEW

FINGER GRIP & SKID
1/8" MED. SHEET BALSA

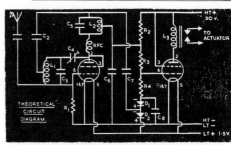

Jetex Delta (*MAN* April 57) typifies the simple sort of experimental model possible with the Jetex 50 or 35. This design by Paul Del Gatto.

Below, variable incidence tailplanes (or, in this case, elevators) were described in detail by Jim Waldron in April 1956 *Aeromodeller*.

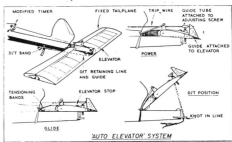

'AUTO ELEVATOR' SYSTEM

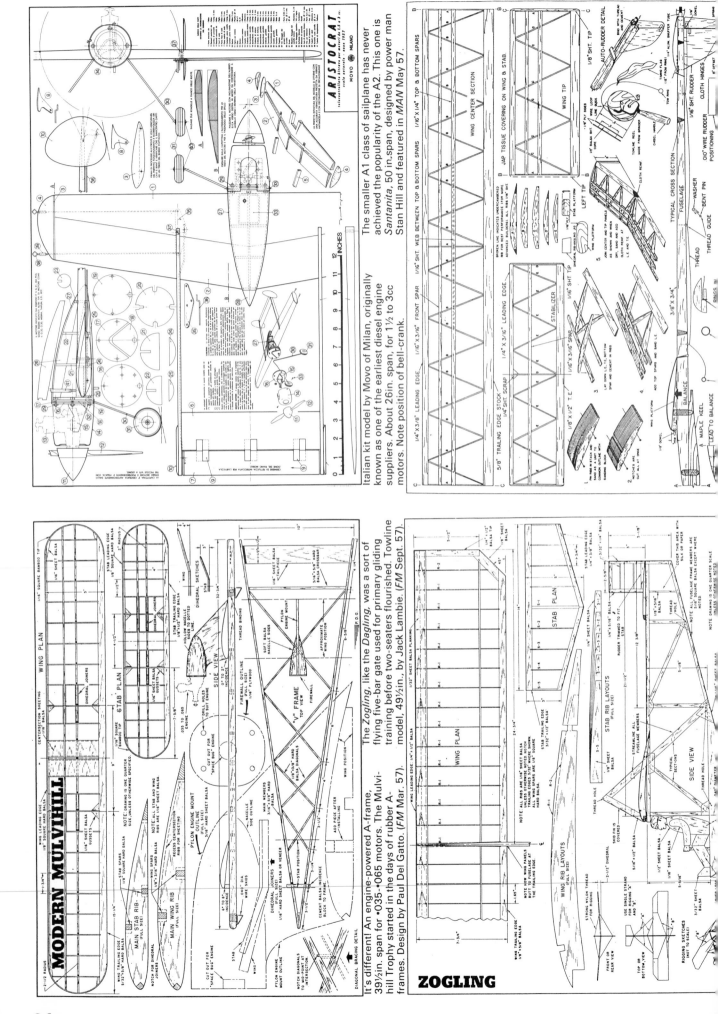

The smaller A1 class of sailplane has never achieved the popularity of the A2. This one is *Santanita*, 50 in. span, designed by power man Stan Hill and featured in *MAN* May 57.

Italian kit model by Movo of Milan, originally known as one of the earliest diesel engine suppliers. About 26 in. span, for 1½ to 3 cc motors. Note position of bell-crank.

It's different! An engine-powered A-frame. 39½ in. span for •035-•065 motors. The Mulvihill Trophy started in the days of rubber A-frames. Design by Paul Del Gatto. (*FM* Mar. 57).

The *Zogling*, like the *Dagling*, was a sort of flying five-bar gate used for primary gliding training before two-seaters flourished. Towline model, 49½ in., by Jack Lambie. (*FM* Sept. 57).

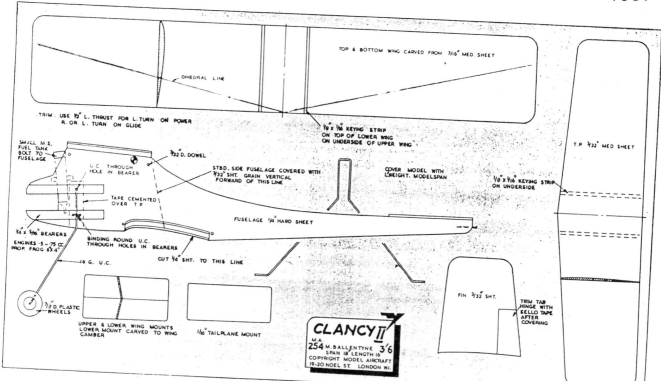

CLANCY II
M.A.
254 M. BALLENTYNE 3'6
SPAN 18 LENGTH 16
COPYRIGHT MODEL AIRCRAFT
19-20 NOEL ST LONDON WI.

Simple all-sheet biplane, 18in. span for •5-•75cc, by M. Ballentyne. Dihedral 2in. each tip. (*Model Aircraft* 1957).

"Galloping Ghost" was a system developed in the U.S.A. which employed a crank which never made a complete revolution but rotated back and forth. The extent of the arc and its centre could be varied by varying the mark/space ratio and the rate of a pulsed signal, thus biasing rudder or elevator, or both, giving proportional control, though with a degree of constant tail-wagging. Widely used in the late 50s. (*AM* July 57).

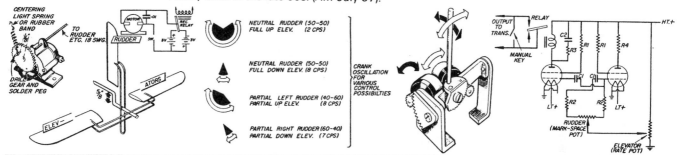

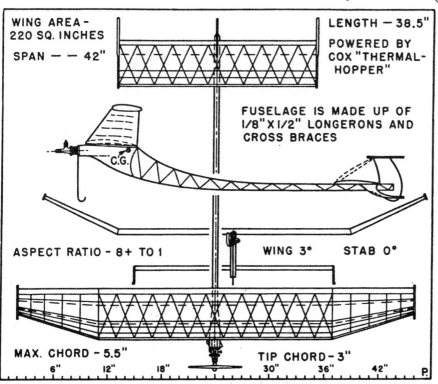

WING AREA - 220 SQ. INCHES

SPAN — — 42"

LENGTH — 38.5"

POWERED BY COX "THERMAL-HOPPER"

FUSELAGE IS MADE UP OF 1/8" X 1/2" LONGERONS AND CROSS BRACES

ASPECT RATIO - 8+ TO 1   WING 3°   STAB 0°

MAX. CHORD - 5.5"   TIP CHORD - 3"

High thrust-line *Jacana* by Don Drury (*American Modeler* Dec. 57), one of twenty variations on a basic theme. The PAAload conversion pod carries a conventional undercarriage but normally model stood on three dowels (top of fin, underneath tailplane tips) for V.T.O., with a wire leg for prop protection on landing. Goldberg airfoil, top surface spars for turbulation.

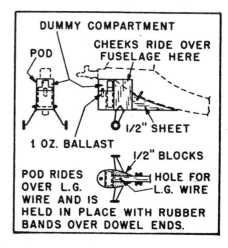

DUMMY COMPARTMENT

CHEEKS RIDE OVER FUSELAGE HERE

POD

1/2" SHEET

1 OZ. BALLAST

1/2" BLOCKS

HOLE FOR L.G. WIRE

POD RIDES OVER L.G. WIRE AND IS HELD IN PLACE WITH RUBBER BANDS OVER DOWEL ENDS.

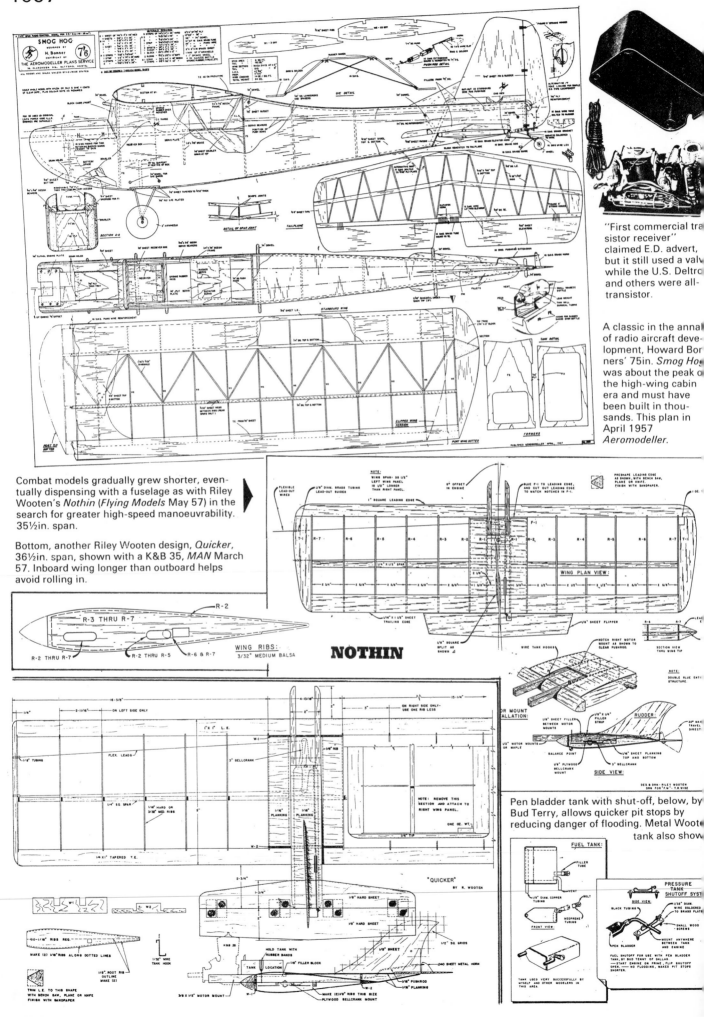

"First commercial transistor receiver" claimed E.D. advert, but it still used a valve while the U.S. Deltro and others were all-transistor.

A classic in the annal of radio aircraft development, Howard Bonners' 75in. *Smog Hog* was about the peak of the high-wing cabin era and must have been built in thousands. This plan in April 1957 *Aeromodeller*.

Combat models gradually grew shorter, eventually dispensing with a fuselage as with Riley Wooten's *Nothin* (*Flying Models* May 57) in the search for greater high-speed manoeuvrability. 35½in. span.

Bottom, another Riley Wooten design, *Quicker*, 36½in. span, shown with a K&B 35, *MAN* March 57. Inboard wing longer than outboard helps avoid rolling in.

Pen bladder tank with shut-off, below, by Bud Terry, allows quicker pit stops by reducing danger of flooding. Metal Wooten tank also show

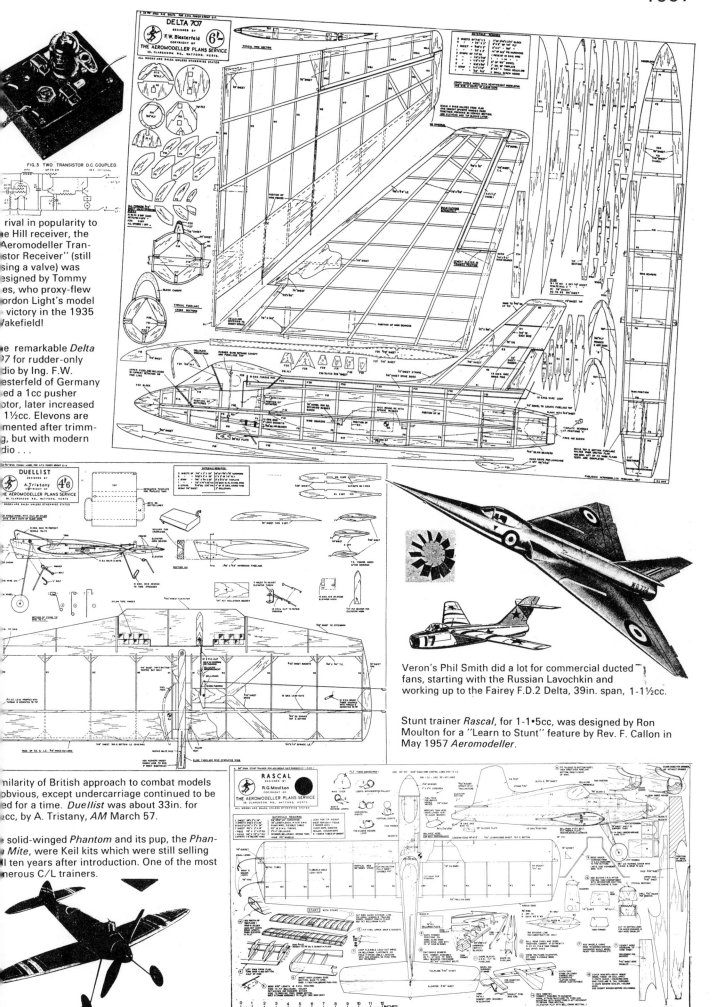

rival in popularity to
e Hill receiver, the
Aeromodeller Tran-
stor Receiver" (still
sing a valve) was
esigned by Tommy
es, who proxy-flew
ordon Light's model
victory in the 1935
Wakefield!

e remarkable *Delta
7* for rudder-only
dio by Ing. F.W.
esterfeld of Germany
ed a 1cc pusher
tor, later increased
1½cc. Elevons are
mented after trimm-
g, but with modern
dio . . .

Veron's Phil Smith did a lot for commercial ducted
fans, starting with the Russian Lavochkin and
working up to the Fairey F.D.2 Delta, 39in. span, 1-1½cc.

Stunt trainer *Rascal*, for 1-1•5cc, was designed by Ron
Moulton for a "Learn to Stunt" feature by Rev. F. Callon in
May 1957 *Aeromodeller*.

milarity of British approach to combat models
obvious, except undercarriage continued to be
ed for a time. *Duellist* was about 33in. for
cc, by A. Tristany, *AM* March 57.

solid-winged *Phantom* and its pup, the *Phan-
Mite*, were Keil kits which were still selling
ll ten years after introduction. One of the most
merous C/L trainers.

1957

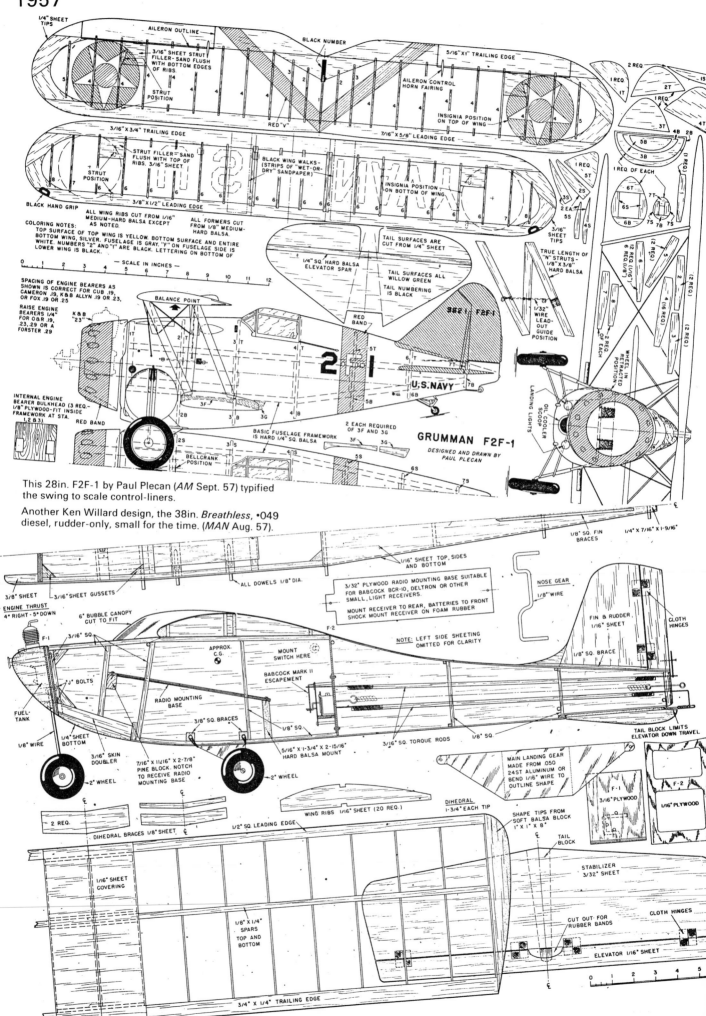

This 28in. F2F-1 by Paul Plecan (*AM* Sept. 57) typified the swing to scale control-liners.

Another Ken Willard design, the 38in. *Breathless*, •049 diesel, rudder-only, small for the time. (*MAN* Aug. 57).

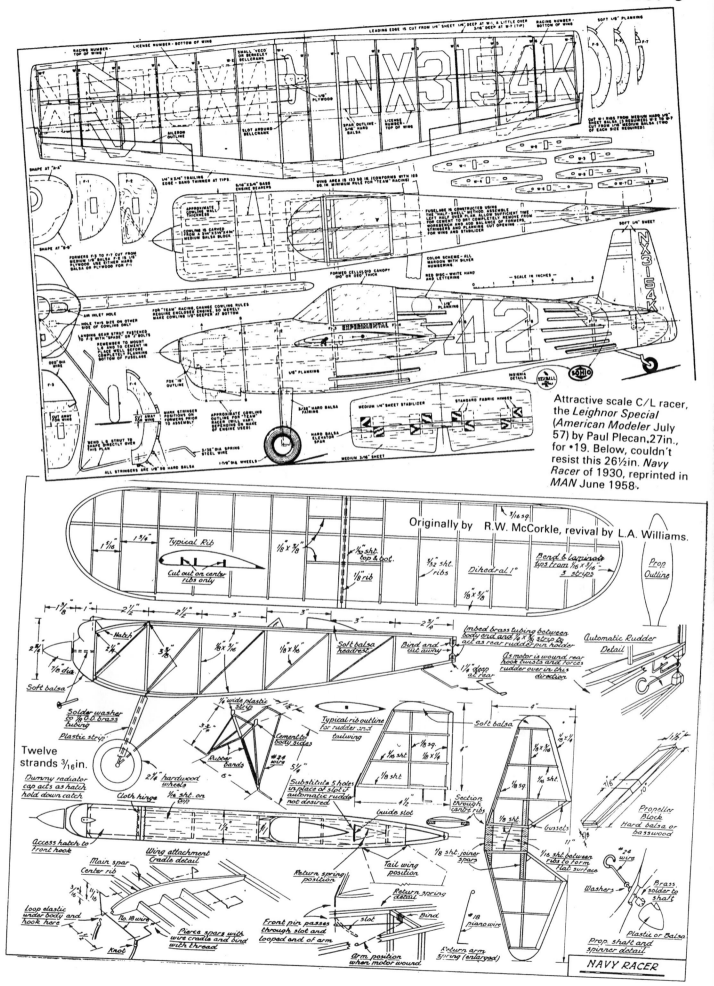

Attractive scale C/L racer, the *Leighnor Special* (*American Modeler* July 57) by Paul Plecan, 27in., for •19. Below, couldn't resist this 26½in. *Navy Racer* of 1930, reprinted in *MAN* June 1958.

Originally by R.W. McCorkle, revival by L.A. Williams.

NAVY RACER

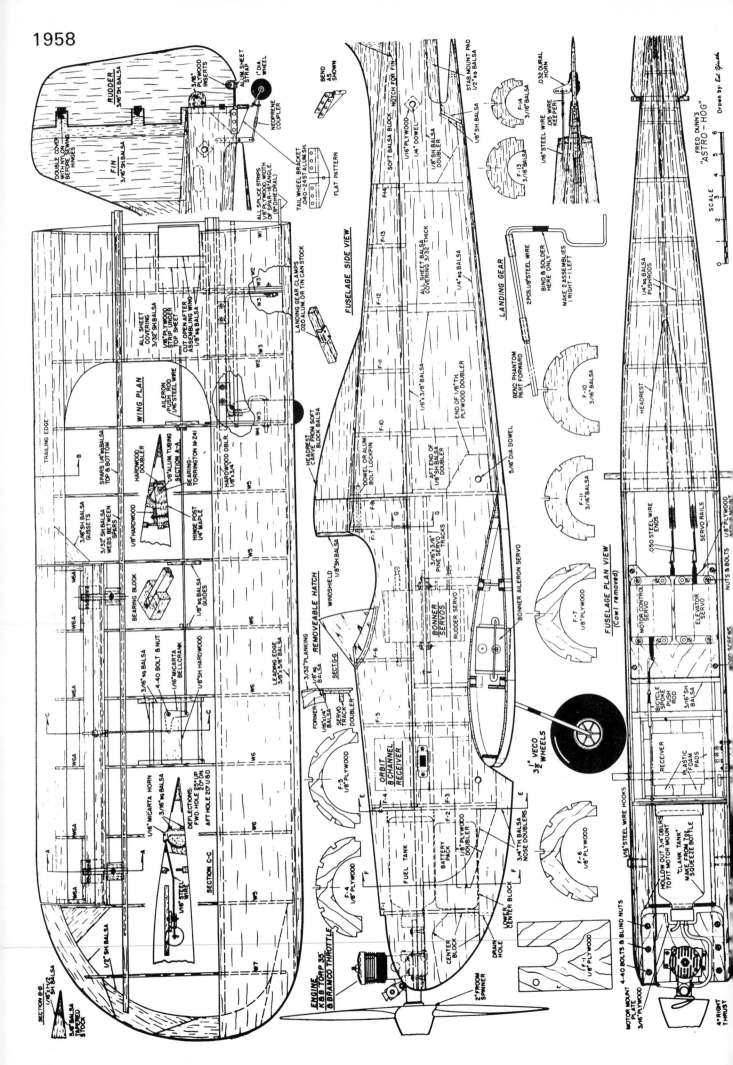

FRED DUNN'S
"ASTRO-HOG"

Drawn by: Ed Yeck

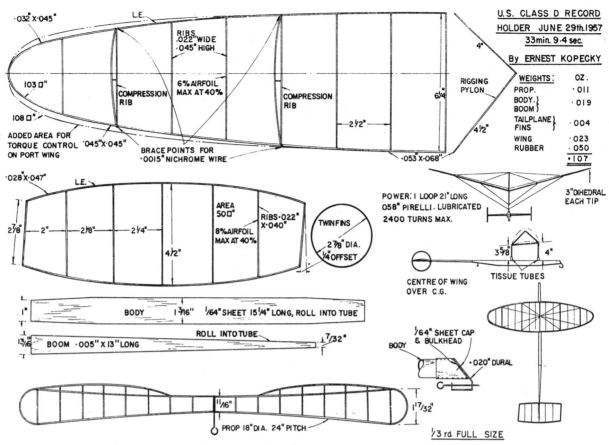

Indoor flying began a revival of interest in GB and Eastern Europe, spurred no doubt by remarkable times being put up in the U.S. and permission to use some excellent facilities.

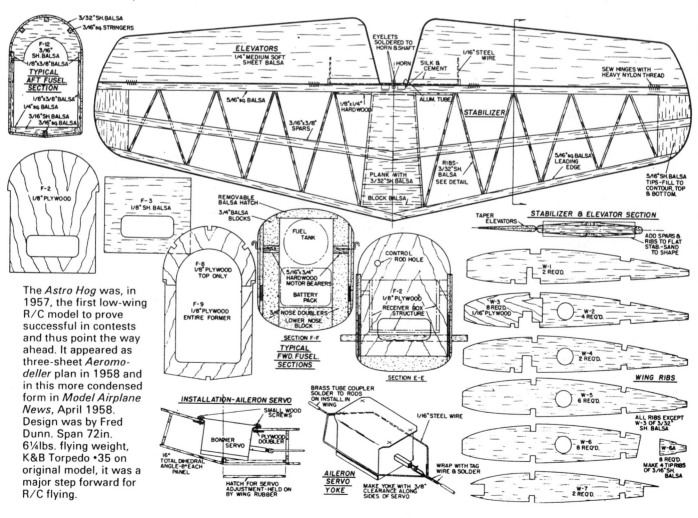

The *Astro Hog* was, in 1957, the first low-wing R/C model to prove successful in contests and thus point the way ahead. It appeared as three-sheet *Aeromodeller* plan in 1958 and in this more condensed form in *Model Airplane News*, April 1958. Design was by Fred Dunn. Span 72in. 6¼lbs. flying weight, K&B Torpedo •35 on original model, it was a major step forward for R/C flying.

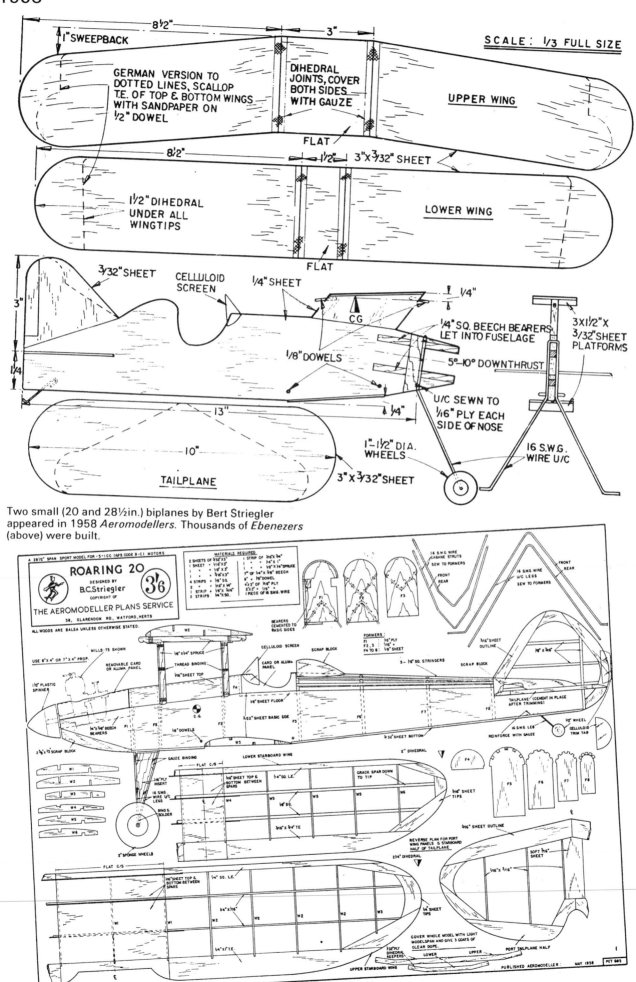

Two small (20 and 28½in.) biplanes by Bert Striegler appeared in 1958 *Aeromodellers*. Thousands of *Ebenezers* (above) were built.

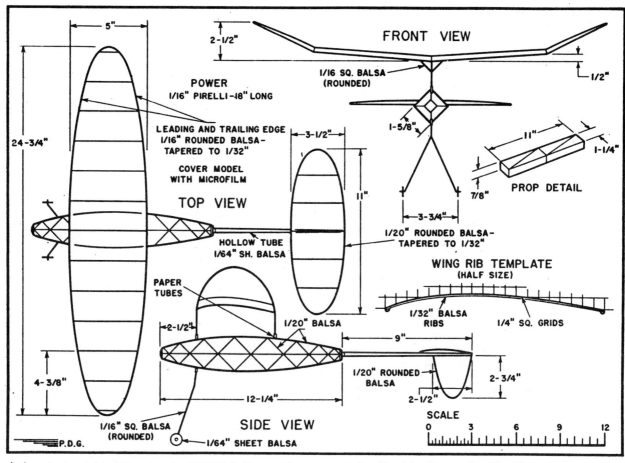

Indoor Junior Cabin Winner at the 1957 U.S. Nats. makes a not-too-hard introduction to microfilm. Flown by Larry Willis.

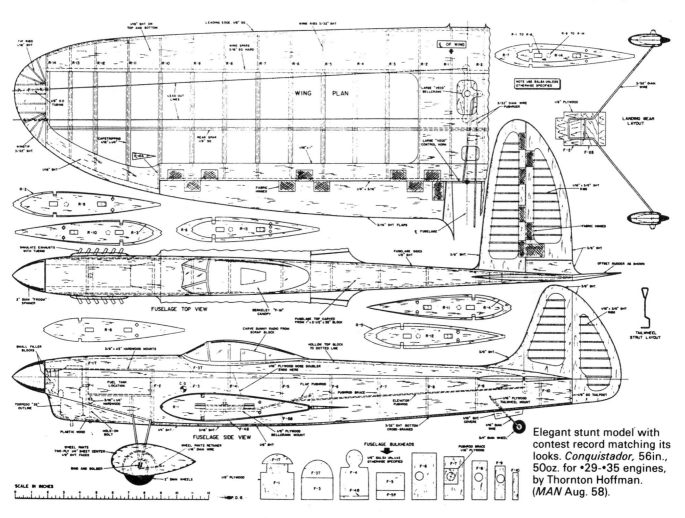

Elegant stunt model with contest record matching its looks. *Conquistador,* 56in., 50oz. for •29-•35 engines, by Thornton Hoffman. *(MAN* Aug. 58).

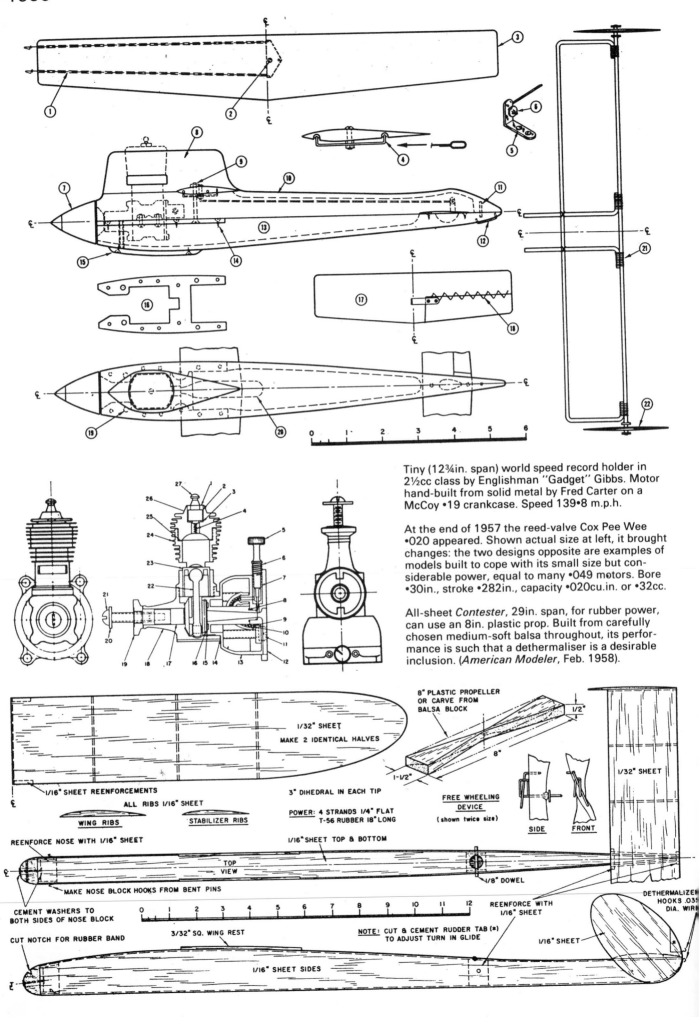

Tiny (12¾in. span) world speed record holder in 2½cc class by Englishman "Gadget" Gibbs. Motor hand-built from solid metal by Fred Carter on a McCoy •19 crankcase. Speed 139•8 m.p.h.

At the end of 1957 the reed-valve Cox Pee Wee •020 appeared. Shown actual size at left, it brought changes: the two designs opposite are examples of models built to cope with its small size but considerable power, equal to many •049 motors. Bore •30in., stroke •282in., capacity •020cu.in. or •32cc.

All-sheet *Contester*, 29in. span, for rubber power, can use an 8in. plastic prop. Built from carefully chosen medium-soft balsa throughout, its performance is such that a dethermaliser is a desirable inclusion. (*American Modeler*, Feb. 1958).

8" PLASTIC PROPELLER OR CARVE FROM BALSA BLOCK

1/32" SHEET
MAKE 2 IDENTICAL HALVES

1/16" SHEET REENFORCEMENTS

3" DIHEDRAL IN EACH TIP

ALL RIBS 1/16" SHEET

WING RIBS   STABILIZER RIBS

POWER: 4 STRANDS 1/4" FLAT T-56 RUBBER 18" LONG

FREE WHEELING DEVICE
(shown twice size)

SIDE   FRONT

1/32" SHEET

REENFORCE NOSE WITH 1/16" SHEET

1/16" SHEET TOP & BOTTOM

TOP VIEW

MAKE NOSE BLOCK HOOKS FROM BENT PINS

1/8" DOWEL

DETHERMALIZER HOOKS .035 DIA. WIRE

CEMENT WASHERS TO BOTH SIDES OF NOSE BLOCK

REENFORCE WITH 1/16" SHEET

CUT NOTCH FOR RUBBER BAND

3/32" SQ. WING REST

NOTE: CUT & CEMENT RUDDER TAB (∗) TO ADJUST TURN IN GLIDE

1/16" SHEET

1/16" SHEET SIDES

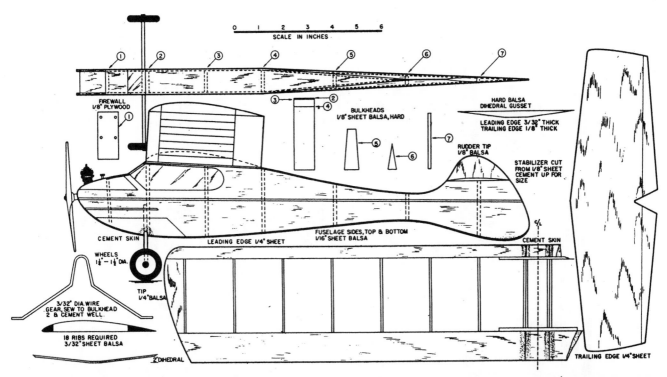

Intended as a fun model for the Pee Wee •020, *Just Right* is a small field performer of rugged construction by Frank Ehling. Inclusion of colour trim lines on profile is confusing – fuselage is flat-sided and what appears a structural item close to the thrust line is a paint guide. (*American Modeler* Nov. 58).

The Pee Wee offered something of a challenge and Howard G. McEntee was clearly tempted to try it for radio. His 24in. span *Mac's Minnie* weighed 5•28ozs. empty and complete with radio outfit just 8•4ozs! Used a Deltron R109 receiver without case, Gem escapement and one 22½v battery. Not a beginner's project by any means.

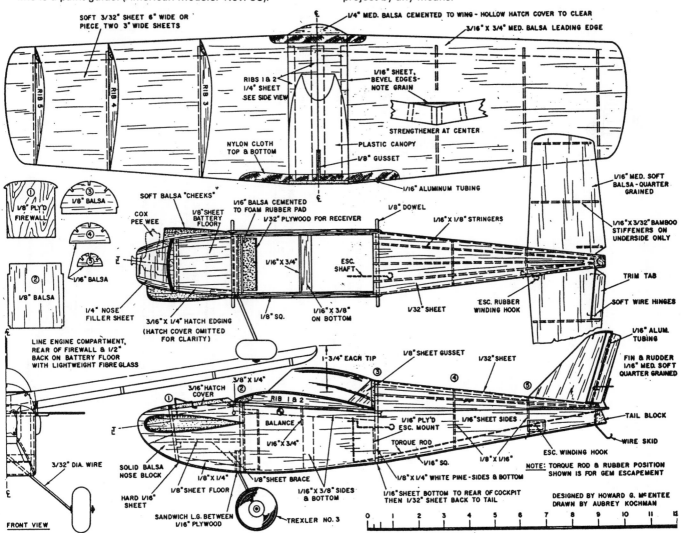

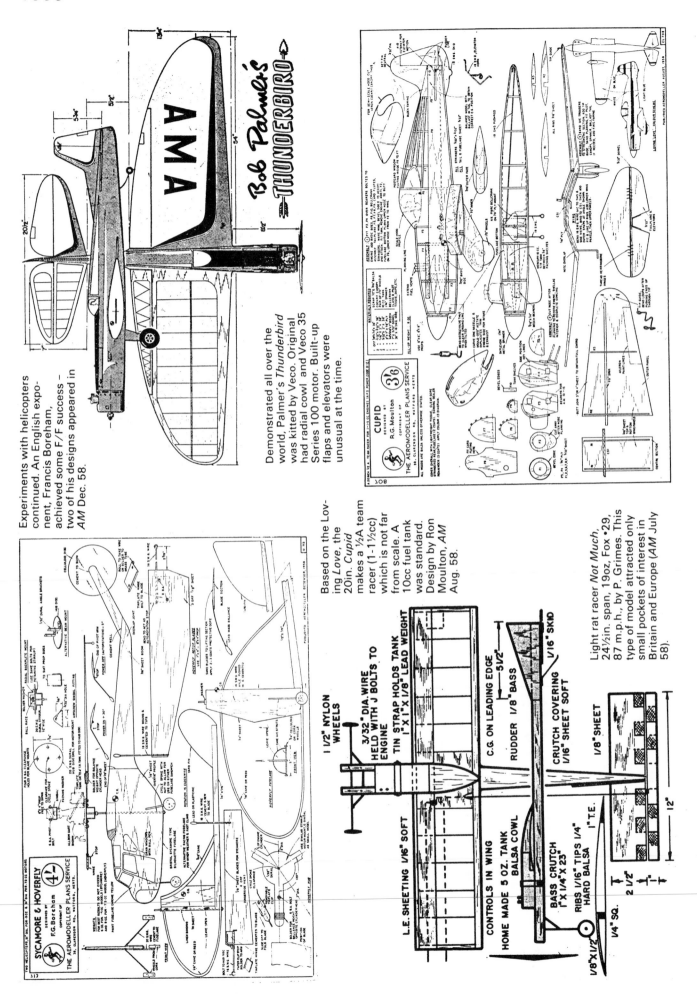

Experiments with helicopters continued. An English exponent, Francis Boreham, achieved some F/F success – two of his designs appeared in *AM* Dec. 58.

Demonstrated all over the world, Palmer's *Thunderbird* was kitted by Veco. Original had radial cowl and Veco 35 Series 100 motor. Built-up flaps and elevators were unusual at the time.

Based on the Loving *Love*, the 20in. *Cupid* makes a ½A team racer (1-1½cc) which is not far from scale. A 10cc fuel tank was standard. Design by Ron Moulton, *AM* Aug. 58.

Light rat racer *Not Much*, 24½in. span, 19oz, Fox •29, 87 m.p.h., by P. Grimes. This type of model attracted only small pockets of interest in Britain and Europe (*AM* July 58).

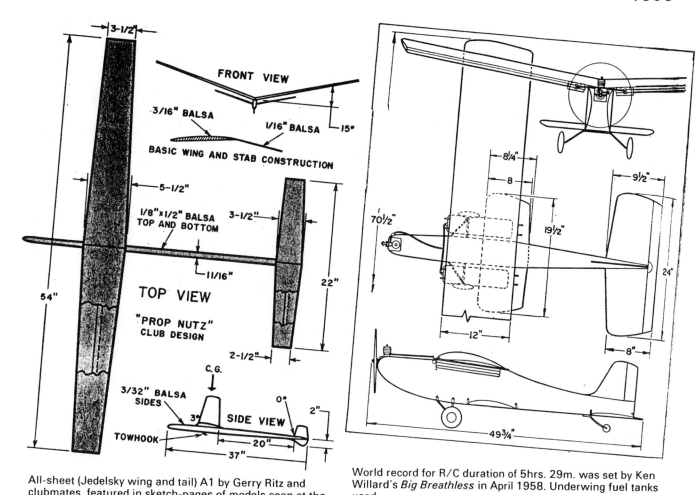

FRONT VIEW

3/16" BALSA

1/16" BALSA

15°

BASIC WING AND STAB CONSTRUCTION

3-1/2"

5-1/2"

1/8"x1/2" BALSA TOP AND BOTTOM

3-1/2"

11/16"

TOP VIEW

"PROP NUTZ" CLUB DESIGN

54"

22"

2-1/2"

C.G.

3/32" BALSA SIDES

3°

0°

SIDE VIEW

2"

TOWHOOK

20"

37"

70½"

8¼"

8

19½"

9½"

24"

12"

8"

49¾"

All-sheet (Jedelsky wing and tail) A1 by Gerry Ritz and clubmates, featured in sketch-pages of models seen at the 1957 U.S. Nats.

World record for R/C duration of 5hrs. 29m. was set by Ken Willard's *Big Breathless* in April 1958. Underwing fuel tanks used.

It takes all sorts! Multi-engined control-liners had a following. This 63in. *Viscount* was for a total 7cc. By J.M. Bodey, *AM* July 58.

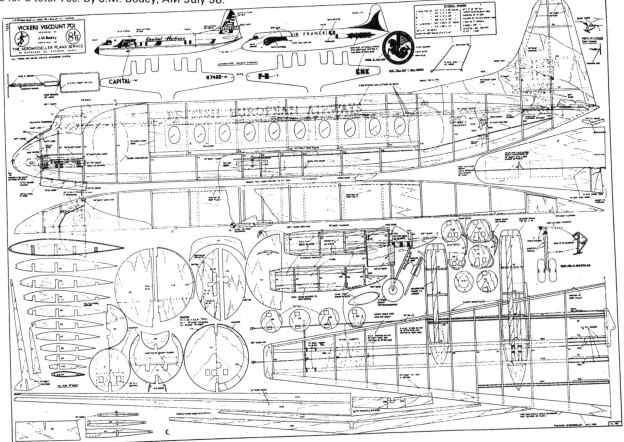

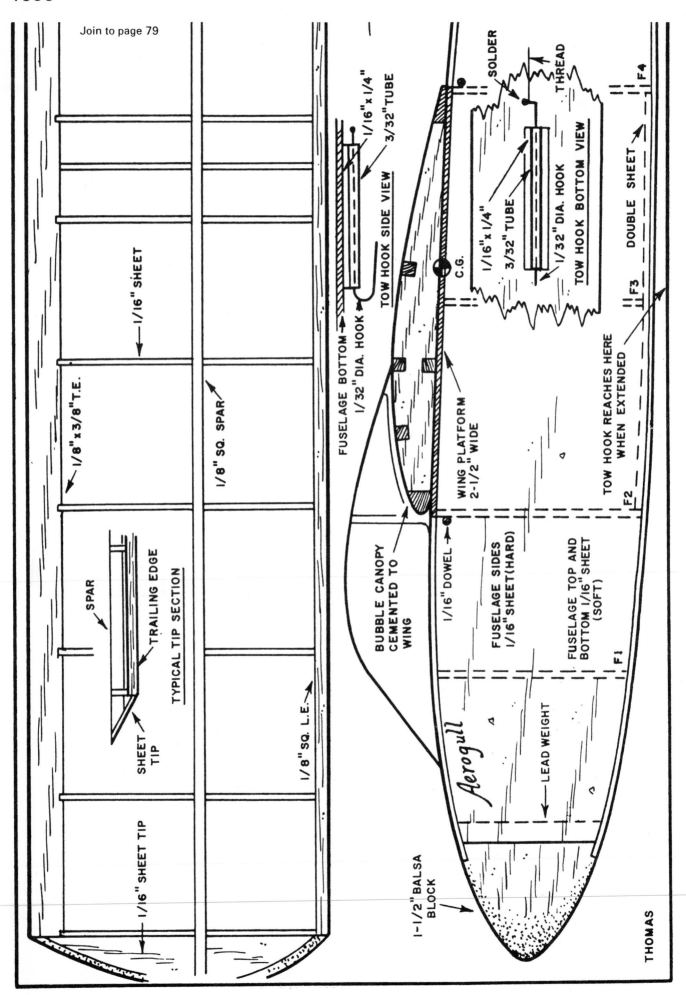

Join to page 79

1/16" SHEET

1/8" x 3/8" T.E.

1/8" SQ. SPAR

SPAR

TRAILING EDGE

TYPICAL TIP SECTION

SHEET TIP

1/16" SHEET TIP

1/8" SQ. L.E.

FUSELAGE BOTTOM

1/32" DIA. HOOK

1/16" x 1/4" TUBE

3/32" TUBE

TOW HOOK SIDE VIEW

SOLDER

THREAD

F4

1/16" x 1/4" TUBE

3/32" TUBE

1/32" DIA. HOOK

TOW HOOK BOTTOM VIEW

C.G.

DOUBLE SHEET

F3

TOW HOOK REACHES HERE WHEN EXTENDED

F2

WING PLATFORM 2-1/2" WIDE

BUBBLE CANOPY CEMENTED TO WING

1/16" DOWEL

FUSELAGE SIDES 1/16" SHEET (HARD)

FUSELAGE TOP AND BOTTOM 1/16" SHEET (SOFT)

F1

Aerogull

LEAD WEIGHT

1-1/2" BALSA BLOCK

THOMAS

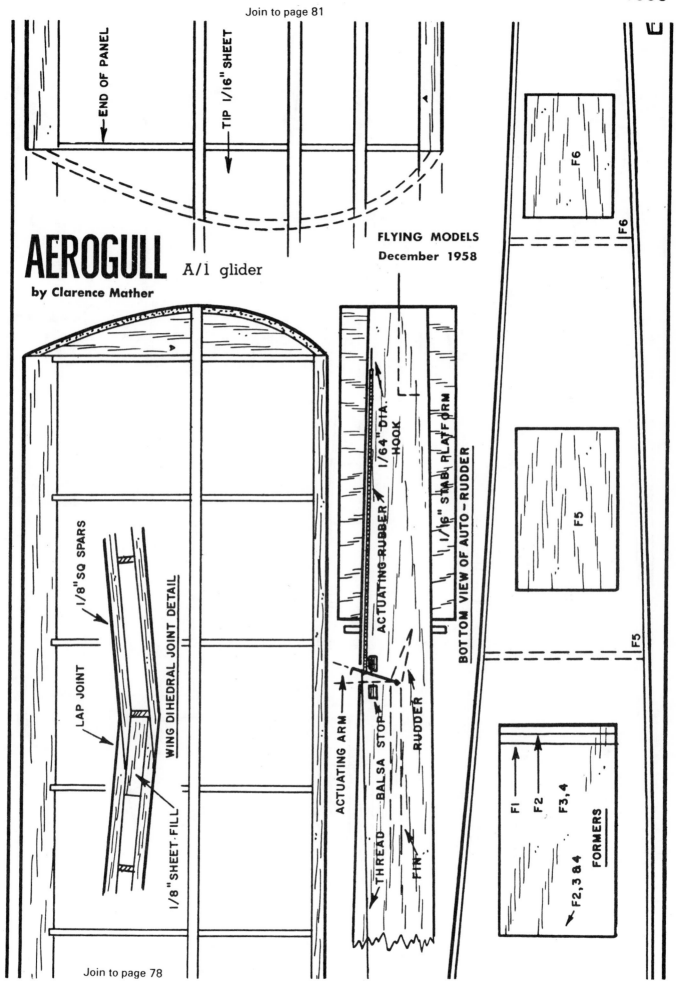

Join to page 81

END OF PANEL

TIP 1/16" SHEET

FLYING MODELS
December 1958

AEROGULL
A/1 glider
by Clarence Mather

1/8" SQ SPARS

LAP JOINT

WING DIHEDRAL JOINT DETAIL

1/8" SHEET FILL

ACTUATING ARM

ACTUATING RUBBER

1/64" DIA.

HOOK

1/16" STAB. PLATFORM

BOTTOM VIEW OF AUTO~RUDDER

THREAD

BALSA STOP

RUDDER

FIN

F6

F6

F5

F5

F5

F1

F2

F3,4

FORMERS

F2,3 & 4

Join to page 78

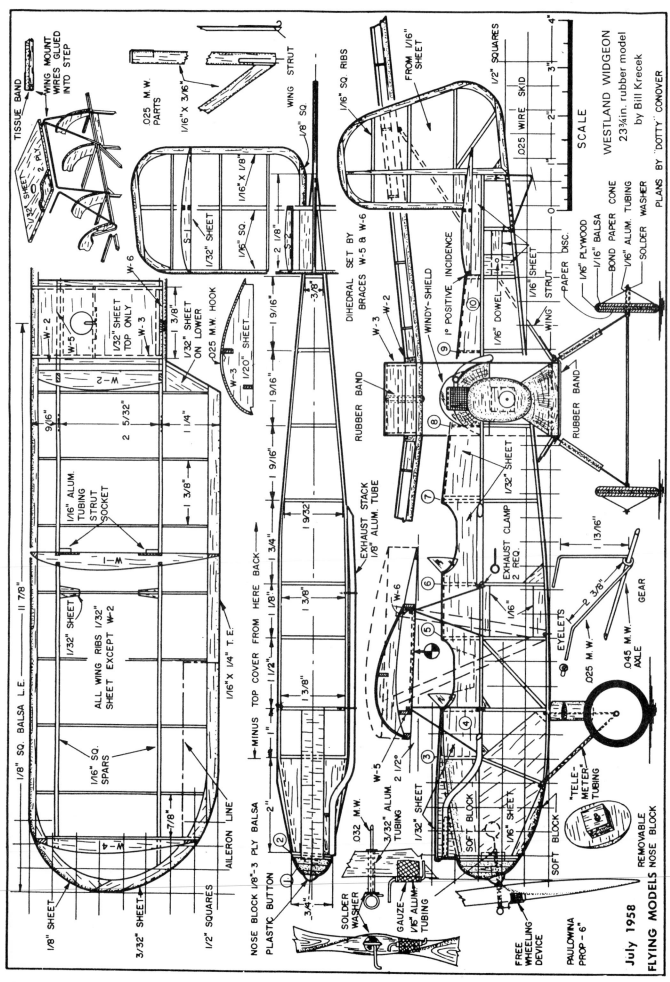

WESTLAND WIDGEON
23¾in. rubber model
by Bill Krecek

PLANS BY "DOTTY" CONOVER

July 1958
FLYING MODELS

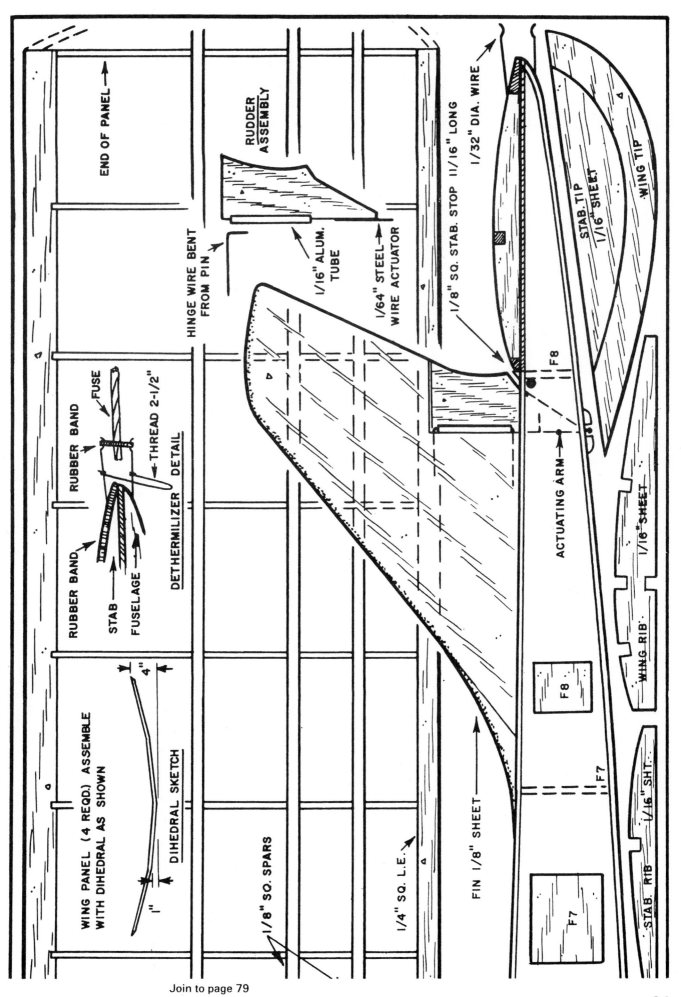

END OF PANEL →

RUDDER ASSEMBLY

HINGE WIRE BENT FROM PIN

1/16" ALUM. TUBE

1/64" STEEL WIRE ACTUATOR

1/8" SQ. STAB. STOP 11/16" LONG

1/32" DIA. WIRE

STAB. TIP 1/16" SHEET

WING TIP

F8

ACTUATING ARM →

1/16" SHEET

WING RIB

F8

F7

FIN 1/8" SHEET

F7

STAB. RIB   1/16" SHT.

RUBBER BAND

FUSE

RUBBER BAND

STAB

FUSELAGE

← THREAD 2-1/2"

DETHERMILIZER DETAIL

WING PANEL (4 REQD.) ASSEMBLE WITH DIHEDRAL AS SHOWN

4"

1"

DIHEDRAL SKETCH

1/8" SQ. SPARS

1/4" SQ. L.E.

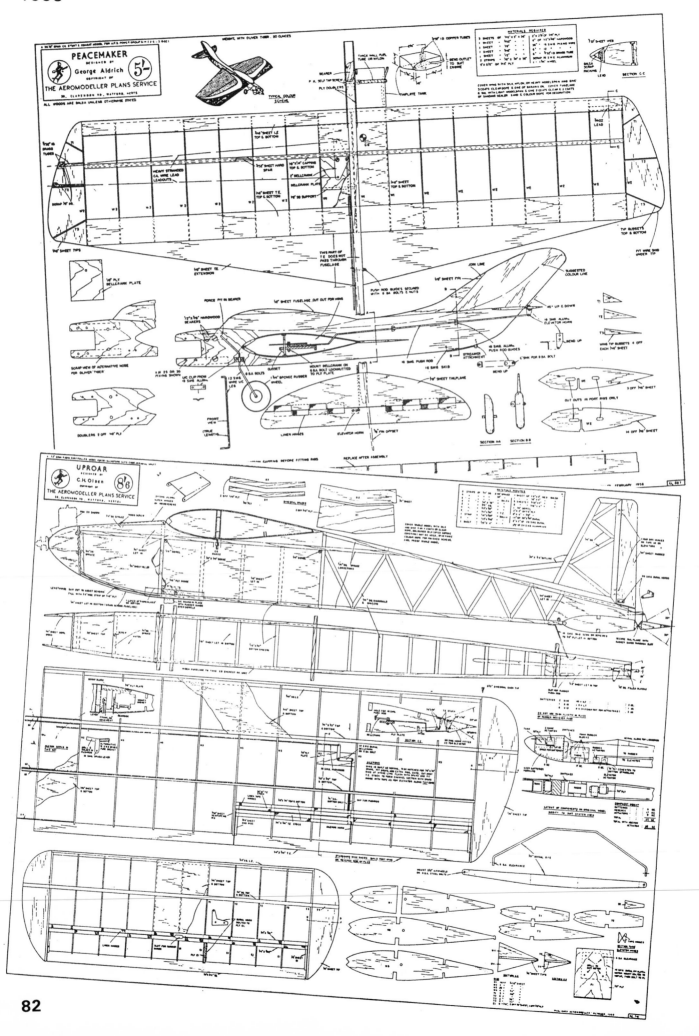

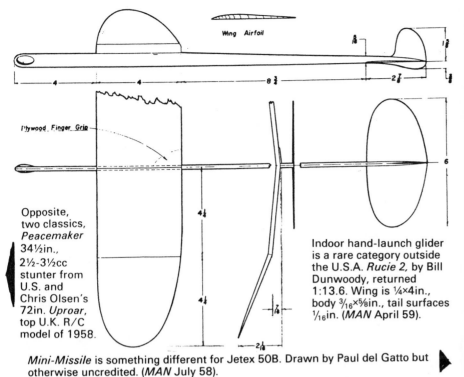

Wing Airfoil

Plywood Finger Grip

Opposite, two classics, *Peacemaker* 34½in., 2½-3½cc stunter from U.S. and Chris Olsen's 72in. *Uproar*, top U.K. R/C model of 1958.

Indoor hand-launch glider is a rare category outside the U.S.A. *Rucie 2*, by Bill Dunwoody, returned 1:13.6. Wing is ¼×4in., body ³⁄₁₆×⅝in., tail surfaces ¹⁄₁₆in. (*MAN* April 59).

Mini-Missile is something different for Jetex 50B. Drawn by Paul del Gatto but otherwise uncredited. (*MAN* July 58).

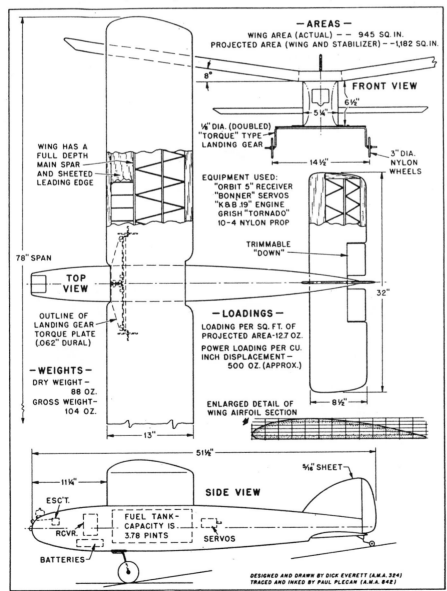

— AREAS —

WING AREA (ACTUAL) – – 945 SQ. IN.
PROJECTED AREA (WING AND STABILIZER) – –1,182 SQ. IN.

FRONT VIEW

WING HAS A FULL DEPTH MAIN SPAR AND SHEETED LEADING EDGE

⅛" DIA. (DOUBLED) "TORQUE" TYPE LANDING GEAR

3" DIA. NYLON WHEELS

EQUIPMENT USED:
"ORBIT 5" RECEIVER
"BONNER" SERVOS
"K&B .19" ENGINE
GRISH "TORNADO" 10-4 NYLON PROP

TRIMMABLE "DOWN"

78" SPAN

TOP VIEW

OUTLINE OF LANDING GEAR TORQUE PLATE (.062" DURAL)

— WEIGHTS —
DRY WEIGHT – 88 OZ.
GROSS WEIGHT– 104 OZ.

— LOADINGS —
LOADING PER SQ. FT. OF PROJECTED AREA–12.7 OZ.
POWER LOADING PER CU. INCH DISPLACEMENT– 500 OZ. (APPROX.)

ENLARGED DETAIL OF WING AIRFOIL SECTION

⁵⁄₁₆" SHEET

SIDE VIEW

ESC'T.
RCVR.
FUEL TANK- CAPACITY IS 3.78 PINTS
SERVOS
BATTERIES

DESIGNED AND DRAWN BY DICK EVERETT (A.M.A. 324)
TRACED AND INKED BY PAUL PLECAN (A.M.A. 842)

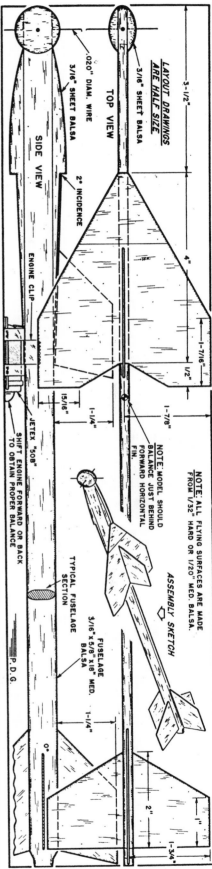

LAYOUT DRAWINGS ARE HALF SIZE

TOP VIEW

SIDE VIEW

.020" DIAM. WIRE
³⁄₁₆" SHEET BALSA
3/16" SHEET BALSA

2° INCIDENCE

ENGINE CLIP

SHIFT ENGINE FORWARD OR BACK TO OBTAIN PROPER BALANCE

JETEX "50B"

NOTE: MODEL SHOULD BALANCE JUST BEHIND FORWARD HORIZONTAL FIN.

NOTE: ALL FLYING SURFACES ARE MADE FROM 1/32" HARD OR 1/20" MED. BALSA.

ASSEMBLY SKETCH

TYPICAL FUSELAGE SECTION

FUSELAGE 3/16" x 5/8" x 18" MED. BALSA

P. D. G.

R/C distance record-setter by Dick Everett; 37•1 miles doesn't sound a lot these days, but . . . Intention was to cover at least 100 miles but weather kept interfering. K&B •19 motor, torsion bar u/c, take-off run only 75ft. at 6½lbs. weight.

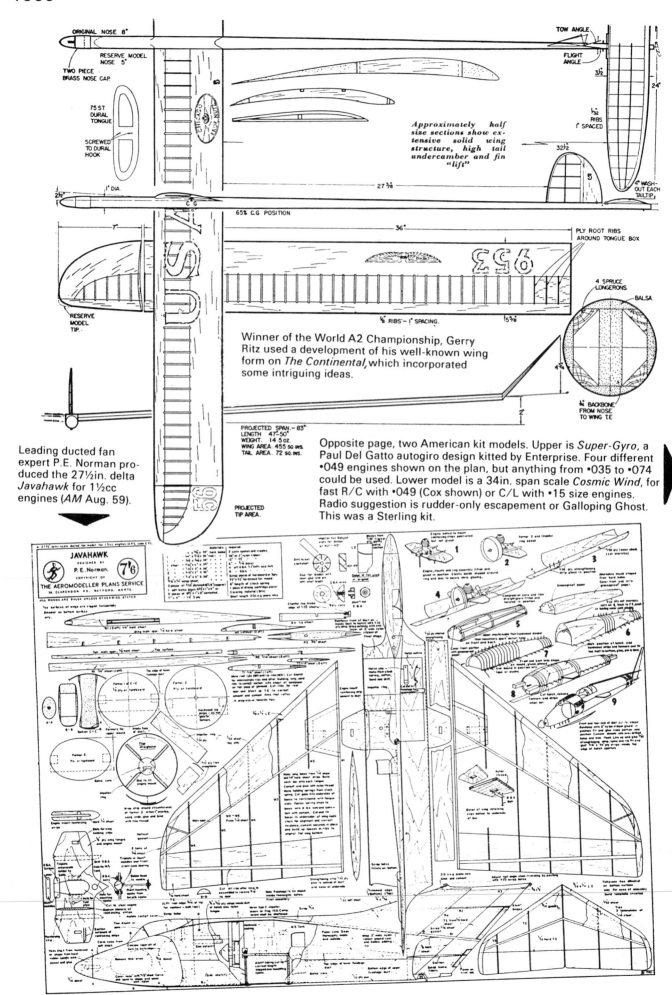

Winner of the World A2 Championship, Gerry Ritz used a development of his well-known wing form on *The Continental*, which incorporated some intriguing ideas.

Leading ducted fan expert P.E. Norman produced the 27½in. delta *Javahawk* for 1½cc engines (*AM* Aug. 59).

Opposite page, two American kit models. Upper is *Super-Gyro*, a Paul Del Gatto autogiro design kitted by Enterprise. Four different •049 engines shown on the plan, but anything from •035 to •074 could be used. Lower model is a 34in. span scale *Cosmic Wind*, for fast R/C with •049 (Cox shown) or C/L with •15 size engines. Radio suggestion is rudder-only escapement or Galloping Ghost. This was a Sterling kit.

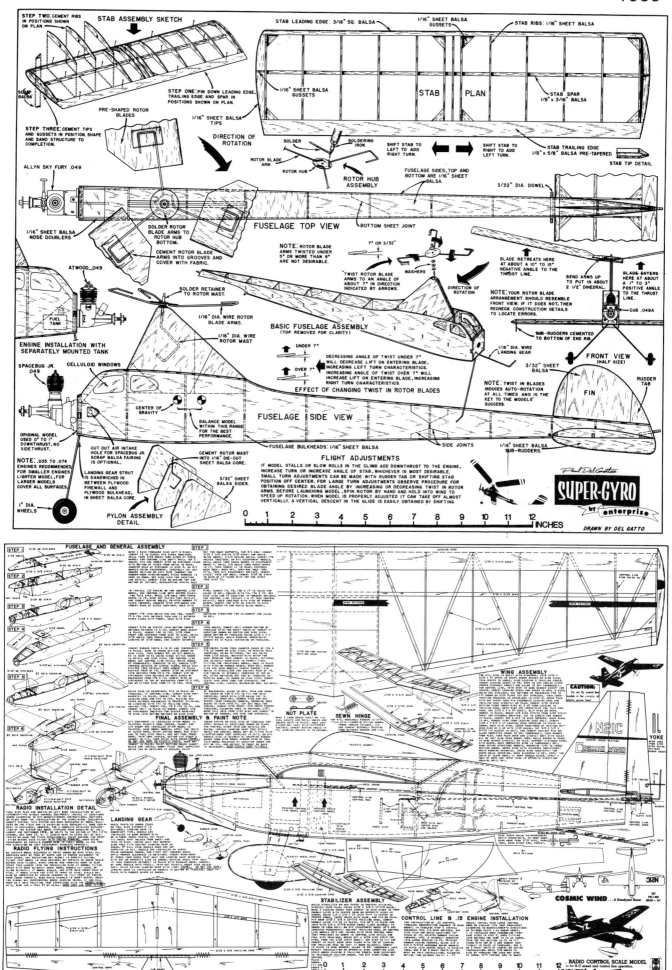

SUPER-GYRO by enterprise

DRAWN BY DEL GATTO

COSMIC WIND ... A Goodyear Racer

RADIO CONTROL SCALE MODEL
—to be R/C speed and control line operation.

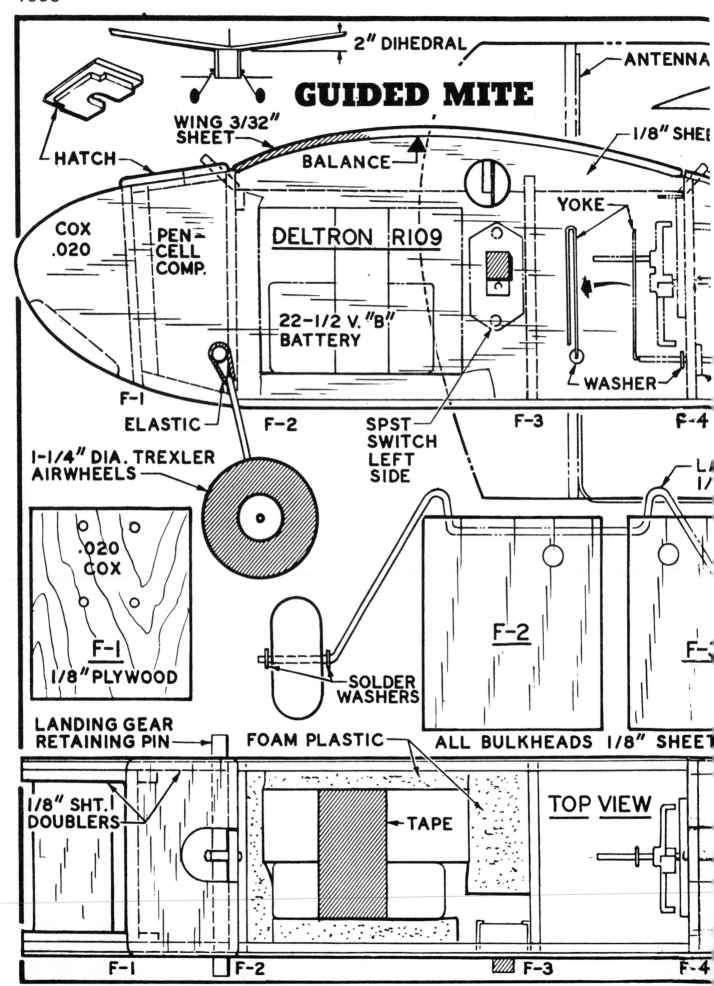

GUIDED MITE

2" DIHEDRAL

ANTENNA

WING 3/32" SHEET

BALANCE

1/8" SHEE

HATCH

COX .020

PEN-CELL COMP.

DELTRON R109

YOKE

22-1/2 V. "B" BATTERY

WASHER

F-1

ELASTIC

F-2

SPST SWITCH LEFT SIDE

F-3

F-4

1-1/4" DIA. TREXLER AIRWHEELS

.020 COX

F-1
1/8" PLYWOOD

SOLDER WASHERS

F-2

F-3

LANDING GEAR RETAINING PIN

FOAM PLASTIC

ALL BULKHEADS 1/8" SHEET

1/8" SHT. DOUBLERS

TAPE

TOP VIEW

F-1

F-2

F-3

F-4

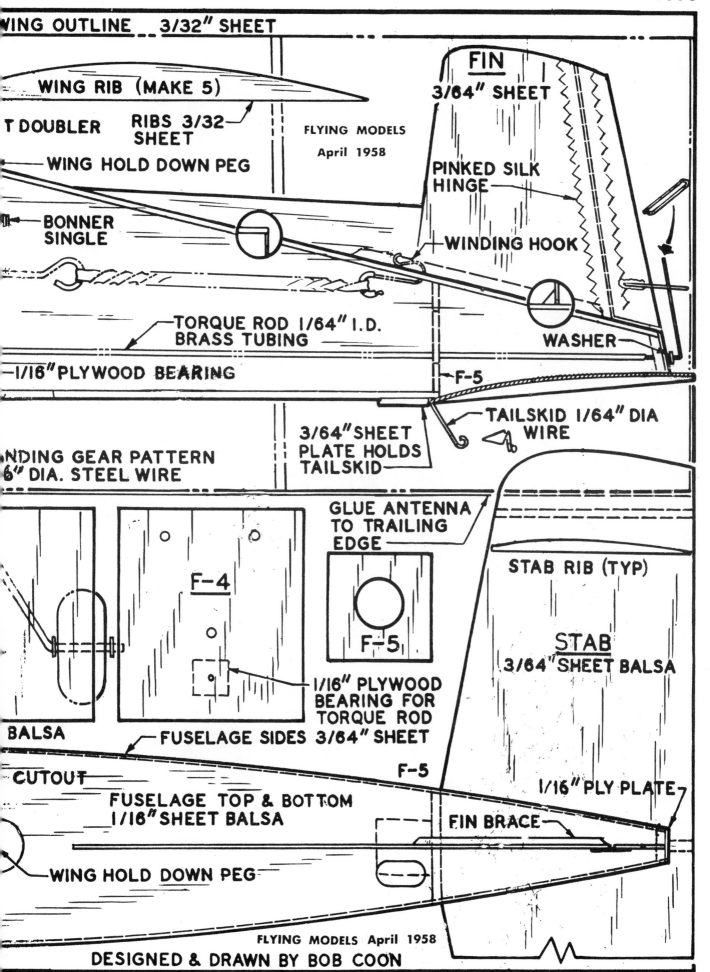

WING OUTLINE __ 3/32" SHEET

WING RIB (MAKE 5)

T DOUBLER   RIBS 3/32 SHEET

FLYING MODELS
April 1958

WING HOLD DOWN PEG

BONNER SINGLE

TORQUE ROD 1/64" I.D. BRASS TUBING

1/16" PLYWOOD BEARING

FIN
3/64" SHEET

PINKED SILK HINGE

WINDING HOOK

WASHER

F-5

TAILSKID 1/64" DIA WIRE

3/64" SHEET PLATE HOLDS TAILSKID

NDING GEAR PATTERN
6" DIA. STEEL WIRE

GLUE ANTENNA TO TRAILING EDGE

F-4

F-5

1/16" PLYWOOD BEARING FOR TORQUE ROD

STAB RIB (TYP)

STAB
3/64" SHEET BALSA

BALSA

FUSELAGE SIDES 3/64" SHEET

CUTOUT

FUSELAGE TOP & BOTTOM
1/16" SHEET BALSA

F-5

1/16" PLY PLATE

FIN BRACE

WING HOLD DOWN PEG

DESIGNED & DRAWN BY BOB COON

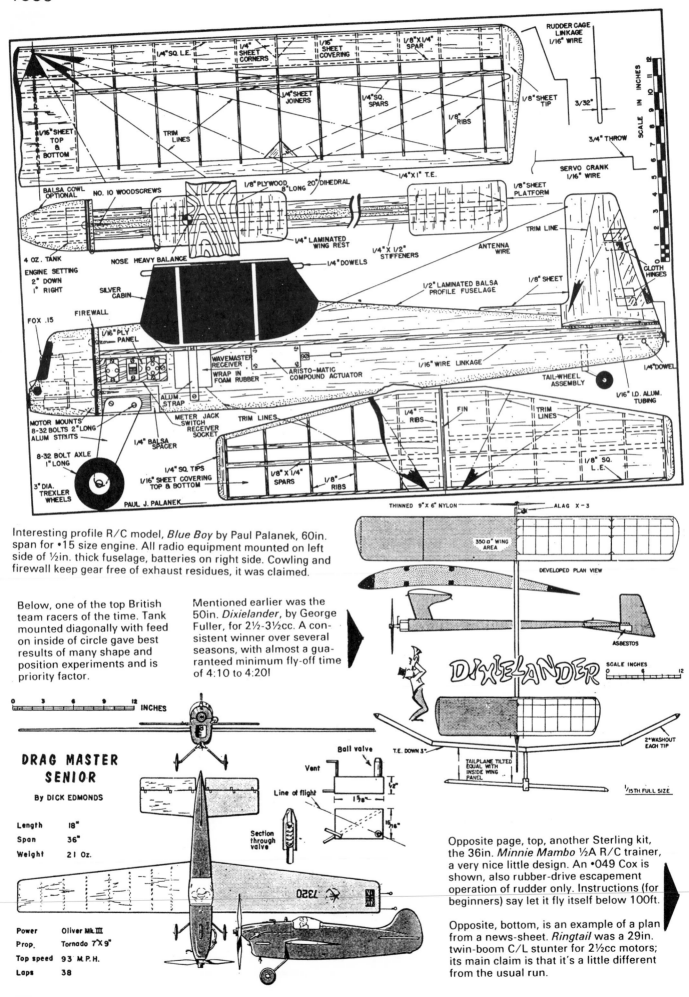

Interesting profile R/C model, *Blue Boy* by Paul Palanek, 60in. span for •15 size engine. All radio equipment mounted on left side of ½in. thick fuselage, batteries on right side. Cowling and firewall keep gear free of exhaust residues, it was claimed.

Below, one of the top British team racers of the time. Tank mounted diagonally with feed on inside of circle gave best results of many shape and position experiments and is priority factor.

Mentioned earlier was the 50in. *Dixielander*, by George Fuller, for 2½-3½cc. A consistent winner over several seasons, with almost a guaranteed minimum fly-off time of 4:10 to 4:20!

DRAG MASTER SENIOR

By DICK EDMONDS

Length	18"
Span	36"
Weight	21 Oz.

Power	Oliver Mk.III
Prop.	Tornado 7"X 9"
Top speed	93 M.P.H.
Laps	38

Opposite page, top, another Sterling kit, the 36in. *Minnie Mambo* ½A R/C trainer, a very nice little design. An •049 Cox is shown, also rubber-drive escapement operation of rudder only. Instructions (for beginners) say let it fly itself below 100ft.

Opposite, bottom, is an example of a plan from a news-sheet. *Ringtail* was a 29in. twin-boom C/L stunter for 2½cc motors; its main claim is that it's a little different from the usual run.

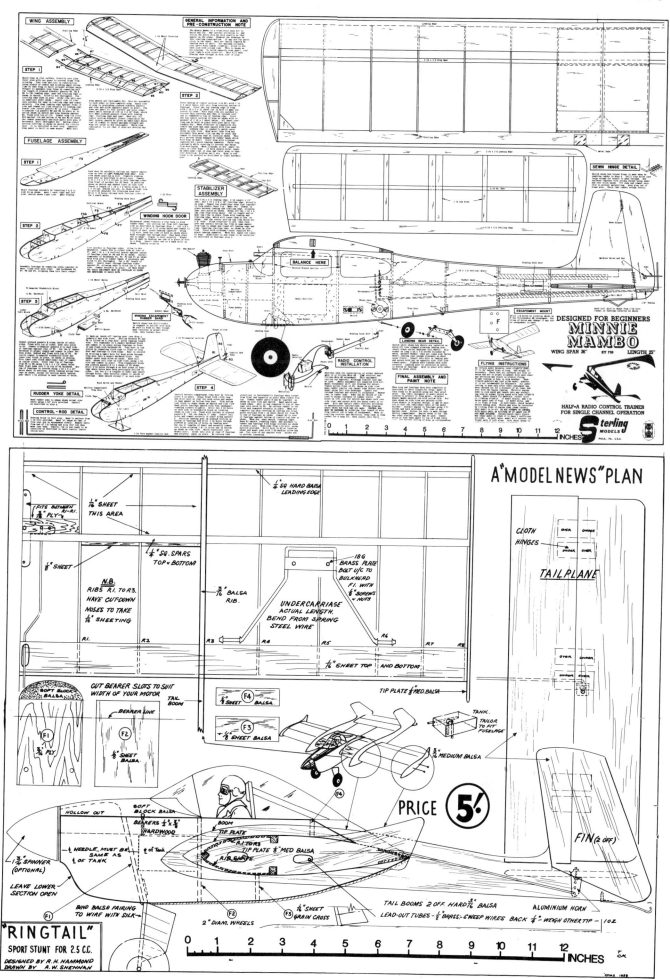

1959

A simple scale F/F model by C.C. Badger (*Aeromodeller* May 1959).

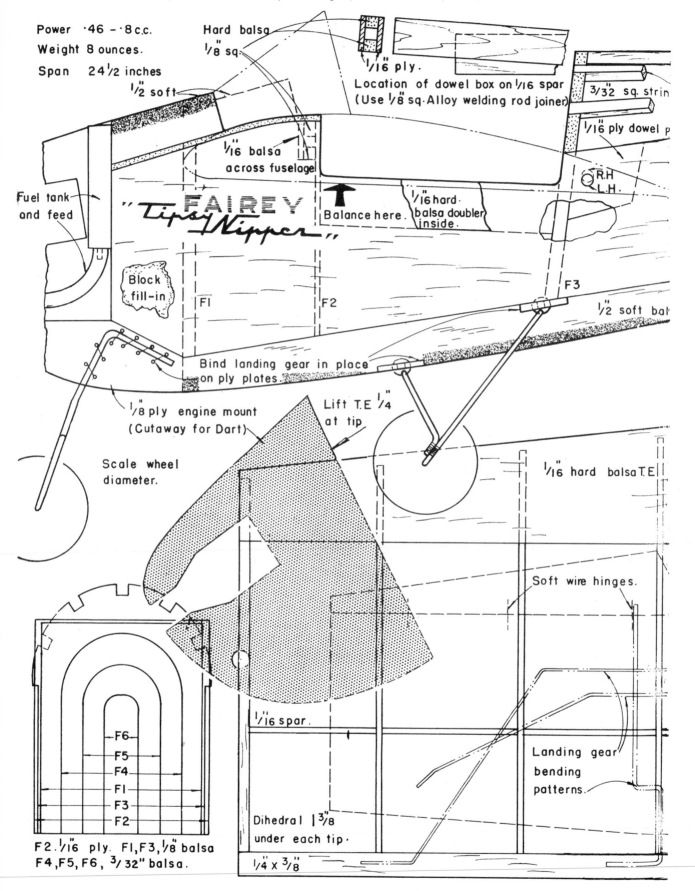

Power ·46 – ·8 c.c.

Weight 8 ounces.

Span 24½ inches

Full-size plans for a 24in., •46-•8cc (•020-•049cu.in.) version. Scale to 36in. for 1cc (•061).

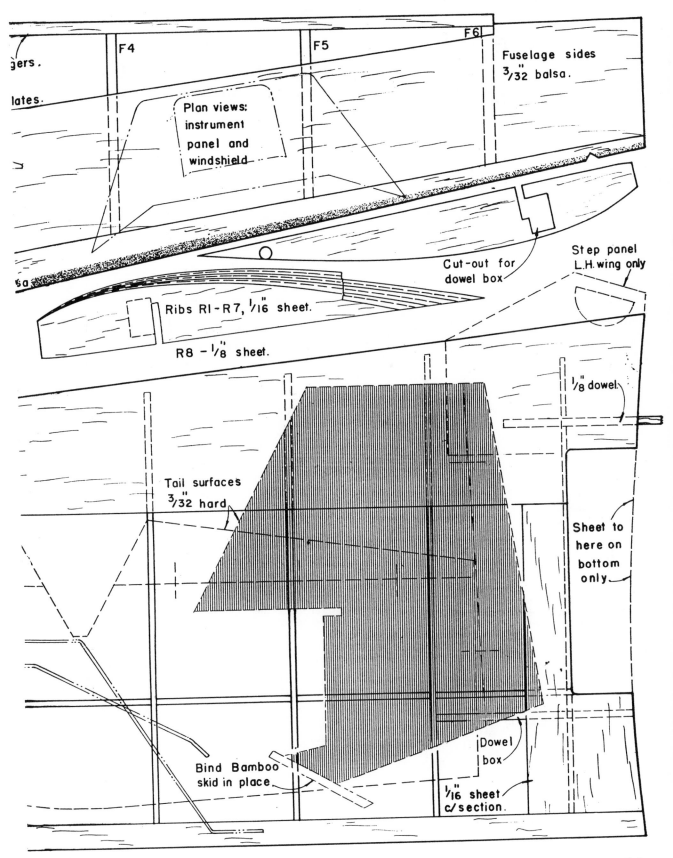

F4 F5 F6

Fuselage sides 3/32" balsa.

Plan views: instrument panel and windshield

Cut-out for dowel box

Step panel L.H. wing only

Ribs RI-R7, 1/16" sheet.

R8 - 1/8" sheet.

1/8" dowel.

Tail surfaces 3/32" hard

Sheet to here on bottom only.

Bind Bamboo skid in place.

Dowel box

1/16" sheet c/section.

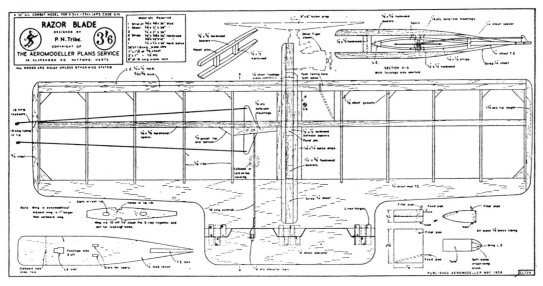

Hottest British combat model of the decade was *Razor Blade*, by P.N. Tribe, 32in. span, for 2½-3½cc, used extensively by the Kenton and North-wood clubs with outstanding success. (*AM* May 59).

A fly-for-fun 22in. span delta by N.D. Peacock, with strip ribs bent over cut spars on an ⅛in. sq. base. Rubber not speci-fied – try two loops of ³⁄₁₆in. or ¼in.

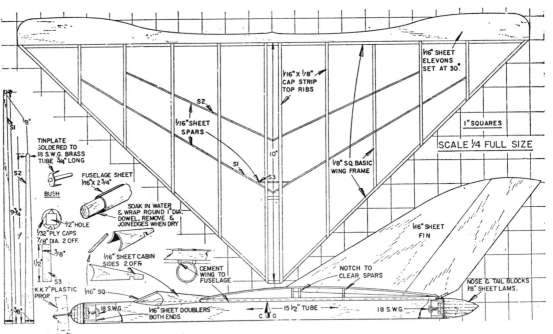

International team racer specifications were altered in 1958 and Ken Long's *Tigress* (below) was one of the first F.A.I. A class designs to appear. One of the most successful, too, in the hands of Wharfedale club members. Span is 38½in. Frequently under 5 min. for 10km, i.e. an average speed of over 85 m.p.h. including pit stops.

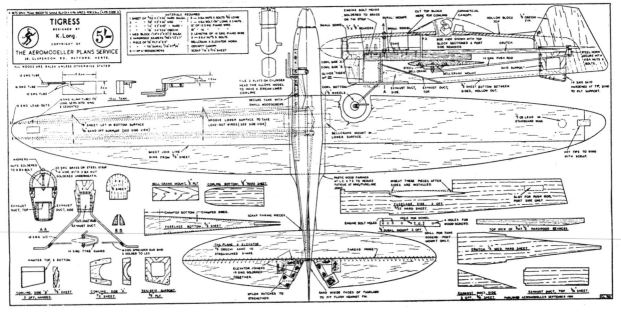

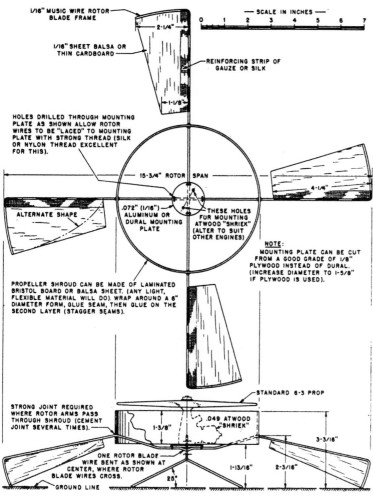

This remarkable "flying saucer" concept was the star of the 1959 German nationals as far as novelty was concerned. Wrap 1⅜in. wide Bristol board round a 6in. saucepan to three thicknesses. Bend a kink in the middle of one of the wires to clear the other, feed through shroud, bending as drawn, secure engine plate very firmly, finally bend outer ends of wires (use a simple jig on a flat table) and fix rotor blades. On a 2 min. motor run it will reach about 1000ft. and descend quite rapidly when the motor cuts.

Pulse jets were usually thought of as for C/L speed only; they were dangerous for free flight because of fire hazard and fuel flow problems arise because of lack of inertia. Paolo Berselli of Bologna showed that stunting was possible with his Zanin-powered model (similar to a Dyna-jet).

Two interesting indoor R/C models by Ken Willard illustrated an article in *MAN* for May 1959. At this time rubber-driven escapements were still the norm but size was quite small and, with transistor development, receivers were light and compact. *Slo' Poke,* top right, was a 33in., 6oz. biplane which required 100×125ft. of space. A lot of downthrust and marked difference in wing/tail incidence gives slow flight (with a deep undercamber) and the model would rock round on rudder due to the dihedral used. *Warpy* was a later model with single-surface wing of similar span but broad chord, using a pusher installation (the Pee Wee engine runs either way) and no undercarriage. Weight was reduced to 3¾ozs. and flight was slow enough to run alongside. Would turn in 30ft. circles.

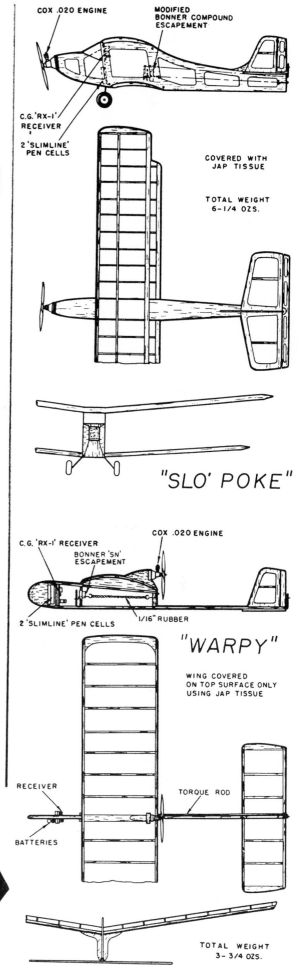

"SLO' POKE"

"WARPY"

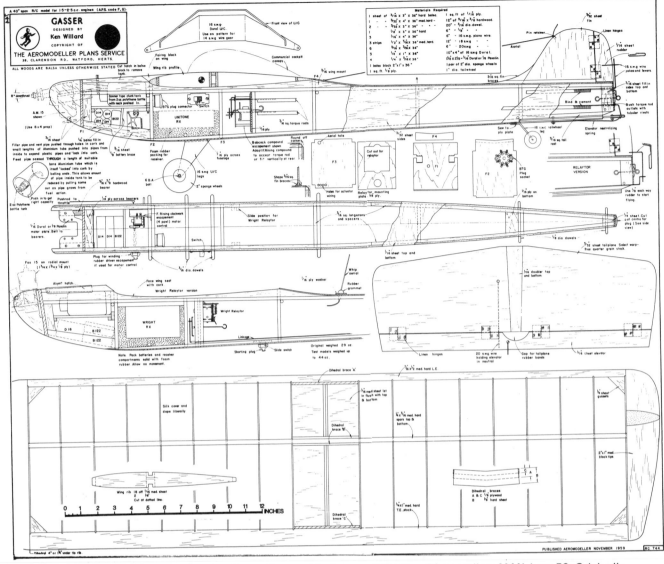

Yet another Ken Willard design, the *Gasser,* featured in *Aeromodeller* Nov. 59 as well as *MAN* June 59. Originally intended as a pylon racer, the design proved excellent for what was called "precision R/C" and Ken won the intermediate class at the 1959 U.S. Nats., this class allowing compound escapements as opposed to rudder-only or multi-channel control. Span 40in., motors 1½-2½cc (K&B Torpedo •09 favoured).

ACKNOWLEDGEMENTS

This book draws heavily on plans published during the 1950s by the leading English language magazines of the time. Several of these publications still continue today though almost all under different ownership and with different editorial and art staff. In acknowledging and thanking their present owners and publishers the compiler and publishers of "Favourites of the Fifties" also express appreciation of the efforts of those who produced the 1950s issues and by so doing advanced the art of flying models while giving enormous pleasure to us all.

The titles providing material and their contemporary owners were:

Air Trails, later 'Air Trails and Hobbies for Young Men', later 'Young Men', then 'American Modeler'.   Street and Smith Publications, Inc., Elizabeth, N.J.

Flying Models (including 'Air World' and 'Flying Aces').   Fifty Crosswords Inc., Silver Spring, Maryland.

Model Airplane News   Air Age Inc., New York.
Aeromodeller   M.A.P. Ltd., Watford.
Model Aircraft   Percival Marshall Ltd., London.
Model Aviation Series   Ian Allan Ltd., Weybridge.
Modele Reduit d'Avion   Publications M.R.A., Paris.

3 GOOD REASONS..

..for subscribing!

Every month, these three informative magazines provide the expertise, advice and inspiration to keep you abreast of developments in the exciting field of model aviation.

With regular new designs to build, practical features that take the mysteries out of construction, reports and detailed descriptions of the techniques and ideas of pioneering aircraft modellers all over the world, they represent three of the very best reasons for taking out a subscription. So that you need never miss a single issue or a single minute of aeromodelling pleasure!

	UK	EUROPE	MIDDLE EAST	FAR EAST	REST OF THE WORLD
Aeromodeller	£22.20	£27.00	£27.20	£29.00	£27.50
Radio Modeller	£14.40	£20.00	£20.20	£22.40	£20.60
RCM&E	£14.40	£20.40	£20.60	£22.90	£21.00

Airmail rates given on request.

Make Cheques Payable to **ASP LTD**
and return to:

Infonet Ltd, 5 River park Estate
BERKHAMSTED, Herts HP4 1HL
Tel: 04427-76661